CUBA'S ACADEMIC ADVANTAGE

Cuba's Academic Advantage

Why Students in Cuba Do Better in School

Martin Carnoy

with Amber K. Gove and Jeffery H. Marshall

STANFORD UNIVERSITY PRESS

STANFORD, CALIFORNIA 2007

Stanford University Press
Stanford, California

Printed in the United States of America on acid-
free, archival-quality paper

Library of Congress Cataloging-in-Publication
Data

Carnoy, Martin.
    Cuba's academic advantage : why students in
Cuba do better in school / Martin Carnoy, with
Amber K. Gove and Jeffrey H. Marshall.
        p.   cm.
    Includes bibliographical references and index.
    ISBN 0-8047-5597-3 (cloth : alk. paper)—
ISBN 0-8047-5598-1 (pbk. : alk. paper)
    1. Education, Elementary—Cuba.   2. Education
and state—Cuba.   3. Education, Elementary—
Latin America.   4. Education and state.   I. Gove,
Amber, K.   II. Marshall, Jeffrey H.   III. Title.

LA487.C36 2007
372'.97291—dc22   2006035228

Typeset by Newgen in 10/14 Janson

Contents

Figures

Tables

Acknowledgments

This research was made possible by the generous support of the Ford Foundation. We would like to thank Janice Petrovich at the Foundation for her unflagging interest in basic research in education.

We would also like to thank Enrique Iglesias and Larry Wolfe of the Inter-American Development Bank, and Ana Luiza Machado, Paula Louzano, and Juan Cassasus of UNESCO Santiago, Jorge Werthein of UNESCO Brazil, and Francisco Lacayo of UNESCO Cuba for their help in accessing the data needed to do this study. Special thanks as well to our colleagues at Stanford, Shelley Goldman and Kim Stevenson, for their generous assistance in helping us interpret curriculum and classroom data.

Most important, we would like to acknowledge our colleagues in Brazil, Chile, and Cuba who were so helpful and so crucial to our research. It was through their experience and patience that we were able to gain so many new insights into the education process. These include Mariana Alwyn (former minister of education), Cristian Cox, and Silvia Elqueta of the Ministry of Education in Chile. Assisting us from the Ministry of Education in Cuba were Luis Gomez Gutierrez, Minister of Education, and Hector Valdés, Victoria Arenciba Sosa, Miguel Angel Ferrer, and Paul Torres Fernandez. Those in Brazil who provided invaluable aid were José Amaral Sobrinho of Fundescola, Carmilva Souza Flores of INEP, and Robert Verhine of the Universidade Federal of Bahia. The views expressed here are the authors' and should not be attributed to the Foundation or to the three countries' ministries of education.

CUBA'S ACADEMIC ADVANTAGE

CHAPTER ONE

Context Matters

Some towns, regions, and countries seem to have better education than others. The students in those schools do better on tests, are more likely to finish high school, and are more likely to seek higher education. We know that these outcomes are not just the result of better teachers and better administered schools, or even more money for supplies and extra programs. The students who go to better schools usually have families who are more highly educated and are hooked into networks that both reinforce the notion that doing well in school is important *and* know the best strategies for succeeding at school.

There is another reason for young people doing better in school that might be just as important as high-quality school personnel, supportive families, and family networks. Some communities, regions, and even countries have created environments and networks that—beyond families—help young people *want* to be academically successful and facilitate strategies that encourage them to achieve success.

This book is about education in one country—Cuba—where even elementary school pupils from rural areas seem to learn more than pupils from middle-class urban families in the rest of Latin America. This achievement is all the more remarkable because Cuba is fairly poor in natural resources and has low levels of material consumption. Yet Cuba has school and social support systems that help a very large percentage of pupils reach high levels of academic achievement.

The reasons for Cuba's academic success that emerge from this study will please some educators but displease others. The reasons certainly conflict with political philosophies stressing individual freedom and decentralized pluralistic democracy. Many of the reasons revolve around a social context of schools that is highly supportive of academic achievement. Most educators, no matter what their political philosophy, realize how important that kind of environment is for a good educational system or school. But Cuba creates this social context mainly through a hierarchical centralized government bureaucracy, not through individual families acting alone or collectively at a local level by attending school board meetings or church services. Indeed, while Cuban classrooms stress a child-centered approach to learning, the Cuban state strictly enforces the implementation of curriculum and these child-centered teaching methods through a chain of command that begins with the minister of education and ends with directors and assistant directors of schools supervising teachers in their classrooms and teachers feeling competent and responsible to deliver a well-defined national curriculum.

The Cuban experience raises important questions for education in all countries, including highly developed ones such as the United States. How responsible should governments be for creating environments that help children focus on academic achievement? How much autonomy should teachers and schools have over what goes on in classrooms? Is there a trade-off between the value that market societies place on individual choice and on the value they place on ensuring that all children—regardless of socioeconomic background—receive high-quality schooling?

Caring about Academic Achievement

Fifty years ago in America, getting good grades in school and scoring high on tests was important but not critical to life chances. Almost everyone who had a "good" job was a white male, so competition for those jobs was not nearly as stiff as it is today. There was also a lot of well-paying manufacturing work around. High school (male, mainly white) graduates and even some dropouts had access to that kind of work, and they earned nearly as much as people who were college trained.

Intellectuals were certainly concerned about the quality of schooling, but they situated academic achievement and attainment, particularly for the poor, in the larger issues of poverty and discrimination. We knew that suburban children went to good schools because their families paid higher property taxes, and we knew that black children in the South went to schools that were segregated, terribly underfunded, and probably not very likely places to pick up advanced mathematics. Thanks to *Blackboard Jungle*, a Glenn Ford-Sidney Poitier film of the 1950s, we also knew that inner-city high schools were rough places, attended by gangs who cared little about anything academic. Everything we thought about education suggested that the main problem was outside the school—the influences of a society in which the middle class could spend more than the less affluent on their children's public education, where whites discriminated against blacks, and where poor city kids were subjected to what sociologists Richard Sennett and Jonathan Cobb called the "hidden injuries of class," resulting in anti-academic, anti-school behavior among urban youth (Sennett and Cobb, 1973).

This view of education has changed. In the past generation, a great urgency has developed over students' school success, and with it, an urgency both to blame the schools for society's ills and to insist on improving how well schools teach pupils what they need to learn. The change results partly from schools' success itself. In the United States and all over the world, a lot more young people are finishing high school and college than ever before. Many more are competing for professional jobs. Once women and minorities began getting hired in jobs previously reserved for white men, everyone became concerned about doing well in school to stay ahead of the game. The other change is that high-paying factory jobs, which did not require much schooling, have been replaced by service jobs (and factory jobs) that demand good reading and interpretation skills and a fairly high level of technical understanding. So increased competition for good incomes from more and more highly educated young people puts ever more emphasis on school success. In the old days, even if you were a high school dropout, you had a chance to get a job that paid a decent wage. Today, at least in the developed countries—the United States, Canada, Europe, Australia, and Japan—simply finishing high school is likely to leave you near the bottom of the economic ladder.

In this environment, despite their success in getting a much higher fraction of students into college, schools as organizations are being increasingly blamed for not teaching children enough. Schools serving low-income pupils are getting the brunt of this criticism, but it is usually couched in more general terms as a condemnation of "bureaucratized" public education and of teachers' unions, with these characterized as the main obstacles to better teaching and learning. Conservative academics and think tanks have done a lot to foster these ideas. They are convinced that schools could be much more "efficient" if they could hire and fire teachers at will, get rid of bureaucratic rules so that teachers and principals could innovate regularly, and replace "constructivist" teaching—teaching that tries to build learning on knowledge and experiences that pupils bring to class—with a focus on basic skills and teacher-driven problem solving—teaching that emphasizes learning a well-defined body of knowledge based on how a pre-set curriculum spells out the learning path.[1]

The claims that schools can do better at teaching children are not restricted to conservatives. Liberal educators are also convinced that schools can improve academic results. Liberals are not as likely to blame bureaucrats and teachers' unions, but they do think that better teaching, smaller class size, better curricula, and more parent participation would increase student learning.

The urgency and the ideas about school improvement have spread to developing countries. In lower-income countries, it seems that there are just not enough good jobs to absorb young people coming out of primary and secondary schools. That does not prevent school systems from expanding. As they expand, the main complaint in most places is the same as in the United States and Europe: the quality of graduates is low, so schools need to raise the amount of learning that goes in every academic year, whether it is in the first few grades, in high school, or at the university. The mantra is that smarter graduates will make the country more competitive and increase economic growth.

The focus on educational "quality" and student performance in school has been fueled by international tests comparing how well young people in different countries perform in math, reading, and science. Countries pay attention to the results, although it is not clear what they can do about them. When Finland scored very high in reading in a recent international test, everyone rushed there to figure out what made Finns such great readers. Finns themselves were not at all sure what made them so successful. One outcome of this puzzlement is that there are as many suggestions for increasing student learning as there are educational analysts, socially involved business executives, and politicians. Reduce class size, improve teacher subject knowledge, stress basic skills, make the curriculum more child centered, get parents more involved, privatize education, eliminate teachers' unions—these are the most common recommendations, but there are many more.

There is little doubt that some schools, communities, and nations do better than others at helping students from similar family backgrounds learn language, mathematics, science, and other subjects considered important. But why is that so? And how important are the differences that can be attributed to the way schools do things compared to differences that are embedded in the social life of communities, regions, and even nations? In developing countries, the answers to these questions may be more obvious because schools differ considerably in the resources they bring to the task at hand. Yet why, for example, do the top 10 percent of students in many developing countries score just at the average of developed countries? Is this a school problem or one with deeper roots?

No matter how sure the many experts are of their ideas, the answers to these questions are not as obvious as we once thought. It is certainly true that thanks to forty years of research and better data, analysts are gaining a clearer understanding of educational productivity—that is, of the key elements driving student performance. But there are still important gaps in our knowledge, and a great deal of controversy exists over what explains and does not explain these differences. Part of the problem is that most research focuses either on the forest or on a single tree, but never brings the two together. One type of research analyzes big data sets gathered in various countries, and another type of research looks only at a single variable or intervention in a few schools, a single community, or a single country.

In this study, we decided to approach the issue in a new way. First, we focus on developing countries, where the answers may be clearer because the variation in educational quality and social conditions is greater. We carried out a comparative analysis of primary schooling in Latin America, focusing on three countries with quite different economic and social conditions and different systemwide management approaches to educational delivery. The three countries are Brazil, Chile, and Cuba, and in all three, third- and fourth-grade children were tested in 1997 in a UNESCO study covering thirteen Latin American countries. The test results, showing that Cuban children scored much higher in math and language than pupils in other Latin American countries, form the backdrop for our analysis.

We went to each of these countries; interviewed officials in the ministries of education in the central government and at the provincial, state, and municipal levels; interviewed teachers, principals, students, and parents; and then filmed math lessons in classrooms. We learned what makes these school systems work the way they do.

Our study is not only comparative. It also uses several different levels of analysis across countries to gain progressively greater understanding of why students seem to learn more in some situations than others. Other researchers have done multiple-level analyses in one country,[2] but as far as we know, our study is unique in using macro (the forest) and micro (the trees) methods of understanding student learning in different educational *systems*.[3]

Our first level of analysis is of the overall impact of family, schooling inputs, and "community" social context differences on student performance in a number of Latin American countries, including our focus group of countries: Brazil, Chile, and Cuba. The second level of analysis is of school system organization in the three focus countries and its links "up" the organizational chain to community social context and "down" the organizational chain to classroom teaching and learning. The third level of analysis is of third-grade mathematics classroom lessons within and across the three countries. This last is the most "micro" of the three levels we use.

Some Background to Our Study

Almost forty years ago, the sociologist James Coleman (Coleman et al., 1966) argued that in the United States, children's home environment was largely responsible for differences in students' academic achievement. Coleman's was the first attempt to explain empirically variation in student achievement among individuals and schools. He also claimed that students' belief that what happens to them is due at least partly to their own efforts, and peer effects, as measured by the social class and racial composition of the school, were important in explaining the persistent gap in achievement between disadvantaged minorities and whites. Skilled or inept school administrators and teachers played a less crucial role (see Jencks and Phillips, 1998, for an update in this controversy).

Others have reassessed and reformulated Coleman's finding that children's family background dominates school outcomes. Economists Samuel Bowles and Henry Levin (Bowles and Levin, 1968) showed that Coleman's estimates could not statistically separate socioeconomic background and school characteristics. The two sets of explanatory variables were too highly correlated to separate their effects. They did not argue that Coleman was wrong in claiming that family background had a major influence on how well children did in school. They just pointed out that his empirical estimates could not *prove* that schooling differences had only a small effect. Because lower-socioeconomic-class children went to schools that also had, on average, fewer and lower-quality resources, explaining academic performance by school differences would give a result similar to the one gained from explaining it by family differences.

French sociologists Pierre Bourdieu and Claude Passeron took this discussion one step further. They claimed that the knowledge children are expected to learn in school is structured to favor particular behavior patterns (including academically oriented activities) and speech modes learned at home—patterns and modes that are much more highly developed in upper-middle-class families. Thus, it might seem that schools try to teach everyone a neutral kind of knowledge, but it turns out that what schools demand from pupils allows schooling to reproduce the class structure from generation to generation (Bourdieu and Passeron, 1977). Bourdieu and Passeron used the term *cultural capital* for the knowledge, behavior, and tastes that families brought to the educational table. They meant that schools were in the business of reproducing a particular culture, especially the way the elites used language, organized their lives, and interacted with each other. For Bourdieu and Passeron, then, the explanation of achievement differences lay in the way schooling *purposefully interacted* with children's education at home, assuring that the values, behavior, interaction with adults, and response to school activities learned in certain home environments were especially favored and reinforced by schools. Any child who did not get the "right" education at home would be unlikely to succeed at school.

However, it is difficult for those interested in education's potential for improving social mobility to accept such a social class–driven analysis of student achievement, especially the idea that schools are organized around skills that pupils with the "wrong" family support systems will find *inherently* difficult to learn. Sufficient exceptions exist to the rule that social class determines outcomes to suggest that better schooling could increase student performance, particularly among the disadvantaged. Knowing that the school is organized around norms of knowledge, language use, and adult-child interaction typical of an upper-middle-class home environment does not tell us why so many lower-middle-class and even lower-class children have succeeded in school, and whether many more could thrive academically under the right circumstances. To answer that puzzle, we need to know why children from a lower social class background or from a disadvantaged minority group do better in some school or classroom environments than in others.

Social scientists have sought the answer to this question in educational "production functions" of the Coleman type. An educational production function models and tries to measure the relationships between students' social class background, school inputs—including teacher characteristics— and student outcomes. Estimating these input-output models, social scientists have tested whether class size, teacher education, and teacher experience make a significant difference in pupils' performance. They have analyzed whether higher spending per pupil produces higher student achievement. And they have estimated the effects on pupil achievement of longer school days, of a longer school year, of summer school, of automatic promotion versus retention, and a host of other educational interventions.

As the databases have become more sophisticated (follow-up surveys of student cohorts, random assignment of students to treatment and control groups), production function analyses have been able to measure more accurately the effects of various policy variables on student outcomes. Literally hundreds of studies have been carried out since the mid-1960s. Economist Eric Hanushek reviewed existing U.S. studies as of the mid-1980s (Hanushek, 1986), but many of the analyses of longitudinal data were done later. In addition, there have been production function studies in Latin

America and in other developing countries (see Carnoy, Sack, and Thias, 1977; Harbison and Hanushek, 1992; and Lockheed and Verspoor, 1991, for references).

Effective schools analysis has been another approach to the same problem. In effective schools analysis, researchers study schools that produce unusually good results—meaning that students of a given socioeconomic background perform much better on tests than production function analysis would predict—and compare them with similar schools whose students are low performing. By studying the characteristics of these schools, the argument goes, we can identify the variables that make students perform better than expected. A typical variable identified in effective schools studies is "leadership" or "instructional leadership," meaning that the principal or a group of teachers make improving instruction the total focus of the school's activities. Another variable usually associated with good student performance is school "cohesion." Cohesion suggests that the school personnel organize themselves as a collective to achieve instructional goals. The opposite of cohesion is "atomization," where teachers pursue goals individually without a common project or school focus (Abelman and Elmore, 1999). Another way of expressing this cohesive characteristic of effective schools is that they are marked by a positive sociopsychological climate. In such a climate, teachers have high expectations; they have a strong sense of belonging to a team; and teachers, parents, and administrators work in harmony (Brookover, 1979; Levinson, 2001; Rutter et al., 1979). Of course, the school focus, or cohesion, may not be around instruction but around some other activity, such as the football or basketball team. This would not necessarily improve academic achievement.

Effective school analysis begins to tell us what to look for that makes schools better places for student learning. But the studies do not tell us how much each of these variables contributes to improving achievement. Often, effective schools analysis is based on a methodological flaw. Unless the research includes a systematic comparison of schools in which students achieve above the predicted norm with schools that perform below the predicted norm, we observe only winners without comparing them to losers. It may be that losers have many of the same traits we identify as contributing to higher achievement, but in the loser schools, they don't contribute.

Besides the studies of student achievement within countries using national data, the steady increase in international test data beginning in the

1980s and accelerating in the 1990s has produced many more *within* country studies trying to explain student achievement, and a new kind of empirical research: comparisons *across* countries (for example, Baker, Riordan, and Schaub, 1995; Heyneman and Loxley, 1982). This comparative approach also spread to effective school studies, which were carried out widely in developing countries (see Lockheed and Levin, 1993, for example).

All these production function and effective school studies were reasonably well formulated theoretically and yielded interesting results but surprisingly few insights into school improvement strategies. For example, one important conclusion of earlier estimates in developing countries was that textbook availability was a high-yield investment. This was a logical result with major policy implications (Lockheed and Verspoor, 1991). Yet, many of the conclusions of such studies were incorrect. Researchers did not understand the limits of an analysis in which student achievement is not measured in gain scores, and researchers do not adjust for selection bias. For example, World Bank researchers concluded that class size does not affect student academic performance for a wide range of students per teacher, approximately twenty to forty-five students (Lockheed and Verspoor, 1991). Later work using data from Tennessee, where students were randomly assigned to normal and small classes and followed over time, showed significant class-size effects (Krueger, 1999).

In our visits to schools in Latin America, we found that schools regarded as "better schools" by students' families were characterized by larger class sizes because they generally filled their classes to the legal limit, whereas "worse schools" had many vacancies and smaller classes. If researchers measured student performance across different schools in that situation, they would likely find that students in classes with more students per teacher were performing as well as or better than students in classes with fewer students. They might conclude that class size made no difference. The flaw is that the students in the larger classes selected themselves into those classes because they wanted to be with other "smart" students. This self-selection confounds the relationship we are interested in, namely, the number of students in the class. Thus, selection bias—students with more motivated families tend to be in larger classes because more motivated families crowd "good" schools—underestimates the true (positive) effect of class size on student performance.

Most of the international production function studies in the 1980s (many done by the World Bank) de-emphasized teacher quality and class size as important factors in explaining variation in student achievement. They concluded that nonsalary resources, such as availability of textbooks, were key. When Coleman and his colleagues published their results from the *High School and Beyond* longitudinal data in the United States showing that Catholic school students scored significantly higher than public school students of similar socioeconomic background (Coleman and Hoffer, 1987; Coleman, Hoffer, and Kilgore 1982), international studies also began to emphasize macro-organizational factors such as private management and school autonomy.

Yet few, if any, of these studies picked up on the social context approach stressed by Bryk, Lee, and Holland (1993) and Coleman himself (Coleman, 1988, 1990). Coleman developed the notion of family and community social capital, which, like all capital, is a source of output of goods and services. Unlike other kinds of capital, which is tangible and benefits primarily its owner, social capital is embedded in *relationships among individuals or among institutions* and benefits all individuals or institutions involved in those relationships by making their work more productive. For example, if a family is particularly cohesive and supportive, and has high expectations for each of its members, that type of family structure can be defined as social capital. If a family or individuals or company employees have well-developed networks, these, too, can be defined as social capital. Family and community cohesiveness, supportiveness, and networking help students that are part of these families and communities to learn more in school and to have higher expectations for themselves, even if they are not contributing very much to the positive relations that benefit them.

Coleman saw Catholic schools as meshing into these networks in ways that public schools do not. He and Bryk, Lee, and Holland argued that the sense of "community" provided in Catholic schools probably explains why inner-city Catholic secondary schools might be more productive academically than inner-city public schools. Such community, they posited, contributes in a major way to learning by stimulating a positive structure in social environments that lacked it. Even though the Catholic school advantage for low-income students is controversial (for a summary, see Benveniste, Carnoy, and Rothstein, 2002), the argument that a sense of a learning-oriented community is important for students' academic achievement has to be taken seriously, and it can be applied on a larger scale.

Coleman's notion of social capital contrasts sharply with Bourdieu and Passeron's idea of cultural capital. Bourdieu and Passeron saw schools as the instrument of a social class. Schools reproduce a social structure controlled by intellectual and bureaucratic elites by reinforcing those elites' cultural capital. Coleman saw social capital as independent of class—families of any social class can accumulate social capital by building networks and putting more effort into their children's education. Institutions such as Catholic schools can also develop social capital by creating community. Coleman does not define social capital in terms of social class but rather in terms of individual, conscious accumulation—a liberal notion of capital, subject to policy intervention, equalization, and all the other possibilities in a society defined as fluid and open to social change. Although we do not agree that social capital is easily acquired, we shall work with Coleman's notion and extend it to include actions by the state. In a sense, just as Coleman turned Bourdieu and Passeron's concept of cultural capital on its head by converting it into an acquirable asset, we will try to re-turn Coleman's notion on *its* head: we suggest that states can generate just as potent a form of social capital in promoting educational achievement as families can, and that state-generated social capital is essential to improving educational achievement for low-income groups—those that have the least cultural capital and the most difficulty in acquiring and accumulating social capital on their own.

The most recent trend in the United States is to build on the school organizational factors literature and to emphasize ways that schooling does impact student achievement, even if this represents only a small portion of total variation in student performance. The quality of teaching has come up as a key variable in these studies, although researchers have not been successful in identifying what it is about "good" teachers that increases student achievement (Bryk and Schneider 2002; Rivkin, Hanushek, and Kain, 2005). In the latest round of international testing and data analysis, attention has turned to curriculum differences among countries (Schmidt et al., 2001), which raises further questions about the capacity of teachers to teach more demanding curricula—questions that we explore further in this study.

This brings us to the present and what we know now about improving schools. We know that student achievement varies greatly among individuals, classrooms, schools, and, somewhat less, among countries. We know that children's experiences in their families, particularly the interaction they have with parents and siblings, have important effects on their academic performance in school. We know that their experiences in school with particular teachers and peers can also influence their achievement gains. Finally, international testing suggests that social and educational conditions in different countries make a difference, yet the challenge continues to be understanding why children in some classrooms, schools, and countries seem to be learning more during each year of school than children in other situations.

We take on this challenge by studying all these levels—individual, classroom, school, and country. We study countries in Latin America, where major differences exist in student achievement on an international test and where major differences exist in the way educational systems are organized. As a first step, we employ a Coleman-type standard production function analysis to estimate input-output relations within each country, but we add a new dimension to this analysis. We define a set of social context variables that differentiate schools' social context within each country and compare differences across countries. We situate this notion of social context in a larger concept of what analysts such as Coleman called *social capital*—the capital created by human actions that creates benefits to others, not just to the person initiating the action. We argue that families and collectivities, such as communities and national governments, create social capital and that this social capital can greatly influence the amount of learning that takes place in schools. This new dimension turns out to be an important explainer of student achievement within and between countries.

We focus on three of the countries—Brazil, Chile, and Cuba—and, based on interviews with teachers and administrators in each country and visits to a large number of schools and several teacher-training institutions, we learn how these three national educational systems operate.

We analyze more than thirty third-grade math lesson videotapes we made in the three countries. This analysis of classroom teaching and content is extremely useful in explaining how national education goals end up being operationalized in the classroom, and to what degree this operationalizing reflects school system organization and how it may impact student learning.

These three levels of the study represent a new approach to understanding the school system as an institution—an approach that is necessarily international and comparative because it attempts to observe systemic institutional differences reflecting different national social environments.

Modeling Student Learning

Student learning is a complex process. We all know that an inspirational teacher can make learning almost anything interesting and fun. But even inspirational teachers cannot reach everyone, and certainly not everyone equally. Other, subtle factors influence students' ability and motivation to learn material that is not particularly interesting from teachers who are not, on average, particularly inspirational. As we have spelled out, social scientists model this process by trying to account for the many factors that can have a significant influence on how much students learn in school. Researchers try to design their models using data from surveys of students, their parents, their teachers, and the principals of their schools.

Most studies of student learning in school are based on data collected in one country or one state or even a single community. The main units of analysis are individual students, their classrooms, and their schools. Social context plays a role in some models, either by defining peer effects in the classroom and school (for example, Betts, Zau, and Rice, 2003), neighborhood effects (Jencks and Mayer, 1990), or group effects (student race/ethnicity) that are rooted in a theory of cultural differences specific to a particular society (see, for example, Ogbu, 1978; Ogbu and Gibson, 1991).

Our model—like most—starts with the premise that a student's family life influences his or her capacity to learn. James Coleman's notion was that families influence their children's learning through human capital (the amount of education parents have) *and* social capital (the amount of effort that parents put into their children's schooling) and that there are also family social capital influences from parents' interactions with neighbors and the community at large (through churchgoing, for example).

The model takes the possible influence of social capital a step further: We extend the notion of social capital to national government policies affecting children's broader social environment—what we call *state-generated social capital*. Thus, there are national social capital or "neighborhood" effects that include state interventions in children's welfare and a national focus on education that can raise educational expectations for all children, particularly the educationally disadvantaged. Governments can therefore generate a cohesive and supportive educational environment on a regional or national scale that creates learning benefits for all students.

Like other studies that focus on the social environment outside schools— whether in family or community—ours considers that social environment is important in shaping what schools and teachers do. There is a structural aspect to social context, in the sense that social and political institutions are powerful shapers of individual behavior and the way that individuals approach institutions, including schools.

Yet we also think that within social-structural contexts, there is considerable leeway to make organizational choices—indeed, choices are made all the time in implementing educational reforms—and these choices can have an important effect on student learning. The results of the academic achievement game are not totally fixed by students' out-of-school conditions. Thus, we still continue to search for answers to the puzzle of student learning by examining what schools do that may have a positive impact on student achievement. One place to search is at the country level: why does one country's educational system teach children to read or do math better than another country's educational system?

In our model, state-generated social capital, as we call it, is crucial to the way the school system is organized (through state regulation or the absence of state regulation). It is also important to the quality of the curriculum, to the opportunity for students to learn various elements of the curriculum, and to the distribution of students by class, race, ethnicity, and gender in schools. Other factors also influence these school structure variables, including students' family background and how well teachers are trained to teach mathematics and language. These factors are influenced by social context and, in turn, influence classroom teaching and teacher expectations.

At the same time, learning can also be greatly influenced by what happens in particular schools and classrooms somewhat independent of social context. In every country—even those with social conditions that are not amenable to student learning—there are those inspiring teachers we mentioned earlier. Every country, including those in which the government does little to help children do well in school, also has some well-run schools attended by mostly low-income students. So student academic success can take place in social contexts that would predict student failure, but such success stories are not usual, and they're not easy to find. The big question is whether effective classrooms and schools can be "scaled up" to make significant improvements in learning for the mass of students in a state or country even in a poor social environment.

Figure 1.1 represents a schematic of an education system. The end point, or outcome, of the flow chart is student learning, and all the other variously shaped boxes are factors that we expect to influence student outcomes. When the arrow points in one direction, it means that there is only a one-way relationship between factors—for example, human and social capital in the family affect children's student learning, but not vice versa. But human capital and social capital in the family both affect and are affected by state-generated social capital, including the amount of resource effort made by the public sector in financing public education. The arrow pointing in both directions represents that interaction between two factors. The center of the flow chart is the educational system, which is the institution we are par-

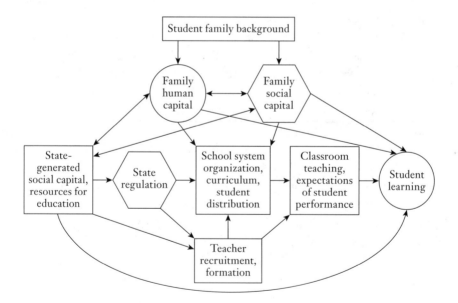

Figure 1.1   Proposed Relationships among Family Resources, Schooling, and Social Context

ticularly interested in. The educational system is represented in Figure 1.1 by two boxes, the organization of the school system and the educational process in the classroom.

Some of the relationships between factors influencing student outcomes are stronger than others, and the relationships vary from school system to school system and even among schools. For example, family background has a weaker relationship with school system organization and expectations of student performance in Cuba than in Brazil or Chile. State regulation is less connected to teacher recruitment and preparation in Brazil and Chile than in Cuba, and probably even less in Brazil than Chile because of more decentralized management of schools in Brazil. Our study is about understanding these differences and what factors seem to have the greatest influence on student learning.

The flow chart also serves as an outline in the chapters that follow for comparing Brazil's, Chile's, and Cuba's educational systems and the possible influences of family, societal organization, educational system organization, and classroom processes on student outcomes.

In the next chapter, we present a general overview of the social context of education in the three countries.

In Chapter 3, we make the case for the importance of the first box, state-generated social capital as expressed through state regulation—the favorable or unfavorable social context for educational achievement created by government social policies.

In Chapter 4, we estimate the relative strength of the relationship of state-driven social capital, school variables, and family background to student outcomes.

Chapter 5 compares educational system organization and teacher recruitment and formation in the three countries and their possible influence on classrooms.

In Chapter 6, we go into classrooms in Brazil, Chile, and Cuba to measure what happens there and how it might relate to school system organization and student outcomes.

Chapter 7 summarizes the lessons learned for educational improvement from our comparative analysis.

CHAPTER TWO

Three Educational Systems in Three Social Contexts

Let's begin our comparative analysis by setting out the *underlying conditions* of education in Brazil, Chile, and Cuba. There are significant differences in the social contexts of their educational systems, and these surely influence the way education is organized. The social contexts, we believe, may also be important in affecting what happens in classrooms. This may be particularly true for children whose parents are less educated, since the education of these children seems to be most affected by how communities are organized and by social policies.

At the same time, all three countries want to improve their educational systems. Brazilian and Chilean policy makers have especially voiced concern about the quality of schooling in their countries; this quality, based on test score results and even casual observation, is not as high as in Cuba. What changes could Brazil and Chile realistically make in the social context of schools and the organization of their educational systems to improve pupil achievement levels? To answer that question, we need to identify the main factors that appear to make academic performance higher in Cuba. Yet we also need to distinguish those that could be adapted to Brazil and Chile from those so embedded in Cuba's social and political system that they could not work in the other two countries unless the countries underwent radical social change.

Are there political and social spaces in the way the educational systems are organized in Brazil and Chile to admit factors that make the Cuban system more effective? Before we get into that, we need to provide some basic background on the three societies and the way they appear to be managing and changing their schools.

Brazil

Brazil is the largest country in Latin America, marked by enormous diversity of population, climate, per capita income, and levels of poverty. The population in the South is more of European origin, and parts of the Northeast are more Afro-Brazilian. The South is more industrialized, with the socioeconomic structure of, say, mid-twentieth-century Europe, and the North is still heavily agricultural, with tenaciously traditional social and political institutions. This is a simplified version of Brazil, as many Southerners migrated from the North, and southern megalopolises have huge pockets of marginalized poor, largely unincorporated into the industrial class structure. These structures are also inserted into a global economy and the information age, giving them a different aspect altogether. Urban slum dwellers, for example, are incorporated into an international drug trade and, through television, into the global media.

From 1964 to the early 1980s, Brazil had a repressive military government, which came to power through a coup d'état intended to "head off" a move to the left by the elected civilian president of the time. The military generally continued the "import substitution" national economic policy that dominated Latin American thinking during this period, but gave it a conservative and nationalistic slant. They supported the development of a local computer industry, small aircraft production, and other industries associated with "national security." And like most other Latin American governments, they borrowed heavily during the 1970s, spurred on by inflation-driven low real rates of interest, to finance this development. In-come distribution, already unequal in 1964, became even more unequal in the 1970s despite economic growth. When Paul Volcker, chair of the U.S. Federal Reserve Board, raised interest rates and the bubble burst in 1981, Brazil had the largest dollar debt in Latin America, plunging it into a steep recession and years of hyperinflation.

The military was forced to step aside in favor of a democratically elected government, but the enormous distance between rich and poor in Brazil was accentuated by lower growth rates and increased unemployment. In the late 1980s and in the 1990s, this situation improved somewhat with the rapid growth of the world economy and considerable debt forgiveness by U.S. and European banks and governments. However, at the same time, Brazilian governments had to dismantle their tariff walls and enter global competition, causing hardship in many industries. Those who were highly educated and fit into the new competitive information economy environment did well. So did workers in internationally competitive industries, of which there were many. The less educated and poor did not do particularly well, and unemployment declined slowly even in periods of rapid economic growth.

Besides having one of the most unequal income distributions in the world, Brazil also had, until very recently, one of the steepest education pyramids. In the early 1990s, about one of three young Brazilians finished basic education (eighth grade), less than one of four completed secondary education, and less than 8 percent graduated with a university degree. The military had expanded the university system in the late 1960s by allowing the formation of many new private institutions that charged tuition, unlike the free public universities. Entrance to public and elite private universities and to faculties of universities required an entrance test (the *vestibular*). Not surprisingly, wealthier and middle-class Brazilians sent their children to private primary and secondary schools to try to gain entrance to pres-tigious universities, mostly public and therefore free. Students with lower entrance test scores could enter the new private universities, paying tuition. Although private universities now receive government subsidies, this is still the prevailing system.

The Cardoso government (1994–2002) greatly expanded secondary edu-cation and implemented financial reforms (FUNDEF) that largely equalized educational spending among states and municipalities on basic education (K–8). By 1998, about 63 percent of entering students finished basic education, and almost one-half completed secondary education. These proportions have continued to grow. FUNDEF established a national yearly per pupil spending floor (beginning in 1998) of 315 reais (about U.S. $200 in 1998), sharply raising spending in poor states and municipalities in a country where spending per pupil varied from U.S. $30 in the poorest rural schools to U.S. $1000 in the wealthier states. The increased spending had a major effect on teachers' salaries in the poorest regions, as 60 percent of FUNDEF resources were earmarked for teacher salaries. Salaries in the Northeast's municipal school systems rose by almost 50 percent adjusted for inflation. Enrollment also increased in basic education in poorer regions as the student funding formula was based on student enrollment, therefore encouraging schools to recruit and retain students to fill places (World Bank, 2001).

Other new initiatives were launched to try to improve educational quality, such as providing federal money for approved school projects in low-income urban schools in poor states (*Fundescola*), subsidizing very low-income families if their children maintain high attendance rates at school (*Bolsa Escola*), and encouraging all uncertified teachers to become certified, with the goal that all basic education teachers should have a university degree by 2007.

Brazilian primary and secondary education is highly decentralized to the state and municipal levels. States and municipalities run separate school systems, in which they control resource allocation decisions and school management, although, in effect, schools and teachers have considerable autonomy in implementing educational decisions. The two public systems are parallel, compete for resources, and are uncoordinated. They also have separate administrations.

Some states and municipalities mandate parent-teacher councils, yet the practice of parent participation depends mainly on each school's teachers and administrators. Autonomy for public schools does not extend to choosing teachers. Teacher assignment to schools is reserved for state and municipal administrations. Teachers bargain collectively with each state or municipality, depending on the system in which they work. Despite the FUNDEF reform, states and municipalities still vary considerably in the resources per pupil they spend on education. State systems also tend to spend more than municipalities, particularly in the poorer regions. This large variation in per pupil spending distinguishes Brazil from the other two countries in our analysis.

An important reform of the Cardoso government was to implement a student evaluation system, based on biannual tests and questionnaires given to a nationally representative sample of fourth-grade, eighth-grade, and third-year secondary (eleventh-grade) students. This standardized student assessment system, known as SAEB, is not a census evaluation, as is the Chilean SIMCE exam, so it cannot be used to compare school-by-school results. But SAEB can allow results to be compared over time by region, by socioeconomic group, and between types of schools, and can show what factors contribute to higher scores (although not to test score *gains*).

Analysis of the SAEB suggests that regional inequalities in Brazil are important. Students in capital cities in poorer regions scored below rural students in some areas of the South (World Bank, 2001, p. 15). We also observe variation in student achievement *gains* from state to state even when differences in student socioeconomic background, average school socioeconomic background, and school resources are accounted for (Carnoy et al., 2006). For example, comparing schools in six low- and middle-income states, we found that basic education students in Pernambuco consistently make lower gains than students in other states. These regional differences are partly the result of an unequal distribution of teacher quality and equipment in the school that persists even after the FUNDEF reform. Analyses of SAEB and other data show that accounting for student SES, student performance increases with teachers' level of education and the availability of school equipment, and that average teachers' education and equipment is lower in poor northeastern regions than in the wealthier Southeast (World Bank, 2001, Table 2.3).

The decentralized system of education affects teacher qualifications and the quality of teacher education. The average level of primary school teacher education is much lower than in comparable Latin American countries, such as Argentina, Chile, and Mexico, especially in the first four grades (World Bank, 2001, Table 3.1). Eight percent of teachers in grades 1–4 in 2000 had completed primary schooling or less, and only 25 percent had a university education. Most (64 percent) were prepared in secondary level normal schools. Even in grades 5–8, in which a university degree in a discipline has been mandated for quite some time, 26 percent of teachers did not have tertiary education. But in the Northeast, only 11 percent of grade 1–4 and 53 percent of grade 5–8 teachers had tertiary education—much lower proportions than in the Southeast (World Bank, 2001, graphs 3.2 and 3.3).

Primary school teachers now teaching in schools have been educated in a variety of institutions, from *magisterio* courses (normal schools) at the secondary level to faculties of education in federal and state universities. The new law requires all primary school teachers to have university degrees by 2007, so normal schools will be phased out, and a teacher with a normal school degree or less will have to acquire a university degree—mainly through special courses being offered to help them upgrade. Many states and municipalities are contracting with universities to provide distance education for large groups of teachers.

Teacher preservice education is also in the process of reform, with a whole set of new institutions, *Institutos Superiores de Educaçao* (ISEs), proposed to train teachers more effectively and more efficiently than in the present system. There is wide agreement that Brazilian teachers are poorly prepared to teach—even those prepared in federal and state universities—and to the present, there is very little control over the quality of teacher education, even though most teachers are educated in public institutions.

The main reform of President Lula da Silva's government (2003–2006) in basic education has focused on equalizing access to schooling by expanding a program, *Bolsa Escola*, begun as a pilot in the Cardoso regime, that gives an income subsidy to the poorest Brazilian families to keep their children in school. Although *Bolsa Escola* has drawn a lot of attention (Mexico has now implemented a similar program), its effects on attendance appear to be small, and on achievement, negligible, according to a recent study in the state of Bahia (Gove, 2005).

Chile

As in Brazil (and Argentina and Uruguay), Chile's government was taken over by the military in a coup d'état, overthrowing an elected civilian government, in 1973. The Chilean military ruled for seventeen years, and as their "antidote" to the leftward shift in Chilean politics in the early 1970s, the military government implemented neoconservative economic and social policies in the context of a repressive, dictatorial political structure. Although Chile suffered through the recession of the 1980s with the rest of Latin America, its debt was much smaller and its growth rates were higher in the 1980s and 1990s than those of many other countries in the region. In many ways, Chile entered the global economy in the late 1970s, instituting International Monetary Fund policies and recommendations before the recession of the 1980s forced these on other countries.

Also like Brazil, the military fostered economic and social policies that increased income and social inequality. One difference is that high economic growth rates and lower population growth in Chile helped reduce poverty levels in the 1990s even in the context of unequal income distribution. And despite almost two decades of military rule, the sixty previous years of democratic governments—the most sustained democracy of any Latin American country—produced a well-developed civil society and relatively efficient civil government bureaucracy that survived the military dictatorship.

Chile's educational system developed in a unique way in this period. In the 1970s and 1980s, the military regime implemented an administrative reform that decentralized formal control of public services, including public education, to more than 300 municipalities. Until 1990, mayors of these municipalities were appointed by the military itself, so the degree of control the mayors had was questionable. But once democracy was restored, mayors were elected. So for the past decade, municipalities have had at least some power to allocate resources and to manage the schools in their jurisdiction. Furthermore, the military implemented a voucher plan in education that gave families the power to choose among privately run, publicly subsidized, or municipality-run schools for their children's education. Private voucher schools and municipalities received the same funding from the central government per student average daily attendance, creating an educational system in which public and private schools compete for students on essentially equal financial footing. Although private school operators complain that municipalities provide "extra" funding to their schools because many municipal school systems run deficits, the differences in per student costs in private subsidized and public schools are not great (McEwan and

Carnoy, 2000). Most of the higher municipal costs per student are the result of higher teacher salaries in public schools, granted largely because of these teachers' greater seniority.

The military also "decentralized" universities, breaking out campuses of the University of Chile into separate regional universities and essentially taking government out of the financing of higher education. All university students were charged tuition that covered more than 70 percent of actual university costs. Although most students continued to attend the major public former campuses of the University of Chile and the various partially subsidized Catholic private universities, the tuition policy led to the creation of many new private universities that received no government funding (Gove, 1997; OECD, 2004).

Rather than restructure financing, the democratic governments of the 1990s formally recognized the overall inequality in the "market system" inherited from the military and have attempted to correct it through compensatory funding of low-income primary schools, isolated rural schools, and more recently, low-income secondary schools. At the university level, the government also underwrites student loan programs based partly on need. Government efforts to move to full-day schools, to implement a more coherent national curriculum with free textbooks for all, and to implement a very extensive program of connecting schools to the Internet (Enlaces) are also heavily influenced by equity goals.

The democratic governments of the 1990s have used a system of educational evaluation based on national testing to pursue their reform goals. Chile has had educational testing since the 1960s, and the military government put in place the beginnings of a censal (all students in a grade) evaluation system with the Catholic University's PER test in 1982–1985. The PER test was supposed to provide information to parents about the "quality" of schools so that they could better choose among them. Thus, in the 1980s, the function of testing was to create better markets for education, to increase competition among schools, and to improve education through competition. There are serious questions about whether PER fulfilled those goals, and by the time its successor, the SIMCE test, came into being in 1988, the goals of the evaluation system were also changing. For example, a main use of SIMCE results from 1988 and 1990 was to identify low-scoring schools to make them eligible for compensatory funding in the

P-900 program. In addition, SIMCE results were released to schools but not directly to parents, and school test scores were not published. In the mid-1990s, the SIMCE also began to be used as a measure of whether the system as a whole was improving, and research using SIMCE data increasingly figured in the largely ideological conflict over whether the Chilean educational market system produced better results than a more traditional public school system. Indeed, most of the evidence suggested that the positive effects of competition were elusive and that despite widely accepted beliefs that private voucher schools were both more effective and more efficient than municipal schools, almost all the studies using SIMCE data suggest that differences are small at best.

More problematic for government policy makers is that average SIMCE scores at both the fourth and eighth grades have not increased significantly since 1996, when the tests were made comparable from year to year. These lackluster results continued with Chile's showing on both the Third International Mathematics and Science Survey (TIMSS) test in 1999 and the OECD's Program for International Student Assessment (PISA) test in 2003. The TIMSS tested samples of eighth-grade students in science and math in a number of developed and developing countries, and the PISA tested samples of fifteen-year-olds in reading, math, and science in OECD countries and non-OECD developing countries. Both assessments showed Chilean students' test scores to be little different from those of students in other large Latin American countries and far below the scores of students in developed countries. Such results have left the government open to considerable criticism. The criticism has come mainly from the conservative opposition, who argue that the fault lies in not allowing educational markets to function to their full extent.

Despite these problems, the educational "market system" inherited from the military has continued to influence Chilean educational policy throughout the 1990s—more than in any other Latin American country. Forty-seven percent of pupils attend private subsidized or private paid schools, and this proportion continues to grow (albeit slowly). Seventy percent of the cost of higher education is financed by private contributions from families. Universities have complete autonomy protected by constitutional law. Private primary and secondary schools also have almost complete autonomy, required—if subsidized—only to keep attendance and to implement the curriculum frameworks developed by the ministry of education. However, beyond this, subsidized private schools have, since 1993, been permitted to select their students (so can many municipal schools) and to charge tuition up to U.S. $150 per month without losing their state subsidy completely. The average tuition in subsidized schools is $13 per month, which is currently about one-third of the value of the monthly voucher amount the government pays schools for each student. Nationwide, these tuition contributions add up to U.S. $200 million per year—an amount large enough that whatever their concerns about the potential equity effects of making selection and tuition payments available to private schools in a system that is already inequitable, ministry officials are reluctant to give up this additional source of funds.

Thus, market thinking has been an important factor in Chilean educational policy making, even after 1990. Nevertheless, Chilean education policy in the past decade has focused mainly on changing the capacity of the system to produce more and better education (OECD, 2004). Secondary education enrollment more than doubled in twelve years, and the number of graduates more than quadrupled. Even if measured educational "quality" has not increased in fourth or eighth or tenth grade (these are the grades in which students are tested), the average level of education of young Chileans has increased substantially. Assuming that a student who graduates from secondary school would score higher on an achievement test in math and language than one who leaves school after only completing eighth or tenth grade, average achievement in the young labor force has increased substantially since 1990.

Yet a succession of governments has also maintained a policy of increasing capacity to produce higher-quality education to students in each grade of school. By correcting the abnormally low level of teacher salaries at the end of the 1980s—a result of several years of recession in the mid-1980s and a policy of letting teacher salaries decline through reducing the real value of the subsidy voucher—the democratic governments of the 1990s have been able to increase the "quality" of high school graduates entering teacher education faculties. By developing a new, more demanding curriculum for all grades, the ministry of education is providing a higher standard for schools to meet in what they teach pupils. By passing a law that all schools must move from a four- to a six-hour day by 2006, and supply the funds to build additional classrooms to meet this goal, the government has also created the capacity to provide more schooling to each pupil in a given day.

The one area that the ministry has not been able to touch effectively, however, is the quality of the initial training that student teachers receive in universities and their insertion into classrooms. A major gap appears to exist in this part of capacity building, and this gap seems to be having a major effect on the implementation of the curricular reform and the overall level of learning in many of Chile's classrooms. The quality of teacher education is currently one of the ministry's principal concerns.

Cuba

Cuba's revolution in the late 1950s led to the installation of a communist government with clear commitment to income equality and mass, high-quality education, universal adult literacy, and universal health care. The commitment to education and health care is consistent with policies in European and Asian countries that had or still have communist regimes (Carnoy and Samoff, 1989).

The Cuban government that emerged from the revolution was undemocratic and hierarchical—by the mid-1960s, Cuba had a one-party state committed to socialist development. In practice, this means that the Communist Party runs the economy and society, allocating resources and, through its economic policies, directly distributing income and other economic benefits, such as housing, food, and social services. Income distribution is highly equalized compared to other Latin American countries, and so are social services. The society is fairly regimented. Lack of housing and tight control over job allocation means little spatial mobility. Because Cuba only has about 10 million people, it is not difficult to keep tabs on all of them. Consumption per capita is low, but few Cubans are "in poverty," in the sense that they cannot get housing, food, health care, and education.

Until 1989 and the collapse of the Soviet Union, the Cuban economy was heavily subsidized by a favorable barter arrangement with the Soviets. The Soviets traded oil for Cuban sugar at an implicit price that was far better than Cubans could have gotten on world markets. As a result, as the rest of Latin America suffered in the recession of the 1980s, the Cuban economy enjoyed moderate growth and Cubans, a rising standard of living—this despite an embargo imposed on Cuba by the United States in the 1960s and carried on throughout the 1970s and 1980s. When the oil for sugar arrangement ended, the Cuban economy went into a deep dive. The 1990s were therefore an especially dark period for Cuba. Pressured economically by the embargo, its political allies in eastern Europe entering into global capitalism, Cuba's socialist project was on the rocks. Nevertheless, it was able to survive by attracting massive numbers of European and now U.S. tourists bucking the embargo. This brought needed hard currency but is necessarily changing Cuban society, creating a parallel dollar economy and a class of Cubans employed by the tourism sector.

From the earliest days of the Cuban revolution, educational decisions were highly centralized in a small group of core members of the new government. One of its first acts was to launch a massive literacy campaign that mobilized university students and was tied into the politics of incorporation, reaching out to the lowest-income and most marginalized groups in Cuban society (Fagan, 1969). In the 1960s and 1970s, a whole series of innovative reforms were tried, all characterized by top-down mobilizations implemented islandwide. "Schools to the countryside," "school in the countryside," the creation of elite secondary schools, curricular reforms, placing secondary school dropouts in the military, and, just recently, reducing class size to twenty in primary schools and fifteen in lower secondary schools— these were all changes decided at the very top of the Cuban political hierarchy and implemented in very short order throughout the country.

An important goal in the 1960s was universal access through lower secondary school. The school system expanded steadily until, by 1980, universal tenth-grade education had been reached (Carnoy and Werthein, 1980). A massive effort was made in the 1960s to *equalize* Cuban education in urban and rural areas and among urban neighborhoods. This has not been an easy task, and by the end of the 1960s it conflicted with the need to produce cadres of highly skilled professionals for the leadership of the Cuban economy and to staff government ministries, hospitals, universities, and research centers.

Yet raising the quality of Cuban education for students from rural and working-class urban neighborhoods has dominated Cuban educational reform since the early 1960s. The effort was aided by a policy that fixed incomes so that they varied little among professions and between workers and professionals. Teaching quickly became a highly desirable profession.

In a revolutionary society, education is a "frontline" activity and teaching in schools a prestigious occupation (Gasperini, 2000).

Special teacher-training schools were created in the first years after the new government took power in 1959. These schools focused on developing teachers to work in isolated rural areas under difficult conditions. In the 1960s, upper secondary teacher-training institutions were founded in each province to train primary school teachers, and postsecondary institutions to train secondary teachers. These institutions were controlled by the central government, and training was always closely tied to the national curriculum.

This drive for equality was also expressed in an ongoing ideological push to "unify" urban and rural populations. This was promoted by a campaign of "schools to the countryside," which brought urban lower secondary (seventh- through tenth-grade) and high school students to rural areas to cut sugarcane and do other agricultural work during school vacations. In the 1970s, this ideological push, combined with concerns about student performance in lower secondary schools, led to the development of boarding schools in rural areas called "schools in the countryside." Each of these schools had 500 students. Large numbers of urban lower secondary students attended these schools, although the government did not build all the 500 schools it had planned, mainly because they were more expensive than expected (Carnoy and Samoff, 1989). In the 1980s and 1990s, upper secondary enrollment expanded, and lower secondary school children were deemed too young to go off to boarding school. The schools in the countryside became upper secondary schools, yet only a fraction of all students attends these schools. The schools in the countryside had a positive effect on student achievement. By putting a significant number of students (about 125,000 in the early 1980s) into a boarding environment, where teachers had close control over student academic work round-the-clock, failure rates went down and grades went up.

Curriculum reform set high standards for student performance. The math curriculum was imported from the German Democratic Republic and translated into Spanish. This curriculum is still the basis for Cuban education today. It is demanding and provides a strong theoretical understanding of math concepts and operations.

The works of Russian educational philosophers, particularly Vygotsky and Makarenko, also have influenced Cuban education. That philosophy is child-centered, and for many years, included agricultural or other manual tasks even at the primary level. Today, the "work" part of the curriculum is reduced, but upper secondary students still do their twenty hours of manual work per week. It is telling that the elite secondary schools, restricted to the very best students in Cuba, are called "vocational schools." Because Cuban education is so child-centered, primary teachers generally stay with their pupils for the first four years of primary school, developing a long-term relationship in which teacher gets to know student very well.

A major recent reform is the extension of child-centered education up to lower secondary school (now seventh through ninth grades). Instead of facing eleven different teachers teaching eleven different subjects beginning in seventh grade, primary school graduates will now have one main teacher in lower secondary school teaching all subjects except English and physical education. Gradually, the entire lower secondary system will be converted over to this form of school organization. The idea behind this reform is that twelve-year-olds are too young to handle so many different teachers and subjects. By making lower secondary school more like primary school, the hope is that young people will have more guidance and supervision and will develop closer relationships with their middle school teacher and therefore learn more effectively.

In Cuba, there has been an absence of labor markets outside of government employment until recently, wages are set by government at very low levels, and the state provides Cubans with basic commodities (shelter, food, and basic human services) at very low prices. Thus, markets—to the extent that they exist—are highly restricted in Cuba. A teacher gets a very low salary, but in most of Cuba, alternative employment at higher wages is practically nonexistent. Individuals are allocated to occupations based on education, taste, and proficiency. Teaching is considered a relatively prestigious profession, and wages (about 300–450 pesos per month, or U.S. $13–18) are only somewhat lower than what physicians earn and about the same as in other professions.

Until recently, this wage structure has assured the Cuban government a steady supply of potentially talented teachers, attracted to teaching mainly on the basis of wanting to work with children and adolescents in a relatively prestigious job. Good secondary school students were likely to choose pedagogical universities for a teaching career as education for other professional jobs because wages were approximately the same. Because Cuban education has been functioning at a reasonably high standard since the 1970s, secondary school average students have received a relatively higher level of math, science, and language training, which they have brought with them into teacher education. By training these student-teachers in government-run pedagogical institutes to teach a well-designed national curriculum, the ministry of education could deliver reasonably "good" teachers trained to teach the required curriculum to every school in Cuba, even rural schools in provinces distant from the capital, Havana.

Now this situation has changed, particularly in two provinces, Havana and Mantanzas, the centers of the rapidly growing tourist industry. Tourists can only pay in U.S. dollars, and a parallel dollar economy has developed in the two provinces. Workers in hotels, transportation, and restaurants receive tips in dollars and can use these dollars to purchase goods not available to other Cubans in special foreign currency stores. A chambermaid in a hotel, for example, may earn $30–$50 in tips per month (or more), double or triple a teacher's salary. Ironically, the competition from tourist industry jobs has drawn off highly skilled labor from teaching, creating shortages in the teaching force.

The shortage is compounded by two major new reforms. The first is class-size reduction, from thirty-five to twenty in primary school (K–6) and from thirty-five to fifteen in lower secondary school (7–9). The second reform is the complete restructuring of lower secondary education from eleven courses taught by eleven specialized teachers taken by students each year to a primary school structure with a single teacher teaching all the core subjects, and specialized teachers only for English and physical education. Cuban decision makers have become convinced that to do well academically, twelve- to fourteen-year-olds need the continued close academic and developmental supervision that forms the basis of Cuban primary school education. This is in response to a sense that student academic growth has been less than optimal in lower secondary. Policy makers also have become convinced that smaller class sizes at both schooling levels will enable students to increase academic gains.

As in California in the late 1990s, when Governor Pete Wilson implemented a class-size reduction in the first four grades of elementary school, Cubans had to build a lot of new classrooms to accommodate this huge reduction in class size. Unlike California, the Cubans built these new classrooms, needed mainly in large cities, with a mass mobilization in less than six months *before* the beginning of the school year. We visited a number of schools in Havana with newly added classrooms.

The Cuban government also had to train thousands of new primary school teachers. Planners recruited bright upper secondary school students with the promise that they could receive a university degree in humanities while teaching in primary school. These recruits entered six- to eight-month teacher education courses, graduating as *emergentes*. *Emergentes* sign up for five years of teaching, taking courses for their university degrees on Saturdays and during the school vacations.

The conversion of lower secondary education into a "continuation" of the primary school model is also using *emergente* training. The prospective teachers receive a one-year teacher education course and are given close supervision by their teacher's college mentor once they are in the classroom. We visited with the first cohort of these lower secondary school *emergentes* at the Salvador Allende Teachers College in Havana. They were being trained by an experienced teacher educator from their province, Matanzas, who had a Ph.D. in science. Once graduated from their year of teacher education, the young teachers were to take over a seventh-grade cohort under the supervision of both their teacher educator and the administrators in the secondary school.

As many of the existing teachers in secondary schools, now teaching specialized courses, are also available to teach in the new structure, the teacher shortage is qualitatively different from that in primary school. The main problem is to convert specialized teachers into multicourse teachers and classroom mentors. A biology teacher, for example, will now have to teach math, language, and other sciences.

Whether this system will work (particularly in secondary school) is still to be seen. We observed *emergentes* teaching in every primary school we visited. Most had had six to eight months of training. All were closely monitored in their daily teaching by school administrators. Cuban pupils are also relatively disciplined to follow rules, to participate, and to respond to the teacher at many levels, making it much easier for young teachers to make rapid progress. Some *emergentes* were already in their second year of teaching, and the difference between first- and second-year *emergentes* was obvious. Thus, strictly supervised on-the-job training seemed to have an important effect. Even so, experienced teachers had much more "presence" in the classrooms we observed than did *emergentes*. Will a significant number stay in teaching after they finish their university degree in five years? Will they become highly productive in two or three years so that the system gets at least two years of high value added from them before many leave teaching?

Student testing in Cuba exists but differs markedly from that in Brazil or Chile. The difference is consistent with the differences in the sociopolitical organization of schooling in the three countries.[1] Cuban municipalities are responsible for testing sixth- and ninth-grade pupils to provide feedback to the ministry of education and to the schools on how well the system is doing. In this sense, the objective of testing is the same as in Brazil or Chile. However, in Cuba the government uses annual test results only for its own internal evaluation. Test results are not released to the public but rather are discussed within the government as the basis for organizational decision making—decisions that are acted on in a particular school or throughout the educational system. In Brazil and Chile, the test results generally serve a much more indirect form of government control. In Brazil, SAEB results function largely as the basis for charting the effectiveness of the overall system and for econometric analysis—a very loose form of accountability and state regulation. In Chile, test results also chart system progress and serve to identify schools that need government assistance. Increasingly, however, they are used as a measure of school output or "profit" in a large government enterprise—as information for parent "investors" to effect "better" choice and as information to government to reward teachers for higher "productivity." This is a more extensive form of regulation, which provides the most information to the public but does not necessarily translate into any meaningful change in the way education is delivered, as educational improvement necessarily depends on *voluntary response* to the information provided. In Cuba, test results can translate much more directly into action, but this action comes straight from the educational bureaucracy, not from parents, who have little school choice or voice. Interestingly, it is the hierarchical bureaucratic system that seems better able to translate the information into more effective education than systems relying on indirect market mechanisms.

Social Context and the Schools

Students everywhere bring their family's educational savvy (or ignorance) and the influence of their family relationships into schools. If children come from a highly educated, loving family that creates high expectations and a learning environment for their children, students' academic performance in school is likely to be higher. Teachers find such students to be "good learners," who do their homework and seem interested in doing well in school. Researchers tend to focus on these student family attributes, and with good reason. They are important. However, the community social environment in which schooling takes place may also be important for academic performance, especially for children living in family situations that are less than favorable.

The contrast between Cuba, Chile, and Brazil brings this influence into sharp relief. Brazilian and Chilean social structures are much more unequal economically and socially than Cuba's. This has important implications for schooling even if, in all three societies, education is viewed ideologically as the great social "equalizer," responsible for transforming class structure into meritocracy and binding pupils from different social classes to each other through the common experience of national education. In Cuba, this ideology is much closer to reality than in Chile or Brazil. The difference is especially evident in Brazil, where, even after a major financial reform in the 1990s, children in low-income regions go to schools with far fewer resources than are found in schools of more affluent areas. Access to schooling is also still more limited than in Chile or Cuba. Thus, for Brazilian education even to *represent* itself as playing an equalizing role, it has to get closer to Chilean educational reality, and Chile's educational reality continues to do an effective job of reproducing inequality when compared to Cuba's.

Cuban society is tightly controlled and regimented. Individual choices exist but are narrower than in Chile or Brazil. The issue of choice is complex, as children in poor families in Brazil and Chile may have more "choice" than rural or low-income urban children in Cuba, but many of those choices are not positive—to work at odd jobs or hang out rather than going to school, to engage in illegal activities, or to join a gang. Poor children in Brazil and Chile may have more choice, but they are also much more likely to be hungry and homeless and in poor health. Cuban children have few of these constraints and little access to the negative choices of drugs, gangs, child prostitution, and child labor. The state in Cuba provides a rigid structure for family and youth choices, much as organized religion does in orthodox religious families and communities. In the Cuban restricted choice model, educational "success" is part of that rigid structure: the state "requires" children to be as successful in school as their ability permits.

In Brazil and Chile, families have considerable educational choice, including whether to allow their children to be absent or not, and, if more than one school is in the vicinity, which school to attend. Schooling is compulsory, but compulsory attendance is enforced largely by school efforts to talk to parents and by state efforts to help students from low-income families with financial subsidization incentives (*Bolsa Escola* in Brazil and *Liceo para Todos* in Chile). In rural and marginal urban areas, school absences are common, both among students and teachers. Chile fully subsidizes private schools, so broad school choice is available beyond the public school system.

Allegedly, school choice creates competition among schools for students, so it creates incentives for schools, and, by implication, for teachers, to work harder for school "quality" to attract parents to their school. Indeed, Brazilian and Chilean parents living in larger urban areas have a choice among a variety of schools that are perceived to be of different "quality." The schools perceived to be of higher quality, in turn, also have choices among students—more apply than there are spaces in classes. Public schools in the two countries must accept students who live in their defined neighborhoods, but if this does not fill classrooms, they can accept students from outside. In Chile, many subsidized private schools locate where they perceive a demand for "better" education than provided by local public schools. Ironically, many of these private schools compete for students mainly on nonacademic grounds, such as greater "safety from the riff-raff" in public schools. Public schools compete back with symbols of modernity, such as increased numbers of computers in the schools.

We visited a public school in Campo Grande, Brazil, the capital of Mato Grosso Sul, near the Paraguayan border, that was considered a "good school." The principal had to turn away many applicants (she had a waiting list) because classes were filled to the legal limit (thirty-four students in each class). The school seemed to be better run than many we visited, but class sizes were also much larger, and the teaching seemed only slightly more consistent. Yet parents who had their children in this school were very satisfied because they had, in many instances, chosen it. Because it was considered a good school, they felt fortunate to live in the neighborhood or to have been accepted from outside the neighborhood.

In turn, school choice places much more responsibility on parents for making the right educational decision. This is especially true in an educational system such as Chile's, where private schools are part of the possibility set available to many families. If you don't like your local public school, send your child to the subsidized private school.

But beyond school choice, parents also have "voice" in Brazil and Chile. They are expected to participate—especially as a result of recent reforms in Brazil—in school councils, and, whether in council or not, to voice their opinions about school policies, teaching, and other educational matters. In other words, parents are supposed to be informed consumers of education and to put pressure on providers to deliver a quality product.

Given this philosophy of parent choice and responsibility, it is not surprising that there is much less "control" coming from the educational system or the larger state generally in Brazil and Chile than in Cuba regarding school success. If a child is not doing well in school in Brazil or Chile, this is treated in practice as a problem for which the *family* has the main responsibility. School personnel meet with the parents, trying to improve the situation, but parents sense no "sanction" other than pupil failure if it does not improve.

In Cuba, a school formally shares responsibility for a child's academic and social progress, and if the school cannot "solve" a problem, municipality personnel enter the discussion. Family difficulties are kept track of by teachers and school administrators, and families must respond to school queries and concerns. The fact that a child has a single teacher from first to fourth grade (which will now be extended to sixth grade) and that the child is in school from eight in the morning until four in the afternoon with that teacher, creates a quasi-parent relationship with the child. Thus, in all three countries, schools have authority over a child's academic progress (and to some degree social development), and parents have control over the bulk of a child's social development and a significant responsibility to support academic development. However, in Cuba, the balance in both areas is definitely greater in favor of the school (as a state institution)—the default mode for defining a child's welfare is state responsibility, whereas in Brazil and Chile, the default mode is family responsibility.

There is yet another side effect of greater choice in Brazil and Chile. As in other capitalist societies, many parents—especially low-income parents—live a relatively precarious economic existence that compels them to change residence in their search for work. Turnover in Brazilian and Chilean schools varies from school to school but is significant, just as in urban schools in the United States. Changing schools for low-income youth has a negative effect on learning, for many reasons (see Coleman, 1988). In Cuba, lack of housing and tight government controls over labor, including changing jobs, practically assure that pupils will stay in the same primary school, then middle school, then high school for all the required years.

We don't want to leave the impression that Brazil and Chile are pure laissez-faire societies when it comes to children's welfare. This is clearly not so. Both Brazil and Chile have had center-left governments in the 1990s, and now Brazil has a president from the Workers' Party, a party with a distinct Leftist philosophy that believes in strong state intervention. These governments have implemented a number of measures to help schools with lower-income students improve their conditions. Brazil has reformed its basic education financing system (FUNDEF) in favor of providing more resources to poor regions; it is also using federal money (*Fundescola*) for school improvement projects in low-income urban schools and provides funds for low-income families to induce them to assure their children's high attendance rates (*Bolsa Escola*). Beginning in the early 1990s, Chile began investing heavily in low-performing schools, having some success in raising academic achievement among low-income students. In the past thirteen years, teacher salaries have tripled, and public spending on education as a percentage of gross domestic product has almost doubled, from 2.4 percent to 4.1 percent. The government is implementing a full-day school reform, extending the school day from four to six hours. With the great expansion of secondary enrollment, compensatory programs have moved up to that level, including a scholarship program for low-income students to help them complete secondary school (*Liceo para Todos*). All these state efforts benefit mainly low-income students.

Chile has also begun to expand its early childhood education to provide preschool for two- to four-year-olds. Although there is mixed evidence internationally on the effect of preschool on children's academic performance in school,[2] there is a sense that children who attend preschool are better socialized to respond to teachers in schools, and that low-income children can get—in high-quality preschools—an enriched academic environment that can help promote their literacy and numeracy once they enter school. Some states and municipalities in Brazil have also started preschool programs, but they are few and far between.

Nevertheless, Brazilian and Chilean state guidance of children's lives is far less than in Cuba. For example, all women in Cuba who work have access to child care and preschool programs for very young children (prekindergarten). The other 60-plus percent of families (in which women with young children are not working) receive instruction from municipal workers on how to provide an enriched environment for children at home in order to promote child cognitive development.

The role of government in Cuba implies a power relationship between individual and state inconsistent with modern notions of democracy and freedom. Yet ironically, in terms of assuring the best opportunity for children to succeed in school, a social context that provides a "moral imperative" for educational success and tight control over family choices is, in this case, much more geared to override social class–based family and youth decisions that reproduce inequality and are inimical to a meritocratic society. The Cuban state is hierarchical and undemocratic and clearly restricts individual freedom. But a Cuban child from a rural or low-income urban family background is much more likely to be successful in school and to have access to a white-collar job than the same child in Brazil or Chile. Perhaps more important, a child in Cuba from a low-income background is assured of a childhood free from fear of hunger, lack of shelter, or isolation.

This moral imperative is akin to the moral structure imposed on families and communities by religious fundamentalism. Religious rules and regulations consciously and specifically restrict individual choices but are consistent with Western notions of political democracy because adhering to religious rules is voluntary, even though community pressures for conforming may be intense. Similarly, in Western democracies, the military is organized hierarchically, consciously limiting choice, and, to a large extent, enforcing its rules outside the state's justice system. It is no accident that schools run by religious orders are associated with greater moral discipline and that families expect such schools to exercise strict control over children's choices. Although children in private religious schools in Chile score higher on tests than children from similar socioeconomic backgrounds in public schools, at least part (if not all) of this difference is due to selection bias. Results in the United States also suggest little if no difference in test scores between students in private and public schools once socioeconomic background differences among students are accounted for. But educational attainment tends to be higher for students in Catholic schools, at least in the United States. Schools on military bases in the United States are much more academically successful with children from disadvantaged minority families than public and private schools on the outside (Smrekar et al., 2001),[3] suggesting that an environment that is much more structured and controlled, with sanctions for parents as well as children, plus a social support system and good health care, has a positive effect on the educational achievement and attainment of children from less-educated families.

The structure of the social environment also differentiates the way schools operate in the three countries. In Chile, the ministry of education develops the national curriculum required in all schools, public and private, that accept government financing. However, the ministry uses only indirect means to enforce the implementation of its curriculum. These indirect means consist of testing students every two years in the fourth, eighth, and tenth grades, publishing the results for each school, and monetarily rewarding the 25 percent of schools (primarily their teachers) that make the largest gains in each region. Principals of schools have the autonomy to take steps to improve their students' performance. Public school principals do not hire and fire teachers (municipalities do that), and public school teachers have tenure contracts, but private school operators (46 percent of students attend private schools) have essentially full power to make staff decisions from year to year. For other matters besides curriculum and teacher hiring and firing, public school principals also have considerable leeway to experiment, mobilize other resources, and be resourceful. On the whole, then, besides being required to teach the subject elements defined by the national curriculum, principals have a great deal of autonomy and decision-making power in Chile.

Whether they know how or choose to use this power to improve instruction is another matter, however. In both public and private schools in Chile, teachers have considerable autonomy in the classroom. Private school teachers can be fired for doing a bad job, but the principal of the school does not necessarily intervene to help them do a better job. There is little culture of the principal as instructional leader, and there is a strong culture of classrooms as teachers' sanctuaries.

In Brazil, the situation is similar to Chile's except that the central government only provides curricular frameworks and approved textbooks. States and municipalities choose the curriculum they will use in locally run schools. As in Chile, school administrators have considerable autonomy in how they run the school, but teachers in public schools are hired and fired by state and municipal governments, not school administrations. The trend in Brazil is to put more emphasis on parent participation in the school (a consumer cooperative model of decision making), on the theory that parents will exert pressure on teachers to exert more effort. Because most parents have little information about how to measure teacher or school quality and do not have the opportunity to observe teachers teaching, parent participation, not surprisingly, has had little effect on instruction or administration.

Chilean and Brazilian education is also marked by large variance in the average social class of students *among schools*—this means that children go to school with children a lot like them socially. With a high degree of choice superimposed on residential segregation, Chilean and Brazilian families tend to sort their children among schools according to socioeconomic background. Seventy percent of families in the bottom two deciles of income earners in Chile, for example, send their children to schools whose students' parents fall into the bottom two deciles of Chilean income earners. More than 80 percent of families in the top two deciles of income send their children to schools whose students come from families with similar incomes (Gonzalez, 2001). Concentrating students of similar socioeconomic background in the same schools segments schools along class lines—this in societies with great inequalities among social classes. The result is highly differentiated schools, with highly differentiated expectations.

In Cuba, schools are also characterized by different social class composi-tions of their students, but much less so than in Chile or Brazil. Some urban schools, such as those in Havana, have high proportions of children from families in which both parents have higher education, but even schools in the outskirts of Havana or in the city center, with a much higher percent-age of working-class Cubans with less education, also have a significant percentage of children with university-educated parents. Rural schools in Cuba can be small and simple. Rural children's parents are less educated. But socioeconomic conditions in rural areas in Cuba are better, on average, than in Brazil or Chile, and rural schools in Cuba have teachers teaching to the same high level as those in the "better" neighborhoods in Havana. To sum up, social distances are much smaller in Cuba, and the schools that cater to students in better urban neighborhoods and those in rural areas certainly have different clientele, but the schools in those different social situations are also less different than similar schools in Brazil or Chile.

The Democratic Dilemma

The contrast in social contexts between Brazil and Chile on the one hand, and Cuba, on the other, points to the advantages teachers and schools have in a social-structural context that enforces a moral imperative protecting children against the excesses of economic inequality and the possibility of negative choices. Cuban families and children are assured a degree of social safety that is far greater than in either Brazil or Cuba, and this is reflected in the way children behave in school, their overall health, their incorporation of high academic expectations, and their desire to succeed academically. Because the Cuban state combines this enforced "child protection" with a sustained emphasis on educational quality and high academic achievement, Cuban children from less-educated families have much greater opportu-nity to succeed academically than their counterparts in Brazil or Chile. Cubans have far fewer social and economic choices and far less political and individual freedom, but they have a far more broad-based opportunity to be highly educated. In Cuban political interpretation, this right to health, security, and knowledge represents what they would call the "true" definition of human freedom.

The Cuban example makes a strong case for a tightly controlled society with limited choices—particularly to protect the interests of children. A surprising number of Chileans—most from the higher social strata, but many from the lower middle class—agree with this notion of limited choices. Many still strongly support the idea that a military government was necessary to correct the democratic excesses of the late 1960s and early 1970s. Indeed, all democratic societies are marked by a tension between movements for greater individual rights and strict social control. However, the degree of political control inherent in the Cuban state over the past forty-five years (plus the almost twenty years of Batista dictatorship before that) is far beyond anything but the more extreme visions of social control (generally coming from a quasi-religious/moralistic version of the state) currently appearing in democratic country political debates.

The counterargument for individual freedom is that despite the high costs at the lower end of the socioeconomic spectrum, a democratic society, relatively free of strictly enforced moral imperatives, whether by organized religion or the state (or a combination of the two), allows for the free expression and creativity necessary for human progress. It is only when individuals are free to pursue their passions and interests, unfettered by the state, that the welfare of society as a whole is maximized.[4] The price of such freedom may be considerable inequality, poverty, and suffering for some, but in the longer run, everyone, including the poor, will end up better off. Empirically, the economic advances made in the Western capitalist democracies sustain this argument, and these are held up to the rest of the world as examples of what can be achieved in free societies. Yet many of these free societies have been marked by considerable state regulation and major swings over the past century in the degree of political freedom accorded citizens.

The relevant question raised by the Cuban system is not whether Brazil and Chile should opt for a one-party or authoritarian state. Rather, it is how countries such as Brazil and Chile can approach the degree of social safety, moral imperative, and educational quality control achieved by Cuba, and do so within the context of political democracy. Are increased school choice, market incentives, and parent participation the best instruments available in Brazil and Chile for improving educational quality? Are greater decentralization and school autonomy effective ways to raise educational quality? Or do these instruments simply reflect a misdirected flight *away* from increased public responsibility for children's welfare and academic improvement?

We can make this point another way. Since the early philosophical discussions of capitalism, the "free market," defined as the epitome of free human expression, has framed the debate over what can and should be done within the context of political democracy. When the Chilean military overturned Chilean political democracy to install a dictatorship, they pushed laissez-faire economic policy. Many in Chile, as well as free-market advocates in the United States, argued that this was tantamount to reestablishing a truly "free" society because economic freedom (read unregulated free markets) is the highest form of human liberty. Thus, movement toward educational choice, parent control of schools, decentralization, and privatization are consistent with this version of democratic ideals—the less state intervention, the better.

However, there are strong indications that unregulated markets and a marketized education system may be inconsistent with the greatest good for the greatest number and, in terms of achieving human progress, human happiness, and, more modestly, increasing student learning in schools may be plain inefficient as well as inequitable.

In the chapters that follow, we try to take a close look at why Cuban children seem to be learning so much more in school than Brazilian and Chilean children and to understand what can be transferred from the Cuban experience to other, very different, political contexts. The comparison among the three systems suggests that there is no *single* factor explaining higher achievement in Cuba. Rather, it is a series of interacting factors building on each other that produces this difference. The issue before us is whether these differences are embedded in the social fabric of societies, or whether factors contributing to higher-quality schooling and therefore higher student achievement are transportable across social contexts.

CHAPTER THREE

Understanding Why School Achievement Varies

Over the past thirty years, when researchers and educators visited class-rooms in Cuba and in other countries, Cuban pupils in every grade seemed to know much more math and seemed to read better. In the late 1990s, an international organization, UNESCO, tested pupils in thirteen Latin American countries. What researchers and educators had believed for years about Cubans was confirmed.

Yet, once having established that high Cuban test scores accord with casual observations, how do we explain *why* Cuban pupils do better aca-demically? Is it because the teachers are more skilled? Are the Cuban pupils' parents a lot more educated, so that the children have a "family advantage" over children in countries where education levels are lower? Is the social environment in Cuba such that children are more motivated to do better in school?

To get answers to these questions, social scientists like to use empirical techniques to relate student learning to family background and the quality of educational resources available to students in the schools they attend. In lower-income, developing countries, we generally measure educational resources by teachers' education and years of classroom experience, the number of students in a classroom (class size), the availability of textbooks for the students, and the availability of supplies for teachers. The idea behind estimating such relationships is that schools, like businesses producing other kinds of services, have a theory of how to produce the most output for the lowest cost. That suggests that schools have a clear idea of how to use the best combination of resources—teacher skills, books, supplies, and so on—to produce the most learning possible for children with different amounts of resources at home.[1] Social scientists usually measure students' learning by achievement test scores, and they try to determine the most effective combinations of resources used by schools through simplified models of school "production."

Many educators criticize this approach to understanding why students achieve better or worse as too broad and overly simplistic. They claim that the variables and the way they are measured are not able to capture what actually goes on in the classroom or the school. Also, test scores may measure only part of student learning.

The critique is well founded. For example, the models social scientists use are not really based on any theory of learning.[2] The scientists assume that if you combine some family characteristics with some teacher characteristics, other classroom inputs, and some school characteristics, they can identify what contributes to student learning and what does not. This implies, for example, that learning occurs just because certain teacher characteristics are present, rather than as a result of a "chemistry" that occurs between teacher and students.

Another sound basis for the critique is that the models are based on an economic theory of organization that assumes schools operate like profit-maximizing firms. Schools are assumed to produce the most output possible using an efficient combination of inputs. Thus, school decision makers are assumed to be buying teacher time, teachers' aides' time, books, supplies, building space, and other inputs at competitive prices in a way that produces the maximum amount of student learning. Whereas school decision makers somewhere in the system do, indeed, hire teachers and buy supplies, it is difficult for them (and for social scientists) to identify the attributes of teachers, other personnel, or school supplies that are consistently related to higher productivity. It is just as difficult (or more difficult) to identify the combination of personnel that is consistently related to a more efficient school.

Recent studies show that good teaching can make a large difference in student achievement, but they cannot pinpoint the particular elements (teacher experience, preschool training, or inservice training) that make for a good teacher. Good teachers just seem to be good teachers. Allegedly, everyone knows who these good teachers are once they have been teaching in a school for a few years, but it seems to be much more difficult to figure out who the good teachers will be before they are hired. Similarly, it is hard to put a finger on why some schools seem to function so well and others, with a similar group of teachers, so poorly. The effective schools analysis, like much of the analysis of effective businesses, generally credits good leadership as the key ingredient in a well-functioning school or business but has a difficult time identifying the precise, reproducible traits of a good leader.

We don't know the answers to these puzzles either. But in Chapter 5 we try to identify some major differences in the ways that educational systems operate in Brazil, Chile, and Cuba. It turns out that there is almost no teacher supervision by school managers (or anyone else) in Chile and Brazil (or in the United States, for that matter), and that teachers operate largely on their own in deciding how to teach the curriculum to their pupils. This gives very good teachers the autonomy to innovate and take responsibility for learning in their classrooms, but it also allows the mass of average and poor teachers just to keep teaching from barely adequately to fairly ineffectively.

The lack of supervision may be a compromise between authorities and teachers in countries where teachers are paid less than other college-trained professionals: teachers agree to teach and get paid low/middle wages but in return, administrators agree to give them the freedom to work on their own, not hassling them with close supervision and high expectations. Thus, autonomy may not be based on any theory of effective teaching but could rather be a consequence of the unwillingness of many governments to pay high enough wages to make greater demands.

Social scientists' estimates of school production models are beset with other problems. One is that students from families with more academic resources at home usually choose to go to schools that also have more academic resources. "Better" teachers usually end up in schools with better performing students. As a result of all these difficulties, this broad approach usually captures only a small part of the variance in student performance even within countries, and many of the "explanations" of student performance are biased because they cannot separate unobserved student academic abilities from contributions to achievement of particular school inputs.

A second problem with these estimates is that schools do much more than focus their efforts on students' academic achievement. Schools and parents are concerned that children learn in school good behavior toward other children and toward adults who are not their parents. For many teachers and parents this is almost as important as becoming good at math and reading, and parents often choose schools because they feel that their children will more likely be safe there or learn proper values, not because of academic excellence. Good behavior and higher test scores may be related, so the two outputs are not necessarily competitive, but they may be. Measuring the values that children acquire in school is difficult, so social scientists rarely even try. Yet leaving this school objective out of the equation misses a lot of what schools are about, including the reasons for hiring certain kinds of teachers rather than others. Ignoring one important output could also seriously bias estimates of how schools produce academic achievement.

The third problem is that school production models have not included factors outside the home and the school that influence student achievement. These outside factors include community resources and public support systems for children. They may be as or more important than parent characteristics or school resources in affecting how much young people are motivated to do well academically. Such "social context" factors have been characterized as "peer effects," or the influence that the collection of students in a school have on each other. Yet students' attitude toward school represent family and community values in the school setting. Peer effects can also occur at a regional or national level if national governments successfully promote certain values about academic achievement and social mobility that motivate a high fraction of students to want to do well in school.

Despite these flaws, if the models are formulated and estimated carefully, even those that use only test scores as the main school outcome and use family and school inputs as the only factors influencing it can give us important clues as to why some groups of students do better in school. For example, students coming to school from families with a lot of academic resources clearly have an advantage over students who have spent the first five or six years of their life in an environment low on cultural capital. One of the main issues in education is whether even "good" schools can overcome this initial gap. Using a broad approach, social scientists have helped us understand the possibilities and limits of schools in closing the learning gap of socioeconomically disadvantaged children (Rothstein, 2004). Many of the results are controversial, but they serve as a basis for discussing important educational issues.

How would we formulate a model to begin to understand the sources of Cuban students' academic advantage? We can look in three main directions: differences in students' families, especially their parents' education and the emphasis in the home on children's academic success; differences in the quantity and quality of academic resources in their school; and differences in the pupil's social environment outside of school.

Resources from students' individual families explain much of the variation in academic performance in both developed and developing countries (Coleman et al., 1966; Lockheed and Verspoor, 1991; OECD, 2003; Rothstein, 2004). Thus, one possibility is that Cuba's children today benefit from two generations of sustained government investment in education. Today, Cuban parents have higher levels of schooling than parents in the rest of Latin America. Beyond the additional human capital that more educated Cuban parents bring to their children's school performance, Cuban families may also be more willing to put more effort into their children's academic achievement, may expect their children to be more "academic" and go further in school, and may move (and change their children's schools) less often than families in other countries. As we discussed in Chapter 1, this family-supportive behavior has been called family "social capital" (Coleman, 1988).

Cubans may have an advantage in school quality, especially teacher quality, which may boost students' academic performance. Cuban schools may be more effective because they are able to recruit better-educated and more able teachers, again because the level of education is higher in Cuba than elsewhere. Its teachers earn wages that, while low in absolute terms, are similar to those of other professions in Cuba, and so recruiting the best and the brightest into teaching is easier than in countries with lower relative wages for teaching. Because Cuban teachers have higher relative social status, teacher (and student) absenteeism may be lower in Cuba than elsewhere in Latin America, giving Cuban children more class time with teachers. Cuban classrooms may also have better physical classroom conditions and more school materials than elsewhere.

It is possible that Cuban children excel because the social context of their schools is more favorable to academic performance than is the case in other Latin American countries. In part, a school's social context represents the aggregate of its students' family characteristics (socioeconomic, or SES,[3] differences), as measured by parents' education, occupation, and income. However, such family differences could have different effects on children's education depending on the "collective meaning" of socioeconomic differences at the level of community, region, or nation. The collective meaning of SES can be strongly influenced by the way individuals and families are organized socially and politically—particularly in the collective commitment to reduce (through the state) the most pernicious effects of socioeconomic differences. Following Coleman's and Robert Putnam's ideas about social networking, we characterize this as "collective social capital." In many contexts, low family SES is associated with greater violence, less access to early childhood education, poorer nutrition, and poorer health care (Brown et al., 2003). Students from low-SES families often face pressure to work outside the home after school (Post, 2002). They may attend schools in which lower-SES students have been concentrated. Lacking sufficiently large groups of peers and parents with higher academic and social aspirations, students and their teachers in such schools are more likely to reinforce the low academic expectations that society assigns to low-income youths (Sennett and Cobb, 1973; Willis, 1981). By contrast, the effect of school-level socioeconomic background on student achievement could be very different in Cuba because its low-income, less-educated families face conditions that are less hostile to children's academic success. Cuban children may benefit not only from more educated parents and better-educated teachers but may also attend school in a social environment that promotes higher academic achievement by middle- and lower-socioeconomic-class children.[4]

In the rest of this chapter, we focus on this third factor—the social capital aspects of schooling. Social capital—especially as it pertains to broader community values, networks, and social controls—has been a blind spot for researchers in understanding student learning. In inter-country, inter-regional, or even inter-community comparisons, family social capital and collective social capital (i.e., the social environment of schools) are probably crucial to understanding student academic achievement differences, especially when contexts vary greatly. Cuba is distinctive in its social organization and, by implication, in the social context of schooling. So before going on, in the next chapter, to estimate the influence of social context on student achievement and to distinguish this influence from the effects of students' family background characteristics and school resources, we need to get a better handle on what it is about social context, or social capital, that makes it so important to academic achievement.

Context Makes a Difference: The Role of Social Capital

Sociologist James Coleman defined social capital as "not a single entity but a variety of different entities, with two elements in common: they all consist of some aspect of social structures, and they facilitate certain actions of actors—whether persons or corporate actors—within the structure. . . . [S]ocial capital inheres in the structure of relations between and among actors. It is not lodged either in the actors themselves or in the physical implements of production" (Coleman, 1988, p. S98). Thus, relationships and networks that enhance individuals' productivity or academic achievement (that in turn enhances productivity) are defined as social capital. Applying this concept to the creation of human capital in the next generation, Coleman argued that a student's family background is "analytically separable into at least three different components: financial capital, human capital, and social capital," with social capital being the "relations between children and parents (and when families include other members, relationships with them as well)" (Coleman, 1988, p. S110). According to Coleman, even if a family has a high level of human capital (parents' education), the child may not get its full benefits if it is not complemented by the family's time and effort to increase children's school achievement and attainment, part of family social capital.

Coleman also discussed social capital outside the family, namely, in the social relations that parents have with other adults in the community and in the relations they have with social institutions.[5] For example, voluntary associations of parents generate social capital by helping to solve community social problems, creating trust, and developing and enforcing social norms for adults and children (see Putnam, 1993, 2000). This gives social capital its character of a public good. Coleman does not discuss peer effects directly, but peer relations also constitute social capital (with both positive and negative implications for academic achievement and attainment). Within neighborhoods, regions, and even countries, the networks and information channels of social organization may contribute to greater collective productivity in a range of activities. These factors include smoothly functioning and equitable legal systems, trust, "intergenerational closure," social norms, and civic cooperation.

The contribution of social capital goes beyond the predictions of individual and family human capital characteristics. Coleman uses the concept of social capital to describe relations in the family and among adults in the community as an important factor explaining educational outcomes. We could extend this concept to include state-generated social capital that influences educational production. State social capital offers a conceptual tool that goes beyond comparing families and communities within countries to comparing political and social contexts across countries. If nation-states can themselves generate social capital, then we would expect to find benefits to lower-SES children who attend schools in those neighborhoods, regions, and even countries that have more socially integrated, safer, cooperative, and coherent social climates, as compared with lower-SES children who attend equally academically resourced schools in less favorable social contexts.

Some of the social capital discussion emphasizes individual or family behavior that produces more favorable social results for family members. Some focus on cooperative institutions in democratic states where individuals *voluntarily* adhere to organizations that promote networks of (democratic) institutions. These networks create better economic and social outcomes for members of those societies in addition to what they produce as individuals (Putnam, 1993, 2000).

States themselves, whether democratic or authoritarian, also help to create social capital. Authoritarian states face difficulties in doing so but can be successful in societies more likely to tolerate authoritarian governance, as long as they deliver improved material and social conditions. Korea, Taiwan, and Singapore, for example, have been governed by authoritarian regimes committed to broad collective improvement. Their policies helped create a social context for high economic growth, high academic achievement, and considerable social mobility (Amsden, 1989; Amsden and Chu, 2003; Evans, 1995).[6]

Authoritarian regimes in socialist countries also have tried to produce social capital. The states of revolutionary Russia, China, Vietnam, and Cuba attempted to generate new social and political structures through collectivizing wealth. These socialist states called on the suppression of individuality for the greater social good, defined by freedom from capitalist exploitation, increases in production, and improved social services (Fagen, 1969; Skocpol, 1979). Socialist states have not been as successful as capitalist societies in linking social capital to individual and collective economic productivity. Contrary to Marxian theory, state socialism is not as good at capitalist accumulation as market capitalism despite a social ideology of individual sacrifice for collective output. China and Vietnam have recently achieved high rates of economic growth, but largely by allowing capitalist markets and relations of production to emerge alongside state enterprises. Socialist values are either not as complementary as individual competition to higher individual productivity, or state-run production is so inefficient that even the presence of socialist values cannot overcome those inefficiencies.

Despite these shortcomings, socialist states have been more successful than capitalist states in developing high-quality mass education, generalized health care, and other social services (Carnoy and Samoff, 1989). Basic and secondary education in these authoritarian socialist states is of high quality because they invested heavily in schooling and because of other social capital generated by the socialist state. The state puts great emphasis on equality and the reduction of social-class differentiation. It aims to insure the health and safety of children and to eliminate child labor. Consequently, families trust in the state's ability to produce high-quality education for all. This, in turn, leads to the development of a youth culture and social norms wherein even lower SES groups value academic success. Socialism complements the delivery of mass education and other social services better than the individuality and individual competition extolled by democratic capitalist societies (Carnoy and Samoff, 1989). At the same time, an authoritarian state committed to high-quality education can enforce the contextual conditions to produce it rather than relying on family-generated social capital or the indirect regulation of individuals' choices.[7]

Earlier, we discussed how Cuba is formally organized around restricted choices, whereas in the rest of Latin America, society is defined as "free and democratic." The Latin American democratic capitalist countries theoretically allow all families a range of choices. These choices include deciding where to work, where to send children to school, and, in many low-income regions, even *whether* to send children to school. Families in Latin America outside Cuba also have more "choice" of where to live and are much more likely to change residences than Cuban families, whose residential movement is restricted. But this means that Cuban children are much more likely to stay in the same school.[8] The state in Cuba constructs a social context for education that supports student success. This is especially the case for the lower-social-class students and their families. In other countries these families might make "choices" detrimental to high academic achievement.

Teachers and administrators in other countries also have greater "choices" than in Cuba, where school personnel are much more closely supervised than elsewhere in Latin America. Teachers have more autonomy in their classrooms to vary their teaching styles and to cover the prescribed curriculum—or not—in other Latin American countries. Although we do not have measures of teacher absenteeism in the countries we cover in this study, from our observations in three of them—Brazil, Chile, and Cuba (and empirical studies in others)—the existence of significant amounts of teacher absenteeism, especially in rural areas, greatly reduces actual class time in most Latin American countries but is not a factor in Cuba (Alcazar et al., 2004; Marshall, 2003; Rogers et al., 2004).

Measuring the impact of either family or collective social capital on student outcomes is not simple. Social capital as it relates to schools is usually discussed in terms of networks among students or among the parents of students who go to the school. Coleman uses indicators of family relations with community (e.g., number of times the family has moved and whether they are churchgoing) to gauge the effect of social capital on the risk of dropping out of high school. Another, more indirect, measure of family social capital effects is the degree of variation of average family SES across neighborhoods and schools and the concentration of academically low- and high-performing students in particular classrooms or schools. This is usually called a "peer effect," which has elements of social capital. It could also be the effect of parent networks (or the lack of parent networks) when highly or less-educated parents are concentrated in different schools (see, for example, Betts et al., 2003; Willms, 1989). More highly educated parents with more income are more likely to be active in their children's schools, in part because they may have more time, and in part because they feel more competent to engage in school-related activities (Benveniste, Carnoy, and Rothstein, 2002). This observation implies that schools with higher-social-class students have higher social capital as well as higher human capital, as the parents in those schools form networks and benefit all students in the school, not just their own.

Our challenge is to go beyond the effect of family social capital to estimate the effects of state-generated social capital. We believe that state-generated social capital in its various forms has a major impact on classroom atmosphere (student behavior) and thus affects the time that teachers spend teaching cognitive skills. It may also shape school organization and strongly influence the management role of school directors, the control that authorities have over teacher and student attendance (Marshall, 2003), the expectations that parents have of teachers (and teachers of parents) in the complex process of educating children, the sense of responsibility and obligation that teachers and school directors feel for improving student learning, and the focus of the school on instruction, especially in low-income schools.

Later in the book, we compare the overall management of Brazilian, Chilean, and Cuban educational systems. We also measure differences in what and how teachers teach in the three countries. But before going into greater detail on what happens in school systems, schools, and classrooms, we will take a look at the big picture as presented by these oversimplified models of how schools produce achievement.

CHAPTER FOUR

Comparing Academic Performance in Cuba and Other Latin American Countries

We now turn to estimating how much of the difference in student performance among Cuba and Brazil and Chile (and other Latin American countries) is related to family background, school, and social context differences among countries.[1]

Just measuring how well children learn what is taught in school is a challenge. Educators argue that we need multiple measures of learning, including tests based on the prescribed curriculum, portfolio assessments of pupils' work, and teacher evaluations. Yet most studies rely on tests alone, and international studies necessarily rely on tests keyed only indirectly to the curriculum taught in any particular country.

In addition, we would like to know what factors in school account for students learning more. To do that well, we should know how much students learn in a *given year of school*—that is, the gain in achievement—so that we can estimate a clearer relation between student performance and teacher attributes and other inputs in that school year. Ideally, we would like to measure student achievement at the beginning and end of the year and be able to have good information on the students' teacher(s) during that year.

Beginning with James Coleman in the mid-1960s (Coleman et al., 1966), sociologists and economists have tried to get at the effect of school inputs on student performance. Generally, they have estimated these relationships for a particular sample of students at a single point in time. They did not have gains for a given year of school. The estimates included such variables as teachers' preservice training and teaching experience, students' family background and situation, and class size. Comparative analysis has usually focused on one particular variable, such as class size, for different groups of students or in different studies (Hanushek, 1986; Krueger, 1999). Because researchers have rarely been able to find surveys that collected the same data across different sets of students in potentially different educational environments, past comparisons necessarily focused on individual student background and school input differences rather than on possible differences in the social context of schools and the impact that this context has on student achievement.[2]

Studies of education using a consistent methodology across countries provide the basis for analyzing such contextual differences. Because of international tests, such as the Third International Mathematics and Science Study (TIMSS), we know that students in Singapore, Korea, and eastern Europe tend to perform far better in mathematics than students in the United States. It is not obvious from the amount or type of resources devoted to education either at home or in school why that should be the case. More detailed comparisons of the educational process in academically highly successful countries and less successful similar countries clearly do not meet the standards of random assignment of students to different situations. Yet, as so-called natural experiments, they may be suggestive of the effect on student performance of different social environments (Knight and Sabot, 1990).

The international survey conducted by UNESCO's Latin American Laboratory of Educational Evaluation (Laboratorio Latinoamericano de Evaluación de la Calidad de la Educación [LLECE]) in 1997–1998 was modeled on earlier and larger international surveys such as the International Educational Assessment (IEA) and the Third International Mathematics and Science Survey (TIMSS). The Laboratorio survey tested third- and fourth-grade students in thirteen Latin American countries. The test was given in math and language (Spanish in all but Brazil, where the students were tested in Portuguese), administered to representative samples (about two thousand urban and two thousand rural) of third and fourth graders, and made comparable through the application of standard psychometric techniques (LLECE, 1998).

Like the TIMSS, the Laboratorio survey sought to address the challenge of evaluating students in countries that used different curricula. In some countries, such as Brazil, the curriculum varies among states and municipalities, whereas in other Latin American countries the curriculum is national. School directors, parents, and teachers answered questionnaires that provided data on the family (e.g., socioeconomic status), individual students (e.g., gender, motivation), teachers (e.g., education and training, expectations), and school (e.g., classroom conditions, textbook availability). The survey did not collect data on the curriculum used and is generally not nearly as detailed as the TIMSS survey. Thus, we cannot compare the type of curriculum in the surveyed Latin American countries.

Further, not all the countries' data sets are of equal "quality." Many questions on the survey were answered sporadically, so that key variables in many countries are missing significant numbers of responses. Thus, when we estimate the basic regression equations, the number of observations is much smaller than four thousand.

It is also reasonable to ask whether the very high test scores in Cuba are the result of picking a select group of schools or a select group of students in the schools surveyed. LLECE researchers returned to Cuba to retest students in five schools selected at random from the original 100 surveyed. They found no significant difference in results. However, this does not answer the question of whether the 100 schools in the survey were representative of Cuban elementary schools. Our own classroom observations in ten schools (rural, urban, and city periphery) suggested to us major differences in the level of performance of Cuban third graders compared to those in Brazilian and Chilean schools. But such classroom observations would not fully answer skeptics' doubts about randomness in the Cuban survey (and randomness of other countries' surveys as well).

Despite these omissions and data issues, the Laboratorio gathered valuable information that we can use to proxy family and collective social capital (what we will refer to as the social context of schooling) in educational production functions. Both types of social capital vary considerably among students and schools within most Latin American countries but much less in Cuba. In turn, Cuban social context (collective social capital) differs significantly from the social context in the rest of Latin America.

The Laboratorio survey is not the first to provide comparison information on student performance in Latin America, but it is the most extensive and complete to date. Although fraught with typical problems of missing data and not as detailed as the TIMSS survey, it appears to be complete enough in seven of the countries (Argentina, Bolivia, Brazil, Chile, Colombia, Cuba, and Mexico) to make possible a reasonable cross-country analysis.[3] Our focus in this analysis is on our three countries of interest—Brazil, Chile, and Cuba—but we also want to see where students in the three are compared to other countries in Latin America.

We made a case for the importance of state-driven social capital to these differences; if it holds, we should be able to show that our indicators of social context are significant correlates of student performance, taking into account family background and school resource differences. We should also be able to show that differences in social context between Cuba and other countries are related to the higher test scores of Cuban students. For Brazil and a number of other countries, this indeed appears to be the case. For Chile, however, social context differences do little to help us understand why Chilean students score so much lower than Cubans.

We create two sets of estimates and compare them. One estimate pools the third and fourth graders into a single sample and controls for the grade in which the student was tested (Willms and Somers, 2001). Even though this approach is not as desirable methodologically as measuring the difference in achievement for the same student at the end of, say, the third grade and the end of the fourth grade, third and fourth grades may be early enough in a student's schooling that the measured classroom characteristics in third and fourth grades should be similar to those in the student's previous two grades.

The second set estimates what we might call a "gain score" by using fourth graders' test results as the dependent variable and the average third-grade score in the same school as an independent variable. The number of fourth graders for whom we have test scores and other information is smaller than for third graders but is adequate for relating fourth graders' achievement to family background, school characteristics, and social context of the school. This approach tends to overestimate "real" fourth-grade individual gains for higher scoring, higher SES pupils. At the same time, it underestimates real gains for lower SES pupils, so the estimated effect of individual SES and family and possibly collective social capital is still biased upward compared to an estimate that measured individual achievement longitudinally. Another problem with these particular data is that in Cuba both third and fourth graders did so well on this (same) test that the difference (gain) was relatively small and had much less meaning than in other countries where third-grade scores were considerably lower. In Cuba, we may be underestimating the "gains" that higher SES pupils would have made had the test been more difficult. Not surprisingly, controlling for third-grade school score essentially eliminates the effect of the average family background of students in the classroom or school on the individual student's performance.[4]

The variables available to measure differences in characteristics of students and students' families are student gender, student self-confidence, parental education, whether the parents read to the student, the parents' expected level of study for their child, and the number of books in the household. These variables are correlated, but as a group, they should capture a significant part of the variation in student background influence on achievement. Following Coleman's analysis, we identify a subgroup of the family background variables as social capital indicators, namely, whether the parents read to the student, the parents' expected level of study for their child, and the number of books in the household. These are correlated with family human capital (parent education) but vary sufficiently to provide an independent measure that can represent social capital. In several of the countries in our sample, there are disadvantaged groups that could, in addition to SES, be identified by indigenous culture or language spoken different from the dominant Spanish (Bolivia, Mexico, Chile, Colombia) or race (Brazil, Cuba). These data are not available in this survey.

The variables we use to measure school resources are whether the student has a textbook in math and language, the student's third- or fourth-grade teacher's education, whether the teacher attends inservice training, the physical condition of the classroom, and the availability of classroom materials. Logically, teacher education and training should be important in explaining differences in student achievement, particularly as subject content knowledge should, in theory, be higher among teachers with higher levels of education.[5] But because we have data only on the student's current teacher, this omission may reduce the teacher effect. Similarly, the "quality" of teacher education and training at, say, the university level, may vary enormously from country to country. For example, many countries may not teach mathematics in teacher education programs. Other, unmeasured, teacher characteristics such as teacher subject content knowledge would then become much more important in describing teaching capacity.

As mentioned, the Laboratorio did not measure time spent on various aspects of a typical third- or fourth-grade math curriculum. This is a definite drawback in trying to determine the contribution of school system and school differences to student performance. The 1995 TIMSS survey did focus on seventh- and eighth-grade math curriculum, and these variables proved to be important in explaining differences in, for example, the performance of U.S. eighth graders compared to those in European and Asian countries (Schmidt et al., 2001). Thus, opportunity to learn is undoubtedly important to how much students actually do learn and would probably explain some of the difference in Cuban test scores. So again, because of lack of more complete data, we are probably underestimating school effects. On the other hand, an analysis of the 1995 TIMSS data using both opportunity to learn variables and social context defined similarly to the way we use it in this paper shows that context is important even when opportunity to learn is included in the estimated model of schooling (Carnoy, Marshall, and Socias, 2004).

We add several other measures of school organization to the model: the degree of principal autonomy in the school, as reported by the principal; whether the school is private or public; and whether the school is urban or rural. It is possible that principal autonomy is a function of the degree of privatization of the school system, and we test for that relationship. Our results suggest that although principals may "feel" autonomous, the effect of autonomy on explaining differences in student performance between countries is greatest in Bolivia, Brazil, and Chile, where either the proportion of students in the sample attending private school is very high (Bolivia and Chile) or the administration of the educational system is highly decentralized (Brazil).

We use four variables as proxies for collective social capital: (1) whether the student attended preschool, (2) whether a student works after school (either inside or outside the home), (3) the number of classroom fights reported by students of each classroom, and (4) the average socioeconomic background of students in the school, taken from principal components factor analysis.[6] Each of these variables indicates something about the social context (state-driven social capital) in which students receive their education. These measures of state-driven social capital go beyond individual parental background and school resource differences. Each proxies some aspect of how much each nation values, controls, and enhances the environment in which children live and learn.

For example, the degree of preschool access reflects how much emphasis localities or nations place on incorporating all young children into a richer educational environment. Although income per capita in the United States is higher than in Europe, the Scandinavian countries and France have invested heavily in universal preschool whereas the United States has not. Scandinavian countries and France have, as societies, opted for early childhood education, reflecting their political view of the state's relationship to families. In the United States, regions vary in the amount of subsidized preschool and day care they provide to low-income families (Loeb et al., 2007). These results suggest that student attendance at preschool is neither a school input nor just a student family choice but a function of more collective public choices, especially in relation to preschool for low-income families.

Similarly, when significant numbers of young children work outside the home, it means that the society is unwilling to provide sufficient material support to reduce the incentive for low-income families to send young children to work for wages.[7] Many analyze the child work decision as a family affair, with good reason—there are important elements of individual family utility functions in the choice of making a child work or not (see, for example, Glewwe and Jacoby, 1994; Post, 2002). However, state social policy—primarily the degree of public sector services, access to schooling (especially in rural areas), and material support to low-income families— also have a major influence on the average frequency of children working outside the home (Post, 2002). As Post has already shown, it is important to distinguish between work outside the home and in the home.[8]

Another proxy of social capital investment is the frequency of student-reported classroom fights (summed across individual students in each school divided by the number of students surveyed in that school). Children living in low-income neighborhoods in all Latin American countries, but less so in Cuba, are exposed to everyday violence, and therefore, we would claim, are more likely to disturb their classroom or fight in school. This is partly associated with the individual student's family characteristics but is also a function of the state's local and national juridical and enforcement apparatuses. Those apparatuses may be unwilling or unable to control violence or are simply part and parcel of the violence culture, as is the case in many Latin American countries.[9]

The school's average student SES variable is a more complex measure of social capital, as we have already discussed. Unlike the other variables we use to proxy social capital, average school SES itself only measures the aggregate of individual student SES in each school.[10] Why would the average school SES affect individual student achievement over and above an average of individuals' family human capital? For one, parents form networks and associations that influence how they relate to their children in terms of academic achievement and attainment expectations, and how they influence teacher performance and expectations: The higher the SES, the more of such social capital parents are likely to generate in the school. Second, peers (even possible young peers in third and fourth grade) form networks and associations that influence how well individual students perform academically: the higher the average SES, the more likely peers are to form academically supportive networks.[11]

Understanding Why Students' Test Scores in Different Countries Differ

Once we estimate the model for each country, we want to estimate the impact on each country's student test performance assuming that its students, schools, and school social context had the same average characteristics as Cuba's. This is called "simulating" student achievement. It answers the question of "what if," say, Brazilian third graders had parents with the same education, went to schools that had the same resources, and studied in the same social environment as third graders in Cuba. How well would Brazilian third graders do academically if Brazilian families, schools, and daily relations were similar to those in Cuba? Our student achievement simulations are one way to approximate such a hypothetical situation.

The simulations reestimate student achievement in each of the other six countries using the estimated coefficients of each country's equation, inserting the average values of the variables in the Cuban survey.[12] This approximates the effect of the difference in "resources" (family education differences, family social capital differences, school input differences, and school social context differences) on student achievement differences.[13] As we discuss later, because the amount of social capital associated with the average socioeconomic background of families in the schools is questionable, we estimate the impact of the Cuban school social context effect, including and not including average school socioeconomic background in our definition of social context.

Means of Variables by Country

Pupils' performance as measured by the mathematics and language tests applied by LLECE varies considerably across countries. Means and standard deviations (when relevant) for each of the variables that derive from the survey questions put to pupils, their parents, and school personnel are detailed in Tables 4.1a and 4.1b; the definitions are listed in Appendix Table A.1. Table 4.1a reports the means of variables for all students in the sample, third and fourth graders. Table 4.1b reports results for fourth graders only; this is the sample we use to make our estimates on test scores of students in fourth grade controlling for average third-grade scores in the same school. Most of the variables are indices, so, for example, parent education is measured on a scale from 0 to 6, and books in the home on a scale from 1 to 4.

Students in Cuba outperform those in other countries by more than one standard deviation in the test of language and about one and one-half standard deviations in math. A one standard deviation difference means that if students in other countries average 50 percent on the test, Cuban students average more than 84 percent. A one and one-half standard deviation

TABLE 4.1A

Means and standard deviations (in parentheses) for variables included in analysis

	COUNTRY							
Variables	Argentina	Bolivia	Brazil	Chile	Colombia	Cuba	Mexico	All 7
Mathematics	276.7	257.5	265.8	259.2	253.7	356.0	257.7	279.4
achievement	(42.0)	(44.1)	(44.3)	(41.2)	(37.9)	(68.2)	(43.0)	(61.9)
Language	290.7	252.2	271.8	280.8	257.1	341.0	255.0	279.6
achievement	(49.9)	(52.4)	(47.3)	(53.0)	(50.1)	(51.0)	(53.9)	(60.4)
Student/Family Characteristics								
Female	0.50	0.51	0.50	0.52	0.49	0.52	0.50	0.50
Student self-	2.46	2.42	2.29	2.32	2.40	2.52	2.40	2.40
confidence	(0.41)	(0.42)	(0.39)	(0.52)	(0.42)	(0.29)	(0.41)	(0.40)
Parental education	3.38	3.10	1.91	3.12	2.55	4.22	2.84	3.07
	(1.58)	(1.65)	(1.52)	(1.44)	(1.49)	(1.27)	(1.40)	(1.63)
Read to child	2.75	2.37	2.65	2.80	2.35	3.60	2.38	2.72
	(1.39)	(1.40)	(1.54)	(1.38)	(1.45)	(0.82)	(1.43)	(1.41)
Expected level	5.28	5.35	4.83	5.14	5.03	5.71	4.45	5.14
of study	(1.24)	(1.26)	(1.56)	(1.21)	(1.38)	(0.80)	(1.68)	(1.37)
Books in	2.93	2.57	2.42	2.66	2.38	2.65	2.33	2.54
household	(0.90)	(0.88)	(0.88)	(0.90)	(0.91)	(0.89)	(0.91)	(0.91)
Teacher/School Characteristics								
Fourth-grade	0.51	0.52	0.48	0.52	0.53	0.50	0.50	0.51
Classroom	7.22	4.35	6.74	7.10	5.01	5.83	6.52	5.95
materials	(2.64)	(3.01)	(2.35)	(2.83)	(2.62)	(1.19)	(2.34)	(2.65)
Student has language								
textbook	0.66	0.69	0.87	0.94	0.70	0.97	0.96	0.84
Student has math								
text	0.43	0.54	0.81	0.87	0.60	0.95	0.92	0.76
Teacher education								
Secondary only	0.40	0.89	0.71	0.26	0.66	0.09	0.60	0.52
University	0.57	0.06	0.29	0.74	0.32	0.91	0.40	0.47
Other	0.03	0.04	0.00	0.0	0.02	0.00	0.00	0.01
Teacher training	7.44	7.42	4.96	3.26	3.85	3.96	4.65	4.98
sessions	(5.40)	(5.93)	(5.61)	(4.64)	(3.24)	(6.79)	(4.30)	(5.54)
Classroom	0.68	0.59	0.69	0.66	0.69	0.77	0.77	0.69
condition	(0.28)	(0.39)	(0.28)	(0.30)	(0.28)	(0.28)	(0.27)	(0.31)
Principal	2.34	2.44	2.41	2.38	2.50	2.42	2.22	2.39
autonomy	(0.36)	(0.42)	(0.38)	(0.36)	(0.32)	(0.32)	(0.43)	(0.38)
Rural school	0.09	0.19	0.18	0.22	0.31	0.38	0.32	0.26
Private school	0.25	0.40	0.20	0.39	0.24	—	0.18	0.23
Social Context								
Student attended								
preschool	0.89	0.73	0.77	0.67	0.69	0.94	0.86	0.79
Work outside	1.48	1.77	1.49	1.50	1.72	1.04	1.62	1.51
the home	(0.18)	(0.29)	(0.20)	(0.22)	(0.29)	(0.11)	(0.25)	(0.34)
Work in the	2.50	2.60	2.50	2.37	2.56	2.72	2.42	2.54
home	(0.17)	(0.14)	(0.15)	(0.14)	(0.17)	(0.14)	(0.13)	(0.17)
Children free	2.18	2.08	2.21	2.21	2.14	1.94	2.06	2.10
from work	(0.21)	(0.17)	(0.16)	(0.16)	(0.26)	(0.28)	(0.21)	(0.23)
Classroom fights	0.30	0.26	0.27	0.26	0.30	0.07	0.28	0.24
	(0.17)	(0.17)	(0.14)	(0.12)	(0.21)	(0.09)	(0.15)	(0.17)
SES factor	0.47	−0.04	−0.47	0.12	−0.37	0.90	−0.22	0.07
(school)	(0.82)	(0.87)	(0.85)	(0.75)	(0.83)	(0.49)	(0.81)	(0.91)
Number of cases								
(language)	1,402	2,825	2,065	2,127	2,451	3,053	2,378	16,311
Number of cases								
(math)	1,402	2,797	1,999	1,305	2,421	3.019	2.305	15,248

TABLE 4.1B
Means and standard deviations (in parentheses) for variables included in fourth-grade-only analysis

Variables		Argentina	Bolivia	Brazil	Chile	Colombia	Cuba	Mexico	All 7
					COUNTRY				
Mathematics		286.0	258.7	277.6	268.9	260.8	357.5	266.1	285.2
achievement		(42.0)	(43.8)	(44.9)	(41.4)	(36.4)	(66.2)	(42.0)	(59.9)
Language		301.3	253.9	283.4	293.1	268.7	343.1	266.4	287.5
achievement		(47.6)	(49.3)	(47.2)	(51.9)	(48.3)	(51.2)	(54.1)	(58.6)
Student/Family Characteristics									
Female		0.51	0.52	0.51	0.51	0.51	0.52	0.48	0.51
Student self-		2.44	2.36	2.29	2.29	2.39	2.52	2.39	2.39
confidence		(0.40)	(0.41)	(0.39)	(0.43)	(0.40)	(0.30)	(0.40)	(0.39)
Parental education		3.32	3.07	1.92	3.05	2.54	4.24	2.81	3.05
		(1.58)	(1.63)	(1.52)	(1.45)	(1.47)	(1.27)	(1.41)	(1.62)
Read to child		2.73	2.38	2.63	2.80	2.38	3.58	2.33	2.71
		(1.39)	(1.41)	(1.57)	(1.37)	(1.45)	(0.87)	(1.42)	(1.42)
Expected level		5.28	5.33	4.77	5.10	5.06	5.68	4.41	5.12
of study		(1.24)	(1.33)	(1.57)	(1.23)	(1.34)	(0.86)	(1.69)	(1.39)
Books in		2.93	2.58	2.44	2.67	2.41	2.66	2.34	2.56
household		(0.90)	(0.88)	(0.88)	(0.92)	(0.91)	(0.90)	(0.90)	(0.91)
Teacher/School Characteristics									
Classroom		7.17	4.26	6.72	7.12	5.05	5.83	6.50	5.92
materials		(2.61)	(3.06)	(2.23)	(2.88)	(2.65)	(1.18)	(2.39)	(2.67)
Student has language									
textbook		0.65	0.69	0.88	0.94	0.69	0.97	0.97	0.84
Student has math									
text		0.48	0.52	0.84	0.89	0.59	0.96	0.93	0.76
Teacher education									
Secondary only		0.40	0.90	0.74	0.25	0.66	0.09	0.59	0.52
University		0.58	0.07	0.26	0.75	0.33	0.91	0.41	0.47
Other		0.02	0.03	0.00	0.0	0.01	0.00	0.00	0.01
Teacher training		7.55	7.75	4.92	3.42	3.86	3.87	4.69	5.05
sessions		(5.76)	(6.26)	(5.78)	(5.85)	(3.09)	(6.92)	(4.56)	(5.86)
Classroom		0.66	0.60	0.68	0.66	0.69	0.78	0.78	0.69
condition		(0.29)	(0.40)	(0.29)	(0.30)	(0.28)	(0.28)	(0.27)	(0.31)
Principal		2.33	2.45	2.41	2.38	2.49	2.43	2.21	2.39
autonomy		(0.35)	(0.42)	(0.38)	(0.36)	(0.32)	(0.32)	(0.42)	(0.38)
Rural school		0.12	0.19	0.18	0.22	0.29	0.39	0.34	0.26
Private school		0.24	0.41	0.19	0.39	0.25	—	0.17	0.23
Social Context									
Student attended									
preschool		0.89	0.70	0.77	0.65	0.70	0.96	0.87	0.79
Work outside		1.49	1.77	1.49	1.50	1.72	1.03	1.63	1.51
the home		(0.17)	(0.28)	(0.19)	(0.22)	(0.28)	(0.12)	(0.25)	(0.34)
Work in the		2.51	2.60	2.50	2.37	2.55	2.73	2.43	2.54
home		(0.17)	(0.14)	(0.15)	(0.15)	(0.17)	(0.14)	(0.14)	(0.19)
Children free		2.17	2.08	2.20	2.22	2.13	1.95	2.06	2.10
from work		(0.22)	(0.17)	(0.16)	(0.17)	(0.25)	(0.27)	(0.21)	(0.23)
Classroom fights		0.30	0.25	0.27	0.25	0.30	0.07	0.28	0.24
		(0.17)	(0.17)	(0.14)	(0.13)	(0.21)	(0.09)	(0.15)	(0.17)
SES factor		0.43	−0.04	−0.49	0.11	−0.36	0.92	−0.26	0.07
(school)		(0.81)	(0.85)	(0.84)	(0.77)	(0.81)	(0.49)	(0.81)	(0.90)
Number of cases									
(language)		718	1,458	983	1,101	1,283	1,550	1,199	8,292
Number of cases									
(math)		718	1,444	948	694	1,269	1,517	1,166	7,756

difference means that Cuban students averaged about 90 percent whereas students in other countries averaged 50 percent. Argentine students also do better than their counterparts in other countries, followed by students in Chile and Brazil.

The resources that might affect student performance also vary among countries. Among the Latin American countries, Cuban students have highly educated parents who are more likely to read to their children and who expect their children to go further in school. Cuban and Mexican pupils are much more likely to have textbooks, and Cuban pupils' teachers generally have a higher level of preservice education. Cuban primary school children are also more likely to attend a rural school, will probably face many fewer incidents of violence in their classrooms, and are much less likely to work outside the home than their counterparts in other Latin American countries.

These differences turn out to be important—especially the differences in family context and the differences in school social context—in explaining at least part of the reason that children in Cuban schools outperform children in other Latin American schools.

Explaining Pupil Achievement in Each Country

The ultimate objective of these estimates is to study the degree to which family and collective social capital and other factors impact *differences* in student achievement among countries, particularly among Cuba, Chile, Brazil, and the other four countries we analyze. To do this, we first need to estimate the relationship between student achievement and these "explanatory" factors in each country. Then we use those estimated relationships to simulate how well students in each country would do if they had similar family and school resources and went to school in a similar social context as Cuban pupils.

The estimates for student achievement in each country suggest the following:[14]

- Student and parent characteristics of individual students are important in explaining student achievement in every country. As is typical, girls in all countries score lower in math than boys (except in Cuba and Mexico) and higher in language (except in Bolivia). Student self-confidence is a highly significant explainer of student achievement but likely reflects how well a student is actually doing in school, so probably should not be interpreted as a contributor to higher student achievement. The positive relation of parents' education to student achievement is also statistically significant in every country. Family social capital, especially parents' expectations of their child's ultimate educational attainment and the index of number of books in the home, generally have significant impact on students' performance in school. Parents' expectations, like student self-confidence, may also be the result of a pupil's better performance in school rather than the cause of it.

• Specific school inputs are generally not very important in explaining student math achievement. But textbooks and classroom materials are significant explainers of achievement in language in certain countries.

• State-driven social capital variables are, like family social capital, important explainers of achievement differences. The different state social capital variables tend to be correlated, so that the variables of importance vary among countries. The apparent impact on individual student achievement of average socioeconomic background of pupils in each classroom/school is large and statistically significant in Argentina, Brazil and Chile; the degree to which a pupil works outside the home has a significantly negative effect in Argentina, Brazil, Colombia, and Mexico; and classroom fights have particularly large effects in all but Chile and Mexico. One reason that work outside the home is significantly related to student achievement in Mexico, but not, for example, in Chile, may be that a higher fraction of young people work in Mexico than in Chile (Post, 2002), in part because the average age of third- and fourth-grade students is somewhat higher in Mexico than in Chile. The same may hold for Brazil and Colombia, although probably not in Argentina. In some countries, attending preschool—or early school inputs—also has a significant effect on third- and fourth-grade achievement. Yet it is evident that responders interpreted the question about preschool as including kindergarten—

hence, the high proportion of pupils with preschool in almost every country (Tables 4.1a and 4.1b), and the probably smaller effect of preschool than were it defined as prekindergarten.

Estimating "Value Added"

A major problem exists in trying to estimate the effect of school inputs on student performance as measured by outcomes in the third and fourth grades combined (see Appendix A for these estimates—Tables A.2 and A.3). Third- and fourth-grade achievement is the result of the cumulative impact of teacher characteristics, school resources, and classroom conditions on students over three to four years in a classroom/school or various classrooms and schools. Thus, achievement as measured on the Laboratorio test is not just a product of third- and fourth-grade teachers and classroom materials. We do account partly for school achievement in earlier grades by controlling for average SES of students in each school's grades three and four. Average SES in a school should be highly correlated with the achievement of students when they entered the school, but this may not be enough to cull out the effects of earlier grades.

In the cases in which students were tested in more than one classroom in a school, it is also impossible to identify the variation in resources across classrooms. Family and social context variables tend to be more invariant over the student's time in school—generally, a student's family background or his or her likelihood of working outside of the home at the age of ten or eleven does not change from the time students are in first or second grade. So these measures tend to be more correlated than, say, teacher quality with a cumulative measure of performance. Thus, the estimates as reported in Appendix Tables A.2 and A.3 probably overestimate the impact of family inputs and state social capital variables and underestimate the impact of school inputs. The nature of the data limits our ability to correct for this source of bias. Longitudinal studies of student performance, in which student test score is measured at two points in time (or more) and the school resources available to the student are identified with each period of time provide much better estimates of the effects of school inputs. Even then, estimates may be biased because more motivated parents get their children into schools with more resources, and students' measured family characteristics may not adequately measure parent motivation.

Although we do not have longitudinal data that measure the gains by individual students, we do have individual fourth-grade test scores and the average scores of third graders in the same school. Assuming that third graders in a school this year scored, on average, about the same that fourth graders scored the year before, including average third-grade score as an independent variable means that the coefficients of the other independent variables in the equation are estimates of the fourth-grade score "net" of the average score in third grade. As far as the individual student and his or her family background variables are concerned, the estimates of their coefficients represent their relationship to individual student fourth-grade scores controlling for the average third-grade test score in each classroom/school. For classroom/school and social context variables, the coefficients represent the relation of each variable to the average fourth-grade test score in the classroom/school controlling for the average third-grade test score in the school—a quasi-school "value added."

As expected, the results for the individual countries suggest that controlling the individual fourth grader's test score for the average third-grade score in his or her school reduces the explanatory importance of family social capital and state social capital variables. Logically, the additional score students achieve in fourth grade is less affected by social capital variables than the absolute level of their academic achievement. The coefficients for classroom fights and work outside the home generally decline in value, yet, in several countries, such as Argentina, Brazil, and Mexico for work, and Argentina, Bolivia, Colombia, and Cuba for fights, they continue to be statistically significant, a finding suggesting that they represent a social capital effect that is more than just the aggregate of individual student SES differences. As expected, the variable measuring average SES of students in the school ceases to be important altogether when we include the average third-grade test score as a control. Unexpectedly, however, school variables generally do not become more important in these "value added" estimates. This may be because we cannot identify fourth-grade students with their teachers, but more likely it is because of poor specification of, say, teacher characteristics that could explain student performance differences. The measures are probably too approximate to explain variation in student outcomes (see Appendix Tables A.4 and A.5).

Simulating Student Achievement by Equalizing Inputs to Cuban Levels

We simulate student scores in each country using the estimated equation for each country and assuming that means of the student/family characteristics, school characteristics, and social context are those of the Cuban students. This implies that family, school, and social context differences between Cuba and the other countries is "eliminated" but that the effect of these variables on student achievement remain specific to each country. Employing this method, we are able to account for a significant part of the gap between Cuban test scores and the scores of students in the

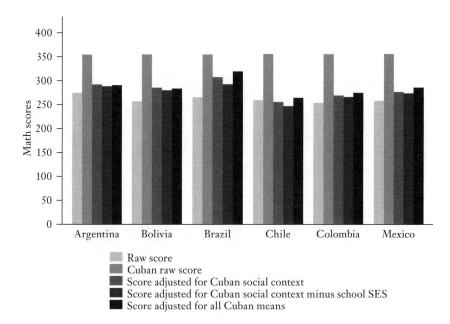

Figure 4.1   Comparison of Cuban Third- and Fourth-Grade Raw Mathematics Scores and Scores Estimated Using Cuban Family, School, and Social Context Characteristics with Raw Mathematics Scores of Selected Other Countries
SOURCE: Table 4.1a and Table A.2.

other countries. We are able to close the gap in the language test scores much more than the gap in the math scores (Figures 4.1 and 4.2). In language, Brazil and Chile close to about one-half a standard deviation below the Cuban score. But in math, even the greatest reduction in the gap—for Brazilian students—leaves them more than one standard deviation below the mean for Cuban students.

The most revealing result, however, is that in both math and language most of the gap is explained by equalizing state social capital to Cuban levels. Most of the gap we are able to close is accounted for by "allowing" other countries' students to work as infrequently as Cuban students and reducing classroom disturbances down to Cuban levels. We assume that lower values of both variables are important indicators of state-generated social capital in Cuba that is largely absent in these other countries. Chile seems to be the one country for which changing social context to Cuban levels does little to close the gap between Chilean and Cuban students' performance.

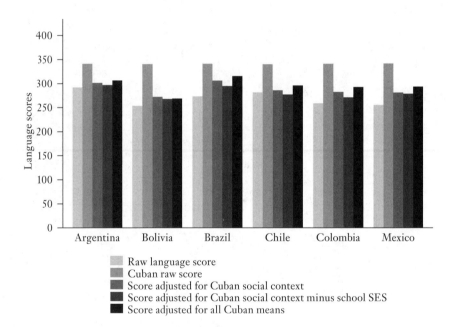

Figure 4.2   Comparison of Cuban Third- and Fourth-Grade Raw Language Scores and Scores Estimated Using Cuban Family, School, and Social Context Characteristics with Raw Language Scores of Selected Other Countries
  SOURCE: Table 4.1a and Table A.3.

This is important because it suggests that for the two countries we are particularly interested in—Brazil and Chile—changing the social context (increasing parent education, reducing school violence, reducing child work outside the home) could have a major impact on pupil achievement in Brazil, but not much in Chile. Apparently, the social conditions for children in Chile, while far from ideal, are so much better than for children in Brazil as to make social policy less of a factor in bringing test scores up to the Cuban level. Implicitly this means that other factors, which we have not been able to capture with our simulation analysis, play a much more important role in explaining lower test scores in Chile. These may be related to schooling or to an interaction between social context and schooling not picked up by the UNESCO data.

When we use the fourth-grade sample of students and the estimates of their scores accounting for average third-grade score, the role of social

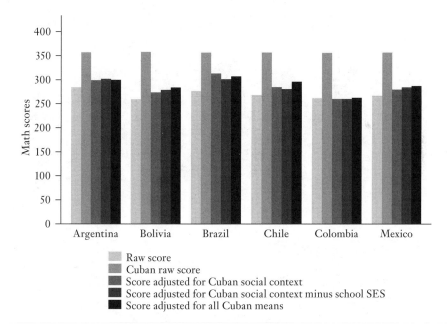

Figure 4.3 Comparison of Cuban Fourth-Grade Raw Mathematics Scores and Scores Estimated Using Cuban Family, School, and Social Context Characteristics with Raw Mathematics Scores of Selected Other Countries, Adjusted for Average Third-Grade School Scores

SOURCE: Table 4.1b and Table A.4.

context variables should be reduced because the average third-grade score should pick up a major part of context differences in each country and among countries. Family effects should also decline, but because individual fourth-grade scores are only being controlled for school averages, family variables may continue to play a similar role. School variables should become more important in explaining differences in the "value added" estimates.

Figures 4.3 and 4.4 suggest that, except in Bolivia and Chile, the effect of simulating fourth-grade "gain scores" using Cuban means for the social context variables, such as working outside the home and classroom fights, has a somewhat smaller impact than when "absolute" performance levels are used. But in most of the countries the effect is still larger on achievement differences than that of family background variables, including that of family social capital. Except in Mexico, family variables continue to have about

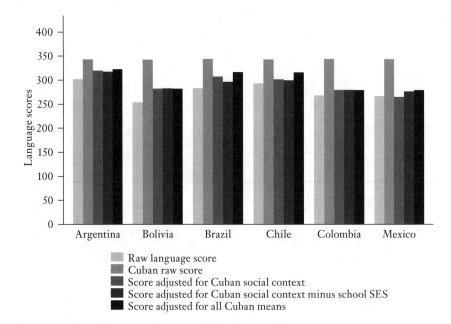

Figure 4.4 Comparison of Cuban Fourth-Grade Raw Language Scores and Scores Estimated Using Cuban Family, School, and Social Context Characteristics with Raw Language Scores of Selected Other Countries, Adjusted for Average Third-Grade School Scores
SOURCE: Table 4.1b and Table A.5.

the same effect on gains, and school variables do generally increase slightly their small overall impact on explaining fourth-grade gain scores.[15]

Summing Up

Estimating relationships between inputs and outputs in education from cross-section survey data is fraught with serious problems. The data from the LLECE survey are hardly perfect. The number of students who took each test varies from country to country. Many of those surveyed did not answer all questions, so the data are laced with missing values, reducing the number of cases "usable" in our regression analyses in many of the countries well below the number of students who took the tests.

Nevertheless, it is possible to gain important insights from such macro-educational analysis into the factors that can affect student performance in developing countries. Our estimated equations and simulations suggest that social context—which we have defined as state-driven social capital—is very important in explaining why students in some countries (especially Cuba) score so much higher than students in other Latin American countries. This is true even when we estimate fourth-grade individual performance controlling for average third-grade performance in the student's school. The continued importance of pupil wage employment and classroom violence in explaining fourth-grade gains in Bolivia, Chile, and Colombia relative to Cuba suggests that the social context of schooling probably affects progress in each grade.

More specifically, our estimates suggest the following:

- The frequency of child labor outside the home, an important indicator of the degree of state-generated social capital, is also an important correlate of academic achievement in Latin America, particularly in Argentina, Brazil, and Mexico. Child labor outside the home is practically nonexistent in Cuba, in sharp contrast with the other countries in our sample this despite the lower income per capita and lower average individual wealth in Cuba. This helps explain at least some of the difference between Cuban students' higher test scores in primary school and the lower test scores of students in other countries.

- Much lower levels of reported classroom fights in Cuba also explain higher student achievement in Cuba, particularly when compared with Argentina, Bolivia, and Colombia. This factor is probably also a proxy for greater poverty and social disorganization rather than classroom management.
- Principal autonomy seems also to be an important, albeit indirect, factor in explaining student performance differences among countries.
- Popular beliefs about the significant positive effects of preschool (measured here as percentage of students with some preschooling) are generally not borne out by our analysis. However, the definition of preschool is vague in the LLECE questionnaire and is probably just measuring whether a pupil attended kindergarten.
- Similarly, popular beliefs about private education (as a whole) as more effective than public are also not borne out, except possibly in the case of Chile's principal autonomy effect on math score gains. We argue that this may be a proxy for a private school effect.

Thus, it appears that although we can explain only part of the difference between Cuban students' test performance and the performance of students in other countries, the part we can explain is as much related to social context differences between Cuba and the other countries as to individual student SES, even in our so-called value added estimates. Further, about one-third to one-half of the effect of students' family background on achievement appears to be related to family social capital. Schooling variables are generally not important in explaining differences among countries, at least not as measured in the LLECE survey, and at least as we can assess through this macro approach to differences among classrooms and schools within the same country.[16]

Much of the difference in test scores between Cuba and other countries remains a mystery, so interaction or unmeasured factors may also play an important role in understanding why students in Cuba do so well. For example, according to our simulations, even if Chile were to have parental education, school resources, and social context as high as those in Cuba, fourth-grade students in Chile's relatively effective school system would score approximately one standard deviation lower than Cuban students in math and 0.4 standard deviations lower in Spanish.

These findings represent major unexplained differences in student performance. The mystery of low math scores in most countries is especially perplexing. Are the Cubans spending more time on teaching mathematics and language than teachers in other countries? The survey question on time on task produced unclear results. Are Cuban teachers better prepared to teach math and language? Is the Cuban curriculum more demanding? Again, the survey does not provide adequate answers to these important questions. For example, reported educational differences among teachers in each country and between countries pick up little of the variation in actual content knowledge and teaching skills.

Nevertheless, the likely importance of family and particularly collective social capital in explaining differences in scores, particularly between Cuba and Brazil, even when these scores are expressed in "value added" terms, is an important contribution to understanding differences in achievement. These results begin to get at what the schools have to deal with in helping to foster social capital in families and what the state must do to foster greater collective social capital in the community and the nation. The findings suggest that *collective social capital*, such as that expressed in reducing the degree of violence in the classroom or reducing the need for young pupils to work outside the home, contributes to student performance differences in classrooms and schools; this notion is important in explaining that raising academic achievement is a function of more than just raising the education levels of parents or increasing the quality of resources used directly by schools.

In the next chapter, we begin to try to get behind these unexplained gaps by using information gathered from local data collection and interviews in schools to assess educational system organization, curriculum, and standards in three of the countries—Brazil, Chile, and Cuba.

CHAPTER FIVE

The Long Road from Curriculum Construction
to Student Learning

We have been studying how governments can affect student achievement by influencing the context of children's lives outside of schooling. A more traditional discussion is how governments can raise student achievement by improving the organization of schooling itself. We now turn to the major differences in how school systems in Brazil, Chile, and Cuba *deliver* education.

The way governments deliver education can make a difference in how much children learn, and sociopolitical context is important in shaping state (public sector) educational policies concerning educational delivery. This context is exemplified by Cuba's reliance on a tightly run public bureaucracy to control the educational process, Chile's emphasis on market incentives, and Brazil's struggle to "correct" its drastically unequal educational system with financial reforms. None of the three policy frameworks is the result of empirical research on how best to approach educational efficiency and equity. Rather, each set of policies results from political views of what constitutes social "efficiency." As we discussed in Chapter 1, the Cuban state believes in a hierarchically directed system for achieving its goals; the Chilean (and Brazilian) state(s) choose to be much more indirect. Nevertheless, educational planners in all three countries are open to a variety of approaches to improving student learning. Ministries make choices within the sociopolitical context, and these strategic choices do matter.

All school systems depend for their "technology" on curricula constructed by the state and on teachers trained to deliver them. Curricula may be national, with a central government printing textbooks based on the required curriculum, or, at the other extreme, schools and teachers may pick curricula by choosing textbooks designed for publishers by educators and content experts. Cuba represents the first option. Over the years since the revolutionary government came to power, the Cuban Ministry of Education developed, with the help of eastern European models, a math and science curriculum to one central standard. The ministry also developed a national Spanish language curriculum, a social studies curriculum that met its socialist and Cuban objectives, and so forth. Chile designed national curricular frameworks, recently (1997) reformed, then private publishers produce textbooks based on these frameworks, hoping to have them adopted by the ministry. The ministry purchases one textbook for each grade in each subject (not necessarily from the same publisher) to be distributed to all publicly subsidized schools in the country. Brazil also has designed curricular frameworks at the federal level, and, as in Chile, private publishers produce textbooks to compete for adoption. The federal government approves the textbook list, and states and municipalities then choose and distribute the books to individual schools in their jurisdictions.

The curriculum that a national school system, a provincial system, or a municipality uses can be coherent and integrative, considered "good" by experts in the field, or can be fairly incoherent and below standard. The United States, for example, has been criticized for a math curriculum that is "a mile wide and an inch deep" (Schmidt et al., 2001) because U.S. commercial textbooks, which tend to define curriculum in most states, try to cover as many subjects as possible to appeal to the largest number of states and school districts. That is the way U.S. publishers sell more textbooks.

No matter how good the curriculum, however, it may be implemented very unevenly unless teachers have the content knowledge and pedagogical training to teach higher-level subject matter to their students. Because teachers in almost every country do not come from the upper stratum of college students, their level of subject matter knowledge, especially in mathematics and science, depends almost entirely on the level of high school math or science required in secondary school for college-bound students. In the United States, for example, high school students need to take much less math than an average student in, say, France, the Czech Republic, Singapore, or Korea. An applicant to a university educational faculty in Brazil and Chile knows less mathematics than an average secondary school graduate in Cuba. Thus, a primary teacher graduating from a pedagogical institute in Cuba is better prepared in math than primary teachers in other Latin American countries. Among the three countries we are studying, this is particularly true in Brazil, where a high percentage of primary school teachers never took math past the eighth grade.

Ideally, teachers also should be familiar with the specific objectives of the curriculum. For new teachers, this means that they should have adequate university training in both the curricular subject matter—say, math and language for primary school teachers—and the best way to teach the specific content. For experienced teachers, for their capacity to remain up to standard, they should have access to professional development and on-the-job assistance.

This is usually not the case. Chile and Brazil differ in the way they organize schooling—Brazil has a federal system; Chile's system is more centralized when it comes to responsibility for reforms, but more decentralized to the school level because of the high percentage of students in private schools. But in both Chile and Brazil, the links between improving the curriculum (the "hardware" of the teaching process) and its effective application are weak.

The Chilean Ministry of Education, for example, is an active interventionist in developing a relatively high-quality national curriculum, in setting requirements for a longer school day, and in revitalizing low-performing schools. Yet the responsibility for implementing these reforms falls to schools and classroom teachers, who have almost total autonomy in doing so. Furthermore, as in many other industries, the initial formation of the labor force for schools—primary teachers—is carried out independently of the employer, in this case the ministry of education, which can only try to influence autonomous universities to train teachers up to standards inherent in the new curriculum.

When we visited a large and highly regarded lower-middle-class public school in the port city of Concepción, Chile, we asked the director whether he regularly visited classrooms to observe his teachers. He answered that his teachers were so competent that he did not need to observe them. Besides, he added, in Chilean school culture, the classroom is the teacher's domain, and the director has to ask permission to enter.

The Chilean and Brazilian situations are typical of most educational systems in this regard. However, as reflected in the voucher plan implemented by the military regime in the early 1980s, Chilean education is deeply influenced by an ideology that places undue faith in market forces to improve teaching and learning. The voucher plan provides the same amount of government funding per student, based on monthly attendance at the school, to all municipal (public) and those private schools willing to accept government subsidies. Until 1993, private schools accepting vouchers could not charge tuition; in 1993, that restriction was relaxed, as was a restriction prohibiting voucher schools from screening students for admission. About 38 percent of all K–12 students now attend private voucher schools, 9 percent private independent (nonvoucher) schools, and 53 percent public schools. Thus active interventionism from the center is largely bound by market mechanisms to implement reform. These market mechanisms, in practice, are generally weak stimulants for educational implementation or improvement, for a number of reasons. The most important is that principals and teachers are not trained to know how to respond to market stimulants in order to increase student learning. Because school directors lack instructional leadership and managerial capacity as well as supervisory authority (often even in private schools), individual teachers end up with most of the responsibility for implementing reforms and improving student learning. High-capacity teachers may be able to carry this off, but low-capacity teachers cannot. Brazil does not have a voucher system, but the highly decentralized public system is plagued by many of the same problems for many of the same reasons as those that are found in systems that use vouchers; because principals in Brazil are highly autonomous yet vary greatly in managerial capacity, schools are often poorly organized and teachers left to their own devices.

There are several reasons that teachers have considerable and, in many instances, total, autonomy in classrooms. One, as mentioned, is the lack of capacity of many school directors to assume instructional leadership. To have a positive influence on what takes place in classrooms, school principals (or assistant principals) would need to be respected by teachers as good instructional "coaches" or "managers," just as in any other line of work. In the absence of this managerial capacity, teachers necessarily take charge of defining how they apply the required curriculum. A second reason for this autonomy is that in many countries teachers are not particularly well paid, and they have necessarily opted for autonomy (less external control on performance) as an offset to what they see as low pay and little prestige. Teachers' unions are usually insistent on the "rights" of teachers to define how they are evaluated as well as their autonomy in the classroom. This is sometimes put forth in the form of teachers' "professional status," a symbol for independence from direct supervision.

A third reason is that when teachers are well trained and know the subject matter well, there can be real advantages in having teacher autonomy. These include *flexibility*, allowing teachers to respond to variations in students' learning styles; and *innovation*, allowing teachers to develop new ways to teach or to use the curriculum and additional materials. When most educators think about teacher autonomy, they have these highly skilled teachers in mind. If all teachers were like them, all children would probably perform academically at a much higher level than they actually do. What do school policy makers do about the reality of teaching quality? Should they continue to act on the basis of an ideal, or should they come up with a plan that confronts the level of existing capacity in the system?

Figure 5.1 outlines the nature of this problem in countries such as Brazil and Chile.[1] *Well-intentioned ministry (or state or municipal) policies, such as defining new and more demanding curriculum frameworks, are weakly coupled to actual school practice because there is little or no supervisory/instructional assistance structure to ensure that the curriculum is being implemented or that teaching practices in the classroom are effective in delivering the curriculum.* Further, teacher education is very important in influencing the nature of school practice, but ministry policies are weakly coupled to teacher education, so university preparation of teachers does not necessarily conform to the improved capacity required by ministry attempts to deliver better education. Finally,

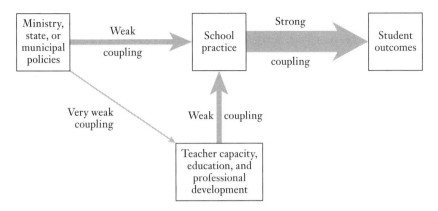

Figure 5.1   Brazil and Chile: Relationships among Components of the Educational System

school practice is important in influencing student outcomes, so the weak implementation of ministry policy results in little improvement in school practice or student outcomes.

In Cuba, on the other hand, the links between the various components of this model are much stronger. Teachers have more content knowledge because of the greater amount of content they learn in primary and secondary school. *The Cuban education system also has the enormous advantage of being able to recruit into teaching young people with relatively high standing in their secondary school cohorts because private markets do not determine Cuban salary structures.* The absence of market pricing of labor services creates problems elsewhere in the Cuban economy, but public services such as education and health care benefit from the artificially low costs of high-quality labor.

In Cuba, ministry reforms and the national curriculum are tightly linked to teacher education and professional development because they are both run directly by the ministry and focus on training teachers to deliver the national curriculum effectively. Beyond teachers' initial education, most teacher training takes place on the job, where new teachers are closely mentored by experienced teachers and school principals and vice principals. The job of these supervisors is *defined* specifically as ensuring that teachers in their school are teaching the required curriculum effectively and that students are learning it.

Our observations of teacher education, teacher supervision (on-the-job training), and school practice in the three systems leads us to conclude that Cuba gives children in its schools more opportunity to learn than either Brazil and Chile, and does it mainly in four ways:

- The Cuban curriculum does not cover as much material as do some textbooks (in Brazil), but essentially all Cuban students cover all the material in the specified Cuban curriculum. In Brazil and Chile, the curriculum coverage varies greatly from school to school. In contrast to Cuba, what is shown in textbooks in Brazil and Chile is not necessarily a measure of what children are exposed to during the academic year.

- Cuban primary school teachers have a higher level of content knowledge, particularly in math, thanks mainly to the higher levels of mathematics they attain in secondary school. This can be labeled the "virtuous circle" effect. Students are better prepared in subject matter knowledge, so the curriculum they teach when they become teachers can be more demanding.

- Teacher education in Cuba is strictly organized around teaching the required national curriculum. Pedagogical theory and child development are also an important part of teacher education, but not at the expense of teaching teachers how to reach curricular objectives.

- Teachers are closely supervised in their classroom teaching by their principals and vice principals. Every Cuban school is focused on instruction, and the primary responsibility of school administrators is to assure that children in the school are reaching clearly specified academic objectives.

As we pointed out earlier, Cuba tests students at the end of primary and lower secondary school, but this test is conducted by the municipality and seems to be used mainly as a way for the ministry to check overall performance of the system. Results are not released to the public. Thus, student testing in Cuba is fundamentally used to evaluate the system internally to the bureaucracy—a means of self-regulation to be used by the ministry for decision making, not as a government mechanism to regulate a decentralized system (Brazil and Chile) or as a measure of output in a marketized system (Chile).

In the rest of this chapter, we elaborate on these points and other features of the school systems that contribute to differences in student performance.

Curriculum

Chile and Cuba both have a required national curriculum that is implemented nationally. All schools in Cuba must follow the national curriculum. All schools in Chile, whether public or private, must deliver at least the national curriculum. Public and subsidized private schools use the ministry-selected (by a panel of experts) textbook in each grade and each subject. Like the departments of education in many U.S. states, the Brazilian Ministry of Education approves a set of textbooks that comply with ministry curriculum frameworks, and then Brazilian state departments, municipal departments, and schools adopt among the approved textbooks. We reviewed national third-grade mathematics textbooks in Cuba and Chile. In Brazil, with its decentralized textbook adoption, we reviewed the third-grade mathematics federal *frameworks* and three of the approved third-grade math textbooks.

The subjects covered in the five third-grade textbooks (three from Brazil) plus the upper-end requirements in the first cycle (grades 1–4) Brazilian frameworks are not very different. All cover somewhat complex subtraction and addition, telling time, and the beginning of multiplication and simple division. They also all cover geometric shapes, and the Cuban and two of the Brazilian textbooks cover parallel and perpendicular line. The Chilean and Brazilian textbooks are different from the Cuban textbook in that they have units on simple fractions. The Brazilian textbooks also begin some work on decimals and operations with fractions. The Cuban textbook does more work on large numbers and on geometry (angles, parallel lines, triangles, and rectangles) than the other books. Two of the Brazilian textbooks introduce division by two numbers with remainders. This is not covered in Chile or Cuba.

These are details, but the main differences lie primarily in three areas: (1) the role of the textbook—in Cuba, the textbook is clearly a supplement to teachers' lessons, providing many problem sets but relatively little detailed explanation, whereas in Chile and Brazil the textbook appears to be a "roadmap" for the teacher and generally much more "user-friendly" for students; (2) the variation in the Brazilian textbooks—the two more recently published ones (Bonjorno and Bonjorno, 2001; Marsico et al., 2004) cover some math operations and subjects that are considerably more advanced than the other Brazilian textbook (Sarquis Soares, 1997); and (3) the lower level of content in the Chilean textbook compared to two of the Brazilian textbooks and to the Cuban textbook.

The Chilean textbook is a Spanish adaptation of an American third-grade textbook originally published by Addison-Wesley in 1991 (Salgó et al., 2001). It has many of the elements of American mathematics curricula: very child-friendly explanations, with clear pictures that illustrate the concept well. In Unit 4, it takes the student through subtraction of numbers requiring "borrowing," then in Unit 5, takes the student into the concept of multiplication. Unit 6 introduces geometric shapes; Unit 7 introduces simple division; Unit 8, time; Unit 9, weights, length, and temperature; and Unit 10, simple fractions explained through pie pieces and collections of cubes.

The Cuban textbook was also published in 1991 (Villalón Incháustegui et al., 1991). It has much simpler drawings that are not as clearly illustrative of the mathematical concept being taught. On the other hand, the math problems the textbook contains are much more difficult from the very beginning. For example, on page 32, the Cuban textbook asks pupils to do conversions from meters to centimeters to millimeters, dividing by 10, 100, and 1000. Division is introduced much earlier; addition problems using columns of three- and four-digit numbers appear by page 60, and borrowing for subtraction, on page 80, about the same time in the academic year as in the Chilean textbook. The problems throughout the Cuban textbook are not nearly as well explained but are much more difficult, and there are many more of them. Multiplication and division are discussed at the same time, as inverses of each other, and the section on geometry is much more advanced than in Chile and somewhat more than in the Brazilian textbooks. Less is covered and more pages are devoted to each subject than in Brazil.

The two most recently published Brazilian textbooks differ somewhat in their approaches. Bonjorno and Bonjorno (2001) is the more traditional, covering number systems in Units 1 and 2, addition in Unit 3, subtraction in Unit 4, multiplication in Unit 5, division in Units 6 and 7, fractions in Units 8 and 9, decimals in Unit 10, measurement (money, distance, mass, capacity, and time) in Units 11–15, and geometry (shapes, angles) in Unit 16.

Marsico et al. (2004) start with number systems in Units 1 and 2; notions of geometry in Unit 3; money in Unit 4; addition, subtraction, multiplication, and division in Unit 5; back to geometry in Unit 6; the notion of math equations in Unit 7; prices and buying and selling in Unit 8; fractions in Unit 9; time in Unit 10; decimals in Unit 11; and measures of length, mass, and capacity in Units 12–14. In both textbooks, a lot of ground is covered in a relatively few pages for each subject.

Thus, although the Chilean and Brazilian textbooks are much more user-friendly, the Cuban textbook spends more time and exercises adding, subtracting, multiplying, and dividing, and more time on geometry. If Brazilian students covered all the subject matter in the two most recently published textbooks, they would be learning more math than third-grade pupils in either Cuba or Chile. And if Cuban pupils covered all the subjects in the Cuban textbook, they would probably be better versed in basic operations with numbers (complex addition and subtraction, multiplication, and simple addition) and in geometry than Chilean or Brazilian pupils, but would not know fractions, decimals, and measurement of time, mass, and capacity.

This suggests that the Cuban curriculum is much more focused on teaching well a limited set of skills than covering a lot of material. Cuban third-grade curriculum covers more than the Chilean national curriculum but is considerably more limited in coverage than two of the Brazilian textbooks. So in terms of the "technology" being used in third-grade classrooms, Cuba's technology is not as "sophisticated" as some of the Brazilian technology. However, it is important to know how much of the textbook is actually applied in the classroom. It is fine to have a high level of available technology, but if workers and managers do not know how to use it or do not use it effectively, productivity is no higher than if the technology were not available at all.

In the next chapter, we confirm that Cuban teachers do, indeed, teach the level of problems represented in the Cuban textbook and appear to cover the whole textbook as a matter of course. Furthermore, research in Chile shows that in some Chilean schools, the math covered in third grade exceeds that in the national textbook, but in other schools, teachers do not cover nearly the entire textbook. In Brazil, assessment of the curriculum is more difficult, as schools can choose among several textbooks to teach third-grade math. We looked at three of those texts and observed many classrooms but were not able to get any data on curriculum coverage or which textbooks are used where. We could confirm that in the classrooms we observed, much less was being taught than in either Chile or Cuba. Nevertheless, we have no doubt that some students in Brazilian public schools have greater opportunity to learn than in Cuba and in most Chilean public schools.

The curricula and their applications are a reflection of these different systems. The Cuban system attempts to prepare all children to a fairly high level of math competence by developing a more limited set of skills and knowledge consistently across all schools. The curriculum used is high level but covers fewer subjects than in Brazil or even Chile. Given the relatively high math skills of Cuban primary school teachers, this relatively solid curriculum is applied rather uniformly in every school. The Chilean curricular reform of the late 1990s aimed at raising knowledge in the system but within the confines of a relatively poorly trained teaching force with more limited math skills than those of Cuban teachers. The average Chilean teacher can meet the demands of the curriculum but many cannot, particularly in lower-income schools. On the other hand, many upper-middle-class schools seem to teach more math in the third grade than covered in the textbook, reflecting the tremendous inequality of student socioeconomic background among Chilean schools. In Brazil, it appears that there is little connection between what teachers can teach or most students can learn and the material presented in the third-grade textbooks. The textbooks seem more like theoretical constructs little related to teacher capacity to teach math (which is very low on average in Brazil) or to classroom practice. This disconnect is inherent in the highly decentralized management of schools. Thus, in the highly unequal Brazilian system, some schools are surely able to cover the curriculum in the two more demanding textbooks, but those schools are a small minority. The vast majority of teachers would cover only a few of the units, and many not at great depth.

Teacher Capacity and Teacher Education

TEACHER CAPACITY

We can view teacher capacity as teacher subject matter knowledge and classroom (pedagogical and management) skills. Few countries measure teacher capacity directly. Teachers are sometimes made to compete for teaching posts by taking exams or are certified by the state in a process that includes a written examination. Mexico has a teacher examination as part of an overall voluntary teacher evaluation system connected to teacher promotion and pay (*Carrera Magisterial*), but neither Brazil nor Chile nor Cuba tests or certifies teachers directly.[2] In Cuba, since the teacher colleges are run directly by the state, graduation is closely connected to certification, but the government does not measure teacher subject matter knowledge or classroom skills in a formal sense. In Brazil and Chile, graduation from a teacher-training institution results in automatic certification without any further government regulation. Neither government sets minimum subject matter standards.

Thus, we have to infer teacher capacity by observing teacher education and classroom teaching or using proxy variables. We originally intended to test third-grade math teachers by giving them a set of problems related to the third-grade curriculum, but this proved difficult because school directors were reluctant to have us test their teachers. Most studies rely on teacher education data (level of education) on the assumption that more highly educated teachers have higher levels of content knowledge. In our empirical analysis of Latin American country third and fourth graders, we used this proxy for teacher capacity.

In two of the countries we studied, Chile and Cuba, about three-fourths of the teachers teaching in primary school had university-level teacher education. In Brazil, only about one-fourth of the teachers in the third- and fourth-grade UNESCO sample had training at that level. Most of the remaining teachers have completed basic education (eighth grade) and three to four years of teacher education at the secondary level (secondary level normal school). Most Brazilian school teachers teaching in grades one to four fit into this category, although some teachers have even less education. In the poorer Northeast, in 2000, 68 percent of first- through fourth-grade teachers were trained at the secondary level normal school, and 20 percent had eight or fewer years of school. In the rural Northeast, 34 percent of teachers in 2000 had eight or fewer years of schooling (World Bank, 2001).

According to our analysis of the UNESCO Laboratorio data, the fact that a teacher was trained at the university level makes a significant difference in student mathematics performance in third and fourth grade in Brazil and Chile, but not in Cuba (see Appendix A). This result makes sense, but *not* because of the excellence of teacher education at universities compared to secondary level normal schools. Rather, from our interviews, we think it is the result of the better basic math skills of teachers in Brazil and Chile who have completed general secondary education, then gone on to teacher training at the university level. Compared with those (older) teachers who finished only eight years of general education and then took their teacher training in secondary level normal schools, university-trained primary teachers in Brazil and Chile have completed four more years of math courses. The teachers with secondary level normal school training are also more likely to teach in lower-income regions and schools. With considerable variation in student performance across regions, particularly in Brazil, part of the variation is therefore probably due to differences in teacher basic math and language skills.

It also makes sense that in Cuba, differences in teacher education do not have a significant effect on student performance in the first four grades of primary school, for two reasons: First, (older) Cuban teachers with a secondary level normal school education may teach in poorer provinces, but the differences in Cuban student performance are much smaller across rural and urban schools and across regions than in Brazil and Chile. Second, even those in Cuba who finished only ninth or tenth grade (these are the minimum levels of education that would permit them to go on to normal schools— teacher training institutions) in the years before the present system was in place) were much better prepared in mathematics and language than eighth graders and possibly even secondary school graduates in Brazil and Chile.

In addition, secondary school graduates who apply to education faculties at universities in Brazil and Chile have traditionally not been as well prepared in subject matter knowledge as those who apply to the disciplinary departments, particularly in math and science. According to a World Bank report on teachers and teacher education in Brazil, "[Secondary school][S]tudents applying for teacher training programs had the lowest *vestibular* (college entrance examination) scores, relative to students applying for other under undergraduate disciplines; attrition rates while in school were high, evidencing low motivation. . . . Today FUNDEF-driven salary increases are changing the picture. . . . [H]igh unemployment rates in other sectors have also turned teaching into a more appealing profession, with large numbers applying to enter the career" (World Bank, 2001, p. 21). Even so, the report goes on, in poorer regions, it is difficult to find enough highly qualified individuals to staff the classrooms needing teachers.

Chile has taken one major step to recruiting higher-ability secondary school graduates into teaching by tripling teacher salaries over the past thirteen years. Thus, teachers' earnings have risen substantially relative to other professional salaries. Subsequently, average college entrance scores of students going into university education faculties began to rise in 1998–2001.[3] If the premise is true that what students learn in high school has a major effect on their subject matter knowledge later as teachers, the subject matter knowledge of new teachers should begin rising as the classes of 2004 and 2005 enter the labor market.

Cuba has had a distinct advantage over Brazil and Chile in being able to recruit higher-achieving secondary school graduates into teacher education. Salary differences in Cuba between teachers and other professionals have been small since the early 1960s. Combined with relatively strong math and science programs in Cuban secondary schools that build on strong mathematics teaching in the lower grades, the subject matter knowledge of Cuban teachers, even those teaching in primary grades, is greater than that of teachers in Brazil and Chile. With the growth of the tourist industry, on which Cuba depends for hard currency, the government's ability to recruit people into teaching is changing, as we pointed out in Chapter 1, but the strong preparation among all students in subject matter knowledge remains.

Pedagogical skills, on the other hand, should be developed in teacher education courses and supervised practice in student teaching and the initial years of classroom work. Let's turn to the differences we observed in the three countries in this kind of capacity building.

TEACHER EDUCATION

Teacher education and professional development systems vary from country to country. Strange as it may seem, teacher education in most countries is run by universities that are autonomous from the state apparatus that operates the educational system. The courses for student teachers are organized by professors of education based on what they think a teacher should know—this includes a healthy dose of "theories" of teaching, curriculum development, the sociology of education, and child psychology. Student teachers usually observe teachers teaching in school as part of their course work, then student teach for a semester in their last year of university or pedagogical college.

On second thought, however, this is not so strange. Professionals in most fields are trained in universities and get degrees without even a semester of practice unless they work during vacations or part-time during the school year. Doctors are an exception, as they intern and then usually go through a supervised residency.

Yet the separation between teacher education and state monitoring of teacher skills creates serious problems in building a level of teacher capacity that would deliver a higher-powered, more demanding curriculum. First, those who teach teachers in universities may be largely unfamiliar with the newest curricula used in the schools. Second, university professors seek prestige, and prestige is associated with abstraction. Teaching abstract reasoning to students studying to be teachers can be very useful, but abstract reasoning divorced from solving classroom teaching problems does not help students become good teachers.

Faculties of education in all three countries are also distinctly separated from other faculties in universities, a division that gives education students relatively little opportunity to take content courses in other departments. So unless teachers are recruited from mathematics, science, or literature departments and given short, specialized teacher training, the level of subject matter knowledge, especially for primary and middle school teachers, is likely to be at the lower end of the spectrum of college graduates. Indeed, most primary school teachers are likely never to have taken a mathematics or science course past high school. Thus, as we discussed earlier, primary and middle school teacher capacity to teach mathematics or science depends greatly on the quality of instruction and the required courses in secondary school. Secondary school teachers are more specialized and better prepared, but because they take their subject matter courses in the education department, they are not being evaluated against university math, language, and science majors. Consequently, they are probably going to have less subject matter knowledge than, say, a physics or math major. This could be acceptable if the education students had to meet the same standards required of students in the disciplinary faculties. Yet that is usually not the case.

Most teachers in Brazil and Chile are currently trained in publicly funded, autonomous universities. A recent evaluation of teacher education in Brazil "characterized initial teacher education (ITE) programs as ineffective: where delivered by normal schools, they are academically weak; and when delivered by universities, they show an excessive theoretical bias. In both cases, school-based *practicums* or internships are limited, with little connection between theory and practice" (World Bank, 2001, p. 22). In a recent visit to Chile, we found that despite efforts by the ministry to assure that universities offering preservice teacher training focus their teacher preparation on using the new national curriculum frameworks, the teaching in these faculties of education remained highly theoretical; subject matter preparation was minimal, particularly for basic education teachers; and the teaching practice component was, in many cases, minimally supervised (OECD, 2003).

We interviewed many students studying to be secondary school teachers in both Chile and Cuba. In Chile, students pointed out that their education provided very limited opportunities to practice and to develop appropriate pedagogies. Their main complaint was that they learned a lot about the theory of teaching (for example, we observed a class studying critical sociology) and about their subject discipline (for example, Spanish literature), but had very little training in teaching the national curriculum. As one fourth-year student in a southern Chile university told us: "I know a lot about the theory of teaching and a lot about Spanish, but almost nothing about *teaching* Spanish." In Cuba, the national curriculum is at the center of teacher education. Students in teacher training colleges learn theory but focus heavily on learning how to teach the curriculum effectively.

The evaluation of Brazil's teacher education also found that pedagogical practice in most teacher training departments is traditional and frontal and, as in Chile, disconnected from the new curriculum guidelines.

As would be expected, Cuba's teacher preservice education is centrally controlled. Although there are teacher education university-level institutes in each province, their curriculum is developed by the ministry of education and constructed around teaching the official primary and secondary school curricula using well-developed teaching techniques based on the educational philosophies of people such as Vygotsky, Makarenko, and Dewey. Teacher educators in these institutes have generally been teachers themselves and have gone on for advanced degrees in education or specific subject matter. There is a clear objective to teacher education: teach student-teachers to deliver the national curriculum; to serve as a social and pedagogical guide for students; and, in the case of those who will be teaching primary school students, to nurture their young pupils, acting as a quasi-parent through the first stage of the young ones' education.

But Cuba faces the same problem as Chile and Brazil regarding the separation of pedagogical institutes from subject matter departments, hence the quality of subject matter preparation of secondary school teachers compared with subject matter majors. Cuba is at an interesting historical moment because of its lower secondary (seventh- to ninth-grade) reform. The ministry is training 4,000 specially recruited[4] new teachers for this level in an intensive two-year program, of which only the first year is all course work; in the second year, courses are combined with supervised classroom practice. The new teachers will be teaching math, science, and language from a demanding European-style curriculum. Many teachers now specializing in teaching one subject will be also converted into multisubject teachers.

Can bright high school graduates be turned into competent lower secondary school teachers with two years of teacher education? The experiment of using short-preparation teachers to speed up the lower secondary reform is potentially fraught with difficulties. These young teachers—not much older than the students they are to teach—are expected to deliver high-quality education in a number of subjects at the middle school level. Older teachers in the same schools that had specialized in one subject now must teach many subjects besides their specialty. The idea behind the reform is to improve quality by using the primary school model of a single teacher for almost all subjects for several years. Whether it will work depends very much on the content knowledge and the success of the short-term preparation strategy being followed by the ministry.

We met some of these *emergente* students at the Salvador Allende Pedagogical Institute in Habana. They are impressive in their enthusiasm, and they are very articulate, just like many of the students we met in Chile. The main difference we noted between Cuba and Chile is that the Cuban students are trained in cadres, with each cadre overseen by a mentor teacher who will follow them into and oversee their student teaching. Another difference is that the training is entirely focused on teaching the required curriculum, so content and pedagogical knowledge is taught using the lower secondary curriculum. Thus, practice, not theory, is at the center of their teachers' education.

It is perfectly understandable that education students intending to become teachers want to study the many wonderful works written about

education from sociological, philosophical, historical, economic, and political perspectives. If teachers are to be intellectual leaders, they have to
prepare themselves intellectually, not just vocationally. We have spoken
with many teachers and all of them like the intellectually loaded courses—
the ones that made them reflect critically on education and the role of the
teacher—most of all. Teachers also found them useful in the sense that
reading these various perspectives helped situate teachers and teaching in a
broader educational and social context.

That said, it appears that teacher education programs in countries such
as Brazil and Chile do not balance these useful and intellectually stimulating courses with sufficient focus on the vocational skills required to be a
good teacher.

Assuring Opportunity to Learn

How much pupils learn in school depends greatly on what concepts they are
exposed to, how much time they spend studying these concepts, and how
effective their teachers are in communicating them. Curriculum coverage
is crucial to opportunity to learn, and so is the "quality" of curriculum coverage. If teachers and students are often absent from school or the teacher
is incapable of explaining key concepts or uses teaching methods that burn
time in the classroom but do little to advance student skills, students will not
learn much. Yet, all these conditions prevail regularly in Latin American
schools. They reflect low expectations and totally inadequate management
of the educational system.

Expectations are strongly influenced by the sociopolitical context of each
country. So is management of the educational system. Attitudes of teachers
and administrators toward lower- and higher-social-class families and their
children depend heavily on a country's social class structure, as do school
personnel's views on different racial groups, indigenous peoples, and gender
roles. But the state controls educational management, so in our study, we
focused on the ways the three countries differed in addressing the management problem. The broad issue is how government approaches guaranteeing
all students a reasonable opportunity to learn. What management system
does government use to implement its curriculum frameworks, and does

this system assure a reasonable opportunity to learn for all students? The main elements of an educational management system concern supervising teacher work and how closely the system monitors student learning.

SUPERVISING TEACHERS' WORK

Many teaching skills are learned on the job while teachers are teaching courses in classrooms. This process starts when a person is a student teacher, continues in the teacher's first job, and continues for a number of years. How teachers are mentored and supervised during these early experiences can make a major difference in a teacher's capacity to teach effectively. The mentoring has two major components: First, assuming that the recommended curriculum is an effective basis for teaching students academic skills, mentoring can be a crucial aid to understanding how to apply the curriculum effectively. Second, "good" teachers and knowledgeable supervisors can help new teachers become better pedagogues and classroom managers by working closely with them over several years.

Where mentoring and instructional supervision is not an integral part of educational management, new teachers have to learn by doing, with little or no feedback. Some of them become effective on their own at delivering the curriculum. They become good teachers based on natural talent, sensitivity to how well they are communicating with students, and a high level of conscientiousness in their practice. But left to learning on their own, most teachers fall into patterns that are not at all effective, and they either do not know that is the case, or do not care. A certain fraction of teachers in every system regard teaching as just another way to get a paycheck, and if they can avoid showing up for work and still get paid, they will do so. For a large-scale educational system to function well, it has to have a management system in place that develops reasonably high levels of teaching skills through experience and guarantees that teachers show up for work and provide the required opportunity to learn to all students.

Our observations in Brazil and Chile indicated that their educational management systems fell far short of this standard. Our observations in Cuba suggested that its management system is much more focused on *instruction*. Further, teachers in Cuba are accustomed to being observed in their classrooms by school administrators and "evaluated" constructively.

Beginning teachers are heavily mentored to assure a "learning transition" into teaching. In Cuban primary schools, a single teacher has traditionally been responsible for a cohort of children from first to fourth grade. In this system there can be little finger pointing at other teachers if a child is not making progress, and greater responsibility is placed on both teachers and supervisors to assure that teachers are implementing the curriculum according to plan, and that children in the cohort are achieving as well as in other cohorts in the same school and in the municipality.

What is it about the organization of schooling in Brazil and Chile that makes teachers in those two countries much less likely to fulfill curriculum goals than teachers in Cuba? The three of us visited about thirty schools in Chile, twenty-five in Brazil, and ten in Cuba, and interviewed principals, vice principals, and teachers in each school. We also visited teacher training colleges and faculties of education in universities in the three countries, and we interviewed teachers' union representatives and ministry officials. Based on the massive amount of qualitative information collected, we identified the following main *organizational* problems, beyond the problems of teacher capacity and education discussed earlier:

- Beginning teachers get mixed supervision in their new schools, mostly no more than the required evaluations by supervisors, often— especially in rural schools—not even that.
- Teachers in Brazil and Chile have won the "right" to have almost total autonomy in their classrooms, hence are rarely observed by administrators.
- School administrators in Brazil and Chile are generally not expected or trained to be instructional leaders. In turn, both because of teacher autonomy and because they lack the capacity to improve instruction effectively, principals and vice principals are reluctant to critique teachers' practice, except in extreme cases.
- The traditional supervision system, imported from Europe, of school "inspection," never reached near the levels of implementation in Brazil or Chile that it did, for example, in France or Italy, where inspectors play an important policy role, but still do not do much supervising. In Chile, *supervisores* have recently replaced inspectors. *Supervisores*, too, play a limited role in actually intervening to improve instruction,

although they could if they were given the power to do so and a different teacher-supervisor relationship prevailed. Thus, in effect, there is no meaningful supervision of teacher practice.

- In the past ten years, both Brazil and Chile have tried to improve teacher effort, curriculum implementation, and quality of classroom practice with forms of "indirect" supervision, namely, testing student performance and, in the case of Brazil, greater parent participation. Chile has used test results since 1995 to pay bonuses to teachers in schools that made the largest gains in each region on the fourth- and eighth-grade SIMCE tests. Undoubtedly, student testing has had a positive effect on teachers' becoming aware that their students' performance on these tests is important (Mizala and Romaguera, 2001). In turn, it may have caused some teachers to improve their teaching. Yet until now, there is no evidence that such teacher incentives improve student performance[5] and some evidence that it does not (Carnoy et al., 2005).

- Thus, whether for ideological reasons, or because educational reformers feel that they cannot strengthen direct supervision, the reliance in Brazil and Chile on testing and other forms of "indirect" supervision (incentives), apparently makes it difficult to improve teaching.

It is symptomatic of the larger supervision and support problem that there is no systematic "induction" of new teachers into classroom practice. A team from the OECD (Organization for Economic Cooperation and Development) reviewing Chile's education system concluded that "there is no formal induction policy, despite the fact that much research indicates the long-term effects of the early formative experiences of the new teacher. While instances occur, no doubt, of senior staff providing some guidance and assistance to teachers beginning their careers, when it occurs it is due to good will rather than any requirement" (OECD 2004, p. 135). Similarly, the World Bank report on teachers in Brazil states:

> Fresh graduates from teacher education programs, few of whom have had adequate classroom exposure, are frequently overwhelmed by the complexity of the decisions to be made in the classroom, the multiplicity of tasks to be performed, and student discipline problems. . . . The lack of a systematic process to mentor or coach beginning teachers during the first year

or two makes this period of their career more difficult than it needs to be, and may have a lasting impact on morale and performance. (World Bank, 2001, pp. 36–37)

The lack of support for new teachers in Brazil and Chile[6] is embedded in a larger tradition of laissez-faire in schools, in which teachers are expected to teach on their own, and school directors are expected to "administer" the day-to-day operations of the school, yet not get involved in teachers' classrooms. This tradition has changed in Chile, but toward systemwide incentives or accountability, and is changing in Brazil in a similar direction. Both countries are avoiding the more direct teacher evaluation and support that is the norm in Cuba. The Chilean strategy, promoted by international agencies such as the World Bank and Inter-American Bank has made improvements, but not to the degree necessary to reach desired outcomes.

The main form of accountability being used in Chile is systemwide student testing, with school average results reported publicly testing results used for rewarding schools financially. As discussed earlier, student test results have served many purposes, but most recently they have become a benchmark of student performance, given parents information in choosing schools (Chile has a nationwide choice system), and acted as an indicator for teacher salary bonuses. However, there are no sanctions on schools or teachers in not making test score gains other than potential parent disfavor.

Despite twenty years of testing, in the typical public school in Chile the new curriculum is applied unevenly, and principals focus on paperwork, not instruction in the classroom. In the typical private school, the principal focuses on student recruitment and meeting the bottom line financially. Although most schools are acutely aware of their test scores, few principals or teachers are able or willing to use the data provided by the ministry to evaluate classroom teaching, except to spot obvious deficiencies. Ultimately, the system relies on school personnel knowing how to make improvements once they are provided with the information on student performance in fourth- and eighth-grade tests. Although some schools mobilize around these test scores, most do no more than exhort teachers to get the scores up without providing roadmaps for doing so.

Schools in Chile also compete with each other for students. Most principals admitted that they tried to attract students by raising test scores, improving the physical plant (including getting more computers per student), and reducing student disturbances. Yet the most important factors attracting families to private schools seemed to be the average socioeconomic class of the peer group (including the absence of the worst-behaved students in private schools) and access to an academic secondary school in the same establishment, with the potential of passing the university entrance examination. The rapid growth of privately managed, publicly funded education slowed during the 1980s but continued into the 1990s, and, as a result, municipal education lost hundreds of thousands of pupils to private competitors, mostly new, "for-profit" schools (meaning that they were run by individuals who derived income from the school) that were created in response to the voucher system. Yet researchers have not been able to find positive effects on student performance in public schools or in all schools taken together in municipalities with a higher density of private schools, hence more competition (Hsieh and Urquiola, 2002; McEwan and Carnoy, 1999).

One reason it is difficult to identify a positive "competition effect" is that the shift from municipal to private voucher schools appears to be marked by "cream skimming," the practice of private schools of enticing easier-to-teach pupils from public schools. "Cream skimming" would tend to lower average test scores over time in municipal schools even as competition might tend to raise scores in those same schools. It is difficult to identify the two separate effects. So competition might be stimulating municipal schools to greater effort, raising test scores, but these same municipal schools might simultaneously be enrolling more difficult-to-teach students.

In 1996, the Chilean Ministry of Education began paying salary premiums to teachers based on several criteria, the most important being student gains from exam year to exam year on the fourth- and eighth-grade SIMCE of the school in which the teachers worked. This program of incentives is called the Sistema Nacional de Evaluación del Desempeño Docente (SNED). The SNED chooses the schools with the highest gains from test year to test year in each region and gives a maximum of 25 percent of the schools in each region an additional subsidy for each student. Ninety percent of this additional subsidy has to be distributed to teachers in the school based on the number of hours taught. The other 10 percent goes to teachers determined by each school to have done an especially good job.

The SNED tries to compare like schools with like schools in assessing which ones should qualify for the premium—the socioeconomic background of students is taken into account as well as the "selectivity" of the school. If a school is more selective in choosing students, it is given less credit for gains from test year to test year. In calculating the SNED score, the average score in the last fourth-, eighth-, and tenth-grade SIMCE is weighted at 37 percent; the difference in the last two SIMCE tests available for each grade counts as 28 percent of the SNED score; the development of a whole list of activities counts as 6 percent of the score; the rate of retention of the students, lack of selectivity, and other attainment and egalitarian measures are weighted as 22 percent of the score; parent participation and opinion of the school counts as 5 percent; and 2 percent is given for equality of opportunity (see Mizala and Romaguera, 2001, for details on the criteria used to assess schools in the SNED).

According to Mizala and Romaguera, a majority of teachers agree that a system of premiums based on teacher performance makes sense. This implies, they argue, that teacher resistance to incentive pay has declined and that the teacher corps is ready to accept some sort of pay variation based on teachers' ability to improve student performance.

Even if this were the case, however, for the SNED to be educationally meaningful, there should be a positive relationship between the incentive pay represented by the SNED awards and student achievement gains from fourth to eighth grades (how much schools improve student performance over the last four years of basic education). For example, say that a group of schools in a region got SNED premiums in 1996 or 1998 or 2000. What was the correlation between the premiums received (between 0 and 3) and how well students did on the eighth-grade test in 2000 relative to the score on the fourth-grade test in 1996? Is there a set of schools that is consistently responding to incentive pay by improving student progress between the fourth grade and the eighth grade, or is the SNED more like a lottery, with some schools doing well one year and another set of schools doing well another year but no relationship to student gains over the fifth, sixth, seventh, and eighth grades? Are teachers in certain schools organized by the director or organizing themselves to get SNED premiums, particularly on the fourth-grade tests?

Despite the existence of the SNED since 1996, average test scores on the SIMCE have not risen significantly. Unless there is a realignment of schools—some steadily rising (the ones that are responding to the SNED)—

and others steadily falling (those not responding to the SNED)—the evidence on SIMCE scores suggests that the SNED is *not* having a systematically positive impact on student performance. The number of awards received is highly correlated with the fourth-grade test score in 1996, but not with school gain in scores between the fourth and eighth grade in 1996–2000. Because SIMCE scores form such an important element in determining SNED rewards, the fact that the reward seems to have had little impact on the gain in SIMCE scores is significant. It appears that schools have an easier time doing well on the fourth-grade test, but not in improving scores between fourth and eighth grades.

The SNED's underlying assumption is that school directors and teachers will innovate, work harder, and generally find ways to improve student performance in order to get more money. However, there could be many reasons that such a system would not work. For example, the system assumes that teachers know how to increase student learning but are not willing to do so unless they get pay premiums. Yet there is little evidence that teachers are actually holding back on fully using their competence because better teachers get paid no more than worse teachers. A second reason is that the school capacity to raise fourth-grade test scores is not the same as the capacity to help students learn more over a four-year period. Besides teaching to the SIMCE test, teachers (and school directors) may not know how to improve learning from grade to grade. Schools are not being evaluated on cohort gains, but rather on the gains *across* cohorts (Carnoy et al., 2005).

This is not to say that there aren't good teachers in Chile or that no principals act as instructional leaders. In Santiago, we visited a public school in a low-income area in the western part of the city. The school has many children with learning difficulties (91 of 646 pupils in grades 1–8 so designated), yet in the past few years, thanks to an energetic principal who is committed to improving learning in the school, test scores rose sharply. The school is able to compete successfully with private primary schools nearby that do not have to take special education students.

The school provided us a good example of the implicit meaning of and limits to using test data and "good" instructional supervision in Chile. One teacher's fourth-grade class (of three fourth-grade classrooms in the school) had much lower math test scores than other fourth-grade classes in the same school but high language results in 2002. The principal and the vice principal in charge of academics told us that they had been aware of the teacher's difficulties with the math curriculum during the school year, which, to their credit, would not have been the case in most Chilean schools. They had asked another teacher to take over the math teaching in the class, but the other teacher declined. The administration apparently did not have the knowledge or power to address directly the original teacher's difficulties teaching math, either through some careful monitoring and assistance, or through inservice courses. A private school in Chile might have fired that teacher at the end of the year, but a public school could not.

We visited a one-room rural public school in a poor region where an experienced teacher was subjecting thirteen children in grades one to six, many obviously bright and eager to learn, to the most irresponsible, ineffective teaching we had seen. The children's parents seemed to be unaware of the low quality of education their children were getting. As far as we could tell, no government agency was providing even the minimum supervision over this abysmally poor delivery of the required curriculum. Yet, five kilometers from this school, we visited another school, this one a subsidized private school, that provided reasonably good instruction and where similar socioeconomic background children were learning a lot more.

We also visited subsidized private primary schools that selected their students and had waiting lists. In one, the principal had implemented innovative approaches in teaching; but even so, the level of writing of students in the early grades was surprisingly poor. This raises another issue: relatively low standards can keep school conceptions of quality in students' work relatively low. Little was being done to improve student performance in that school because by Chilean standards as measured by the SIMCE test, children in the school performed well, and applications greatly exceeded available places.

In Brazil, indirect evaluation or "accountability" on the Chilean model, either through incentives provided by competition or monetary rewards for higher test scores, is practically nonexistent. The *Sistema Nacional de Avaliação da Educação Básica* (SAEB) test is given to a sample of students in each state, so individual schools are not evaluated by the test. The SAEB results are published, indicating national improvement or lack of improvement over time, and regional differences. This is useful for national and regional benchmarking but not for ensuring that teachers are doing the best possible job in delivering curriculum to students.

The highly decentralized nature of Brazilian education has placed much of the responsibility for designing and implementing instructional improvement plans on states and municipalities. In Minas Gerais, for example, where we filmed several classrooms, school governance is highly decentralized, and schools are highly autonomous. Teachers and the community select principals from a list of candidates screened by the state secretariat of education. An elected council composed of student, teacher, and community representatives manages the school. They have choices as to pedagogy and curriculum, and some discretionary funds to innovate in both areas. In theory, this should improve teaching, but teachers in Minas Gerais also have a lot of autonomy in their classrooms. Just as in the rest of Brazil, they are compelled to change their teaching only if someone actually observes them teaching and has the capacity and legitimacy to help them change. This is not a regular activity of the school councils. The notion that, based on clearly understood criteria of effective teaching, school councils can sanction or reward teachers, or even recommend that teachers seek professional development assistance, is not part of the school governance culture.

The inspectorate system still exists as the main form of supervision. Inspectors come to the school, perhaps reviewing school plans and observing a few classrooms, but providing almost no training and/or support. A form of external supervisor is being created in some states. This supervisor is more like a "facilitator." He or she brings materials to the school, conducts workshops, and so forth. One trend appears to be to upgrade supervisory personnel, requiring them to have a higher education degree and to have taught at least two years. They also they have to compete for the position.

The school director is responsible for problems in the school. The supervisors do not check teacher attendance—this is the director's responsibility. Another trend is to do a better job preparing directors for supervising and serving as instructional leaders, but as it stands now, Brazilian directors, like their Chilean counterparts, are basically bureaucrats who stay in their offices and deal with administrative details.

The pedagogical coordinator in Brazil is the closest thing to an in-house supervisor and/or teacher trainer. However, our experience in schools concurs with researchers we interviewed and the World Bank report on teaching in Brazil (2001) that the pedagogical coordinators are of limited utility and do not appear to spend any time in classrooms. Instead they organize workshops with the whole group of teachers. Or as one of us found, they are the ones to answer the phone when someone calls the school.

We visited one urban middle-class school in a lower- to middle-income state considered good enough by parents that children attending came from many different parts of the city. The pedagogical coordinator admitted to us that she rarely observed teachers in their classroom. We filmed two language classes in that school and observed teaching that was obviously ineffective— very little learning was taking place. In one class, pupils wandered around while the teacher wrote text on the board, her back to the class, for children to copy and discuss. A pedagogical coordinator interested in improving the quality of teaching in the school could have easily helped these teachers do much better. Yet that was apparently not how this and most pedagogical coordinators interpreted their job.

Nevertheless, as in Chile, the situation in Brazil is hardly static. Many states and municipalities are engaged in various improvement efforts, such as the Fundescola program in poorer states. Fundescola provides limited funds to schools for planning, some equipment purchases, and staff development. But these programs do not deal at all with improving classroom teaching. The national legislature passed a resolution in March 1997 providing that incentives over and above automatic seniority and qualification pay increases should be tied to teacher quality standards and evaluations of teacher competencies (known as the PCC). But "implementation of the PCC requirement has proven difficult . . . due partly . . . to a lack of consensus among stakeholders" (World Bank, 2001, p. 37).

The closest thing to a program that directly addresses teaching quality is in Ceará. That state created a pedagogical support system in 1998—a set of regional centers where pedagogical coordinators meet to plan visits to schools, evaluate ongoing professional development programs, and offer a mentoring program for *interested* teachers. "A cutting-edge feature is that the teachers in the network who exhibit most improvement in their practice may, in turn, become mentors and instructors at the regional centers, and then return to their school, a practice shown to have strong impact on teacher learning and performance in other countries" (World Bank, 2001, Box 4.4, p. 40).

In sum, Brazil and Chile rely largely on teachers delivering the required curriculum effectively without any institutional mechanisms in place to assure that they do so or even systematically to assist them in achieving this crucial goal. In both countries, there are many talented teachers, and they teach effectively, although even in those cases, they are likely to have lower standards than effective (and many ineffective) teachers in highly developed countries. Chile has relied on competition among schools and indirect monetary incentives to induce teachers to improve learning in schools. But because no sanctions are imposed on schools that make low or no test score gains, teachers do not have to respond to competition or incentives, and most do not change how they teach unless their students are doing much worse than others in the school. Even then, as we suggested, public schools are not likely to be able to fire or move their teachers.

The administrative team in a Cuban school is *required by the political system* to act as instructional leaders. This translates into a school culture of directly supervising and assisting teachers in their early years to improve their teaching. It also puts much greater direct responsibility on every primary school teacher for the learning of a cohort of children. We observed this in every school we visited—in schools catering to children of relatively highly educated parents, to schools in the more "proletarian" suburbs of Habana to rural two- or three-room schools in the provinces.

This culture of supervision and teacher responsibility is undoubtedly embedded in the hierarchical governance structure of Cuban politics and society. But it is also embedded in a strategy in which the state takes primary responsibility for assuring opportunity to learn for every child in the society. Teachers in Cuba are considered professionals and responsible for delivering the state curriculum, but their professionalism does not include autonomy at the expense of student learning. The organization of schools in Cuba is subject to the categorical imperative of achieving the goals of the curriculum in every classroom, and school principals and vice principals share responsibility with teachers to assure that the teachers in their school are doing their job. Municipality officials, in turn, share responsibility for student performance in schools in their district. Teachers know that if they do not act responsibly to assure that the children in their charge learn the material, they will be relieved of their duties; at the same time, the teachers we talk to believed in their work and had real affection for the children they taught.

We don't want to idealize this system of supervision because it is hardly flawless. Not every teacher in Cuba is effective, and we are sure that a lot of poor teaching slips through the cracks. However, as we show in the next chapter, classroom teaching is, on average, more effective in Cuba than in Brazil or Chile; and from what we observed, at least part of this greater effectiveness is due to a much more pervasive system of administrative involvement in and vigilance toward the quality of instruction. Our interviews with principals, vice principals, and teachers in Cuba centered on that issue. A principal of a primary school with 400–600 pupils could name every child with learning difficulties and the steps that were being taken to help the child, including sending a teacher home to speak with the parents, checking on issues with the family, and trying to work on particular parts of the curriculum with which the child was encountering difficulties.

At the same time, most teachers in Cuba have been empowered by very good training and constructive supervision to be effective in their job—they are not only made to feel responsible for the children they teach, but they are given the skills to turn those feelings of responsibility into high levels of student learning.

Teacher and Student Attendance

The supervision issue plays out most clearly in teacher and student attendance. Teacher attendance is a chronic problem in Latin America and in the developing countries more generally. An eight-country research study found 15 percent teacher absentee rates in Peru and Ecuador, and 25 percent in India (Kremer et al., 2004, Table 2). In another recent study, Marshall found that of 140 "official" days of school in Guatemala (already a low figure compared to many other countries), school was held an average of only 110 days in his sample of almost 60 rural schools (Marshall, 2003). In Argentina in the late 1990s, government officials in various provinces claimed that about 20 percent of teachers were absent more than five days per month from their classrooms (Carnoy, Cox, Cosse, and Martinez, 2004). Teachers' unions denied this, but many provinces implemented salary penalties for frequent absences anyway. In Brazil and Chile, one of the most common complaints we heard from public school principals was the number of medical absences. In Chile, this is partially provoked by a poor pension system that leaves many older teachers without sufficient pension to survive should they retire, so they keep teaching into their late sixties and seventies, when indeed health becomes an issue.

Teacher absences are related to student absences, and the two together lead to lower student achievement. This seems obvious, but it is not simple to prove. Marshall's research in Guatemala uses complex econometric methods and some of the best data collection ever done in rural schools to show that teacher attendance (the actual number of days the teacher meets with students during the school year) can be taken as a proxy for school quality, and Guatemalan parents seem to react to lower school quality by sending their children less often to school. This is particularly true in the case of boys. Marshall (2003) also shows that ten more school days per year (one standard deviation from a mean of 110 days) is associated with an increase of one-third of a standard deviation in student achievement.

Teacher absences in rural schools are provoked by isolated conditions, the unwillingness of teachers to live at the school, and the lack of support by the educational system to make rural education more tolerable and stimulating (Marshall, 2003). Colombia implemented the *Escuela Nueva* program in the 1980s. It features monthly get-togethers for rural teachers with workshops and lots of special materials. Careful evaluations of *Escuela Nueva* indicate that the system has worked to increase teacher and student attendance and achievement (McEwan, 1998).

In Brazil, the World Bank has been pushing more of an accountability approach to rural absenteeism: greater parent participation in evaluating rural teachers, with salary consequences for lower attendance, based on the apparent success of the EDUCO project in El Salvador. This, too, is an appealing solution to the days-of-schooling issue, although there are conflicting appraisals of the results from EDUCO (Jimenez and Sawada, 1999).

Teacher absenteeism, unfortunately, is a persistent problem with roots in notions of civic duty, trust, and obligation, as well as lack of adequate supervision and accountability. Student absenteeism, which as long been situated in family decisions about the value of children's work relative to the value of additional schooling, now can be also related to parents' perception of school quality (hence a more nuanced conception of the value of schooling). Teacher absenteeism is an important variable affecting school quality, parents react by keeping their children home, and student achievement and attainment suffer.

In the countries we studied, teacher and student absenteeism is probably most frequent in Brazil and least frequent in Cuba. Chile has some problem with absenteeism, but it is small compared to the absenteeism in most Latin American countries. For example, self-reported student absences survey by the TIMSS in Chile showed about the same level as that in many developed countries. Obviously, this varies among regions. In some rural areas absences are high, particularly in periods of bad weather. In Cuba, absenteeism appears very low, in part because if children are sick for more than a day or two, a teacher usually stops by the house to make sure everything is all right. We interviewed a kindergarten teacher in a tiny (29 pupils) rural school in Piñar del Rio province; one of her six kindergartners had been out for a second day, and she sent someone to inquire about the child.

One could argue that in Cuba teachers avoid absences out of fear. That may be so, but it is just as likely that teachers in both Cuba and Chile and in many schools in Brazil show up regularly because they are socialized to do their jobs on a day-to-day basis. We got the sense that especially in Cuba, teachers are taught to feel responsible for their students and how much they learn. The social context of teaching, teachers' view of themselves as responsible or not responsible for their students, and the degree of control by someone (principal, municipality, or central government) of teacher behavior are all important factors in influencing teacher presence or absence in the classroom on a day-to-day basis. Without these elements, teacher (and student) absenteeism is likely to be a serious problem in schools—a problem that must be solved for the school system to work effectively.

We need to mention one other difference between Cuban schools and schools in Chile and Brazil. Cuba has long had a full day of school—from 8:15 in the morning until 4:20 in the afternoon, with an hour and a half break for lunch. Chilean schools have only begun to move to a six-hour day (*jornada completa*) since 1998. Brazilian schools generally operate on a double shift, and even a triple shift, with night school. To be fair, Cuban schools and those with a full day program in Chile do little academic work after lunch. Cuba has some educational television programs that all relevant classes must watch for forty-five minutes each afternoon, but that is it; the rest is almost all recess and quiet time. The same is now true in Chile. Afternoon activities are mostly extracurricular. What effect the extra hours have on academic performance is unknown, although some studies of longer school days show positive results (Aronson, Zimmerman, and Carlos, 1998).

Summing Up

In terms of the main variables connecting curriculum construction to curriculum delivery—teacher acquired capacity through teacher education, new teacher induction, and teacher supervision and development on the job—Brazil and Chile do not do nearly as good a job as Cuba, and this appears to account for much of the difference in students' performance in the three countries. Cuban teachers come out of secondary school with better subject matter knowledge, they get a teacher education that focuses on practical instruction methods using the national curriculum, and they are supervised and trained in the early years of their career by school administrators and mentor teachers. Almost all schools are specifically organized around instruction, a focus that differs from that of most schools in Brazil and Chile.

The main effects of poor supervision systems in Brazil and Chile are that many teachers never learn to teach effectively and are unable to do a good job delivering the required curriculum. As a result, much of the curriculum content is never made accessible to many students, and they and their parents often do not know how little students have learned compared to what they might have learned given the chance.

The extreme end of the effects of poor supervision in these countries is teacher absenteeism. From our observations and interviews, Brazil's system, among the three, is particularly vulnerable to absenteeism, although we have no comprehensive study to support this claim. At this extreme, students are assured less coverage of the material and marginalization from modern society. Unlike "hidden" low quality, where the teacher appears but delivers low-quality education, when teachers are absent, parents apparently understand that the quality is low and respond by reducing the pressure on their children to attend school.

Are these differences embedded in sociopolitical contexts? Partly, yes. It is impossible to study the three systems and observe the way schools function in them without concluding that great differences exist in the *ambiente* surrounding educational delivery in each. It is much easier for a teacher to deliver high-quality education in a society where essentially all children come to school at the "right" age and are well nourished, where educational success is believed to be important by most families, and where families consider the teachers and the school to be dedicated to high-quality education for their children.

But partly, no. Many private Brazilian and Chilean firms operate efficiently, competing in world markets, supervising their employees and managers, helping them to increase productivity, tracking output and profits, conveying information to employees that helps the firms increase profits. Why shouldn't the educational system be able to employ the same techniques in its schools as used by private companies in the same society? This should be especially true in Chile, where more than 45 percent of students attend privately managed schools. Yet Brazilian and Chilean schools do not emulate their counterparts in other industries, whereas in Cuba, ironically, government-run schools are organized to function like many traditional private firms in capitalist societies. They supervise their "employee-managers," helping them increase productivity, know their clients well, and monitor school output carefully. Municipalities (and states) in Brazil and Chile could adopt these methods—at least some of them—even within the current sociopolitical context. They could also certify graduating teachers and intervene in a host of ways to try to improve teacher attendance in rural schools.

Brazil and Chile could begin focusing on factors that work in Cuba without becoming authoritarian states or incorporating fully Cuban society's moral (revolutionary) ideology. We will expand on the implications of this point in the last chapter.

CHAPTER SIX

Opportunity to Learn and Teaching Patterns

The quality of an educational system depends ultimately on the quality of students' classroom experiences. In previous chapters we argued that Cuban third and fourth graders know more mathematics and read better than expected, even taking into account their parents' higher level of education. The reasons are that they live in a social environment that is more favorable to academic achievement, their teachers tend to be better trained, and classroom practices are more consistently supervised. Simply put, Cuban pupils attend schools where the quality is better controlled than in the other two countries examined. Yet to claim that these factors are related to higher achievement, we should be able to observe Cuban pupils' classroom experiences as qualitatively different from those of pupils in Brazil or Chile—that better-trained teachers and quality control produce a different process at the classroom level. Ideally, we would want to go one step further to demonstrate that these differences in classroom experiences actually make Cuban pupils' learning more productive. But—as we discuss later in this chapter—we cannot go that next step with the information we have.

Are Cuban pupils' classroom experiences really different? To find out, we compared teaching practices using data from Brazil, Chile, and Cuba. The data included our own observations and videotapes we made of ten to twelve third-grade mathematics classes from each country. The classes were all about fifty minutes long. We analyzed the videotapes using an observation instrument that focused on the structure of the lesson, the level of student engagement, and other indicators of the teaching process. We used a second instrument to assess the concept of the lesson, the level of cognitive demand, and the interaction between the teacher and his or her pupils. The two instruments helped us understand differences in teaching practices among the three countries. We wanted to know whether such differences reflect the broader conclusions we reached about the organization of the educational systems in Cuba and the other two countries.

Classroom visits provided an intimate glimpse into the core of each country's educational system. Of course, teachers knew we were observing them and recording their classes, so they were more likely to put on a show. But the show could never exceed what each teacher considered to be a good teaching performance. That performance varied greatly from classroom to classroom and even from country to country. The most consistently well-organized classrooms were in Cuba, where the (eight-year-old) children seemed the most focused and most responsive to their teachers. The Cuban teachers, in turn, were the most confident in what they were supposed to be showing us that day. Not surprisingly, this was less true in an unplanned visit we made to the classroom of a young Cuban teacher who had begun his career just two months earlier. We also saw very well-run classrooms in Chile and Brazil. But there was less consistency, and some classes—especially in Brazil—were classic examples of bad teaching. We did not observe "bad teaching" in Cuba, even in the several classrooms taught by novice teachers.

Teachers in Chilean public schools and in some of the classrooms we observed in Brazil used what is known in education circles as the "constructivist" method of teaching.[1] Theoretically, this means that teachers engage their students by allowing them to direct their goals, to have control over their learning, and to construct knowledge based on what they already understand or experience in everyday life. The idea is that if students can relate new knowledge to what they already know and also participate actively in classroom activities, they will become better problem solvers and will like learning. They will also learn to reason rather than just memorizing meaningless facts.

Constructivism is all the rage in Latin America because it is seen as an antidote to "chalk and talk" methods of teaching—a traditional pedagogy in which the teacher writes something on the blackboard and then talks about it to the class. Chalk and talk can be very boring for students, especially if the teacher is not naturally engaging and doesn't know much about the subject she or he is teaching. In the worst of cases, the teacher writes long passages with his or her back to the classroom while students entertain themselves by talking to their friends or drawing pictures (we observed this in classrooms we filmed in Brazil). As it is interpreted in Chile, constructivism takes the chalk out of the teacher's hand and puts the students at tables working in groups, with manipulables (for example, number blocks, dominoes, or pieces of paper with numbers written on them that can be added to each other to form sums), or on special projects. Mostly, teachers just get students to participate more than they did in the past.

We were surprised that the Chilean private schools we visited, aside from an elite private school where students paid full tuition unsubsidized by vouchers, tended to use more traditional chalk and talk methods (teacher directed rather than student directed), and less group work. Students also tended to be more self-disciplined in those schools, often in classes with more students per teacher than in public schools.

In Cuba, the teaching method can best be described as participative but very directed. As in France and many other European countries, students in Cuba spend much of their time working individually on math problems handed out by the teacher on duplicated sheets. Once these are completed, the teacher goes over the problems with the students, asking those students who did not get the right answer how they did the problem and then discussing with the rest of the class and the individual student the source of the error. Students are expected to participate in these discussions, and they do. At the time of our visit, elementary school students in Cuba tended to stay with the same teacher for four years (there was talk of increasing this to six years), so the third graders and teachers we observed knew one another well. We often asked the teacher questions about individual students, and though our first visit came early in the year, he or she could tell us everything about them—their strong points, weak points, personal situation at home, and so on.

In both Cuba and Chile, students in all the schools we visited had access to computers and computer software—in Cuba, even to a computer specialist in each school. In Chile, all but the rural schools had access to the Internet; in Cuba, no Internet, but a closed-circuit television in every school, with educational television programs after lunch aimed to reinforce one or another lesson for one of the grades either in math or language. Some schools in Brazil also had computers, but these were not part of a national initiative to provide computer access for all, as in Chile and Cuba.

Beyond trying to draw contrasts among teaching practices in the three countries, we quantified our observations to making more systematic analyses of what we had seen at the classroom level. We present these results in the rest of the chapter. Although more technical and boring than telling stories about our experiences visiting schools, it gets past the "he said, she said" aspect of most classroom descriptions. We cannot, however, connect our quantified observations directly to student performance, mainly because we would have had to sample many more classrooms and test the children in those classrooms in order to make that connection. This is definitely a major flaw in our analysis.

That said, if the teaching we observed was at all representative of teaching in most classrooms in each of these countries, we were convinced that Cuban children, on average, are exposed to better teaching and higher expectations on how much math they *can* learn than are children in either Brazil or Chile. Part of this difference is undoubtedly a result of the better health and nourishment of the average Cuban third grader—the level of focus in Cuban classrooms rivals that of high-income countries. We did find some support, in comparing Chile with Brazil, to indicate that a greater emphasis on student-directed learning creates better learning opportunities for children than mechanistic chalk and copy methods used in many Brazilian classrooms. But there seems to be little evidence from our observations that pedagogy associated with group work is particularly effective in producing high academic achievement. In another study in rural Guatemala, Jeffery Marshall (2003) showed that seat work (working individually on problem sets, for example) is positively related to higher test scores and that group work is uncorrelated with higher scores. If we could be sure from our study that seat work is more effective in raising math test scores, we could argue that the differences we observed among Cuban, Chilean, and Brazilian classrooms helps explain why Cuban pupils scored higher than students in the other two countries. However, we cannot make this claim—our work is only suggestive.

Sample, Variables, and Methods

SAMPLE AND TAPING PROCEDURE

The schools we visited in each country were selected in a semi-random fashion. For Chile, nine of the ten urban schools were part of a larger sample of schools in greater Santiago being studied by a Chilean Ministry of Education project on curriculum and teaching practices (Ministerio de Educación, 2002). These schools comprised both voucher and public schools. One additional "pure" private (nonvoucher) school was chosen at random. All tapes were made during August 2000. In Brazil, Rio state school personnel chose three state schools for us in Niteroi (about twenty minutes outside of Rio de Janeiro). We chose four state schools in greater Salvador da Bahia from a list of state schools drawn up by state school personnel. We also chose at random one rural school outside of Brasília and two schools belonging to the *Escola Ativa* project in the rural environs outside of Salvador da Bahia. Finally, one municipal and one state school in Belo Horizonte were chosen at random by local officials. The Brazilian classrooms were filmed during August 2001 and July 2002. In Cuba we visited two classrooms in one school in Havana in November 2002, and seven schools in the Havana area and two rural schools in the Piñar del Rio district (about two hours west of Havana) during February 2003. We designated the kinds of schools we wanted to visit (Habana, urban outside Habana, and rural in a different province), and the Ministry selected the schools within these categories. Table 6.1 provides a breakdown of the sample.

The tapes come from one lesson of a third-grade mathematics class in each school (except for one school in Havana where we videotaped two lessons).

TABLE 6.1
Overview of sample schools in Brazil, Chile, and Cuba

Country/school type	Number (percentage of total)
Brazilian Sample	
State schools (urban)	
Niteroi (Rio de Janeiro state)	3 (25.0)
Salvador da Bahia (Bahia state)	4 (33.3)
Belo Horizonte	1 (8.3)
State schools (rural)	
Brasília (federal district)	1 (8.3)
Municipal schools (rural)	
Cawacari (Pernambuco state)	2 (16.7)
Belo Horizonte	1 (8.3)
Chilean Sample	
Public schools (urban)	
Santiago	6 (60.0)
Private voucher schools (urban)	
Santiago	3 (30.0)
Private paid schools (urban)	
Santiago	1 (10.0)
Cuban Sample	
Public schools (urban)	
Havana	8 (80.0)
Public schools (rural)	
Piñar del Rio	2 (20.0)

In most cases it was possible to film the entire class from start to finish, but in others the class had already begun or our sixty-minute tape ran out before the end of the class session. We obtained consent from school directors and teachers before each taping session. To make the taping procedure as unobtrusive as possible, we stood off in one corner for most of the class. In most cases the schools had received prior notice that someone was coming to film a classroom. This was especially necessary in Chile where schools have considerable autonomy, and in Cuba where a very centralized system dictates that permission to visit schools be obtained from multiple authorities in the educational bureaucracy. In Brazil it was sometimes possible simply to show up at the school, but in most cases the schools were notified beforehand. It was not possible to select a teacher at random to observe in every case. Sometimes the school directors allowed us to indicate which section (when multiple sections were available) we wanted to work with. But in most instances we were taken to a classroom that was already chosen. This, again, was the predominant mode in Chile and particularly in Cuba.

DATA AND VARIABLES

A copy of the observation instrument used for evaluating the classroom activities on tape is available in Appendix B. The first part of the instrument consists of a series of categories that are used to divide the class into time segments. This approach borrows heavily from the "time-on-task" framework pioneered in the 1960s by educational psychologist John Carroll (1963). Burns (1984) and Karweit and Slavin (1981), among many others, have done empirical applications of this method in developed countries.

We first used the instrument to ask a simple question: how does each class spend its time? The five primary categories are (1) *seat work*, when the students work individually; (2) *recitation*, which usually involves whole class activities; (3) *group work*, when students work together or are at least grouped together; (4) *whole-class activities*, characterized by teacher-centered actions (lecturing, writing on chalkboard); and (5) *transitions and interruptions*, marked by no organized learning activity. For the first three categories we used a series of subcategories to further specify the kind of segment that was taking place. Each fifteen-second segment was marked with a check in the appropriate box. The total number of checks was then added up, and each segment was measured as a percentage of total time.

There are several limitations to this time-on-task framework. First, it would be important to measure the degree of student engagement in each type of task, but the segments are not easily weighted according to engagement. The same is true for the kinds of questions and materials used by teachers, the order in which the instruction plan moved from topic to topic, or the overall classroom "climate." Segments also say very little, if anything, about the level of content or curriculum that is being covered.

An additional limitation is that the time segment approach to studying the classroom is not rooted in any theory of best teaching practices. Within each of the four main "delivery" systems (seat work, recitation, group work, and whole-class activities [teacher-centered actions]), there is a range of possible activities, and it is difficult to state, a priori, what are the best teaching strategies. So our comparisons of teaching by school types and countries are more descriptive than confirming specific hypotheses about the kinds of teaching we expect to see. Nevertheless, the results from the time segment analysis give us insights into the patterns of teaching and learning processes in these different national contexts and allow us to speculate about what they imply for student learning.

To address the limitations in our analysis, we added other components to the basic segment classification scheme. First, we classified the overall classroom level of student engagement every ten minutes along a four-point scale ranging from "Not Engaged" to "Very Engaged." The kinds of questions teachers asked during each class were also measured, and the degree of discipline in the classroom was judged along a four-point scale. Student-initiated activity was accounted for with a scale ranging from "Teacher-centered" class to "Student-centered" class. We measured the use of materials by a checklist of different kinds of handouts, textbooks, and learning materials. Finally, we also measured the physical condition of the classroom along four dimensions together with the presence of student-made materials on the walls. The inclusion of these various components broadens the comparative framework and makes it possible to make more specific judgments about teaching quality.[2] For more details and definitions for each of these components, see Appendix B.

The second instrument we used to analyze the videotapes is a rubric containing four main elements: *mathematical proficiency of lesson*, *level of cognitive demand*, *format or goal of lesson*, and *level of support*. The first of these components, *mathematical proficiency*, was derived from the Mathematics Learning Study Committee, National Research Council's study of mathematics instruction, *Adding It Up* (2001). *Mathematical proficiency* is a term that encompasses expertise, knowledge, and facility in mathematics. It captures what we believe to be necessary for anyone to learn (and by implication, to teach) mathematics. We identified five key strands of mathematical proficiency, as follows:

- *Conceptual understanding*—comprehension of mathematical concepts, operations, and relations
- *Procedural fluency*—skill in carrying out procedures flexibly, accurately, efficiently, and appropriately
- *Strategic competence*—ability to formulate, represent, and solve mathematical problems
- *Adaptive reasoning*—capacity for logical thought, reflection, explanation, and justification

- *Productive disposition*—habitual inclination to see mathematics as sensible, useful, and worthwhile, coupled with a belief in diligence and one's own efficacy (Mathematics Learning Study Committee, 2001, p. 117).

These strands are not taken as individual goals but as an interdependent and interwoven definition of proficiency. If any one of the five elements is missing, the learning process is not considered complete. We rated each of the lessons based on these five strands, identifying which strands were lacking in any given mathematics lesson.

The content analysis also evaluated the level of cognitive demand required by the lesson. For this component we derived a rubric from Stein et al.'s *Implementing Standards-Based Mathematics Instruction* (2000), which classifies lessons by higher or lower cognitive demand, including memorization and procedures without connections (lower-level demands) and procedures with connections and "doing mathematics" (higher-level demands). The third element of the rubric evaluated each lesson for the level of teacher interaction or support given to students, including group versus individual work or teacher providing answers, or teacher defining the concept or goal of the lesson. Last, we evaluated the curriculum content or concept being taught using definitions from the National Council of Teachers of Mathematics' *Principles and Standards for School Mathematics* (2000). Together, these elements formed our rubric for understanding the content of the lesson.

METHODS

Our statistical analysis was very basic. We tested whether the differences in the average time spent on various activities in the classrooms we observed were significantly different from one another statistically. Our small samples made it more difficult to get statistically significant differences. The problem was exacerbated when we tried to control for differences in types of schools (for example, urban/rural) in each sample. So we made statistical comparisons for only two groupings of schools: the whole sample of schools in each country and urban schools. We also divided the Chilean sample into private and public schools, as four of the schools we observed were private.[3]

In analyzing content, we used a rubric derived from the sources described earlier to rank and categorize the lessons taught in each school.

We compared schools along two dimensions: mathematical proficiency and cognitive demand of the lesson. Because of the qualitative nature of the final two types of assessment, we indicated the descriptions of lesson goals and level of support by individual classroom lesson.

Time Segment Analysis

Table 6.2 provides an overview of the time segment results for each sample of schools. However, before turning to those results we should address the large differences in class size shown in the first row of Table 6.2. These class size differences between Cuba and the other countries have important implications for our interpreting not only the rest of the findings but also for understanding our larger "purpose" with this analysis. When UNESCO's Latin American Laboratorio applied standardized exams in 1997, the average class size for Cuban schools was close to the whole sample average (about 33). Our earlier analysis in Chapter 4 of Cuban student performance compared to students in other countries was based on this larger Cuban class size. Since then the Cubans have implemented a class reduction policy similar to recent initiatives in California mandating that classrooms in grades 1–4 have twenty or fewer children (in Cuba, this policy applied to grades 1–6). Of all the variables we observed in this qualitative analysis, this is the one variable that is likely to be much different in the current educational context in Cuba compared to the situation when the students actually took the *Laboratorio* exams.

The differences in class size between Cuba and the other countries could have influenced the teaching practices we observed in Cuba and therefore our comparison of teaching practices among countries. As already mentioned, our intention here is not to use classroom observations to explain test score results from the 1997 UNESCO test. We cannot relate classroom observations to student outcomes in this study. Rather, we focus on the large differences in test scores between Cuban students and those in other Latin American countries as a departure point for comparing three very different education systems. As the class reduction policy was inaugurated in 2001, it is not likely that its effects on teaching practices have spread through the entire system. Further, Cuban officials and teachers assured us that

TABLE 6.2
Basic overview of classrooms

Variable	COUNTRY COMPARISON			URBAN ONLY			
	Brazil	Chile	Cuba	Brazil	Chile public	Chile private	Cuba
Number of students in classroom	27.9	37.1***	17.9***	28.0	36.2**	38.5**	19.8***
Main segments (% of time)							
Seat work	22.5	· 6.5**	40.9***	22.5	0.6***	15.3	36.2**
Recitation	22.5	34.6*	26.2	27.2	38.6	28.6	27.0
Group work	29.6	34.4	11.3*	18.3	38.3*	28.9	13.8
Whole class teacher-led	17.8	16.6	17.1	23.0	16.4	16.9	17.8
Transition/ interruption	7.5	7.9	4.8	8.7	6.1	10.7	5.3

NOTES: For main segments numbers refer to percentage of total time. Due to rounding, these numbers do not always add up to 100 percent. Segments refer to the predominant activity during each 15-minute period. Seat work describes students seated and working individually. Recitation involves questions and answers, work at chalkboard, whole class responses, and other forms of student recitation. Group work requires students to be arranged in groups, although as seen below they are not necessarily working together on the same problem. Whole class teacher-led describes teachers giving instructions, lecturing, or solving examples at the board without input from students. Transitions and interruptions refer to work stoppages that occur due changing activity, disciplining a student, or being interrupted from the outside. See text and Appendix B for more details on segment definition. Statistical comparisons are between each group and the rest of the sample, either for all schools (country comparison) or urban schools only.

*Statistically significant at 0.10 level (two-tail)
**Statistically significant at 0.05 level (two-tail)
***Statistically significant at 0.01 level (two-tail)

teaching methods have not changed in the past two years. Nevertheless, smaller class size could influence our comparison, especially between Cuba and Chile, where average class size differences are large.

The rest of the data in Table 6.2 refer to category averages with each category interpreted as the average percentage of each class period devoted to a particular activity. Only a handful of these averages are significantly different from the rest of the sample. The results show that Chilean students spend very little time working in individual seat work, which is the predominant mode in Cuba. Chilean students do spend a lot of time in individual seat work while in groups (see the group work segment). We discuss the meaning of group work in more detail later. This difference between Chile and Cuba is particularly pronounced in the public schools. Private schools in Chile spend (comparatively) more time in individual seat work than their public counterparts. Table 6.2 also provides some evidence

TABLE 6.3
Seat work segment in more detail

Variable	COUNTRY COMPARISON			URBAN ONLY			
	Brazil	Chile	Cuba	Brazil	Chile public	Chile private	Cuba
Total seat work	22.5	6.5**	40.9***	22.5	0.6***	15.3	36.2**
By seat work subsegment							
Copying instructions/problems	6.8*	1.3	2.1	4.8*	0.6	2.3	1.1
Solving problems individually (teacher circulating)	12.1	2.2**	33.8***	15.3	0.0**	5.5	34.4***
Solving problems individually (teacher on other task)	1.3	0.0	4.1	1.0**	0.0	0.0	0.0
Checking work individually (working)	0.8	1.5	0.9	0.0	0.0	3.4**	0.8
Checking work individually (stopped)	1.5	1.7	0.5	1.9	0.0	4.1*	0.6

NOTE: Seat work describes students seated and working individually. Segments refer to the predominant activity during each 15-minute period, and seat work subsegments are measured as percentage of total time, not total seat work. Due to rounding, these numbers do not always add up to the total for the segment. See text and Appendix B for more details on segment and subsegment definition. Statistical comparisons are between each group and the rest of the sample, either for all schools (country comparison) or urban schools only.

*Statistically significant at 0.10 level (two-tail)
**Statistically significant at 0.05 level (two-tail)
***Statistically significant at 0.01 level (two-tail)

that Cuban classrooms are more "efficient" than those in Chile or Brazil, as less time (as a percentage) is spent in transitions and interruptions. These differences are not statistically significant, so they should be interpreted cautiously. The positive correlation between average class size and time spent in transitions highlights one of many likely effects of class size on observable differences in classrooms. Chilean private schools have the largest student-teacher ratios, and they also spend more time moving from activity to activity. This makes sense. Chilean classrooms make the most use of group work, and shifting from other activities into group work involves more transition time.

Table 6.3 focuses on the seat work segment and presents the percentage of the total class time spent in each of the subsegments. The first row contains the Total Seat work segment averages from Table 6.2. The results show that of all the seat work subsegments, the predominant mode is individual problem solving with the teacher circulating. In Cuban classrooms the emphasis in many of the classrooms we visited was on "ejercitación," or problem solving. In most cases the students were seated individually, and the activity usually required them to work through a series of problems that were either prepared on a sheet (called "Hojas de Trabajo") or in their workbooks. In the other countries there was less of this, although it was not uncommon in Chile for students to be in groups but working individually in a very similar fashion (and with prepared activities). Another significant difference is between Chilean private schools and the rest of the sample for the teacher to check work while students are seated individually. In two of the four Chilean private schools there was a great deal of emphasis on checking work. Chilean private schools appear to share this feature with Cuban schools. Given the large number of students in Chilean classrooms, this takes longer to do.

Brazilian students spend significantly more time copying instructions. In our visits to many other Brazilian classrooms that we did not videotape, we observed the same activities we saw in our videotaped classrooms: Very few Brazilian schools made use of prepared activities, something that was fairly common in Chile and Cuba. Having to copy math problems from the board before beginning to solve them obviously affects time use in the class. This difference also points to a theme that develops throughout this comparative analysis, namely, that Chilean and Cuban schools—especially Chilean private schools—often have more resources available for teachers to use. Social class composition may also explain these differences: The Brazilian children in our sample were of relatively low socioeconomic status, and they may either need more time to write out the problems or their teachers have less access to paper and copying equipment to prepare worksheets. It is interesting that Cuba is known to be short of resources, but that "hojas de trabajo" and other school supplies are more available there than in Brazil, particularly for low-income children.

Table 6.2 revealed few differences between the three countries regarding whole class recitation. Table 6.4 builds on these summary results and presents the averages for the Recitation subsegments. Significant differences were found for two of these more specific subsegments. For example, Cuban teachers made far more use of individual recitation, which is defined as individual students' responding to questions put to the whole class. This compares with more use in the Chilean classrooms of whole-class responses

TABLE 6.4
Recitation segment in more detail

Variable	COUNTRY COMPARISON			URBAN ONLY			
	Brazil	Chile	Cuba	Brazil	Chile public	Chile private	Cuba
Total recitation	22.5	34.6*	26.2	27.2	38.6	28.6	27.0
By recitation subsegment							
Q-A whole class							
individual	2.0***	7.7	14.1***	2.4**	5.0	11.6	16.1***
Q-A whole class chorus	13.3	14.8	2.6**	17.1	17.9	10.2	2.8**
Individual/whole class							
Read orally	2.9	1.1	1.7	2.0	1.5	0.7	1.8
Solve at blackboard	4.0	10.0	7.7	2.0	13.2	5.5	6.4

NOTE: Recitation involves questions and answers, work at chalkboard, whole class responses, and other forms of student recitation. Segments refer to the predominant activity during each 15-minute period, and recitation subsegments are measured as percentage of total time, not total recitation. Due to rounding, these numbers do not always add up to the total for the segment. See text and Appendix B for more details on segment and subsegment definition. Statistical comparisons are between each group and the rest of the sample, either for all schools (country comparison) or urban schools only.

*Statistically significant at 0.10 level (two-tail)

**Statistically significant at 0.05 level (two-tail)

***Statistically significant at 0.01 level (two-tail)

(called "Chorus"). This result may, once again, be driven by class size differences, as Chilean teachers may realize that involving every student is impossible unless group responses are allowed. It may also reflect a more homogeneous group of students in the Cuban classrooms. Chilean private schools, with larger class size, use almost as much individual response to questions as do Cuban schools. In one of the Chilean private schools, the teacher went around the room putting simple review questions to each student (more than forty students). In Brazilian classrooms, by contrast, usually only a handful of students were called on individually and in many instances a group of students was far behind their counterparts in the activities. Note that few of the reported differences in Table 6.4 are statistically significant.

Table 6.5 analyzes group work in more detail and presents most of the subsegment averages by school category. Once again we see that Cuban classrooms make comparatively less use of group work, whereas in Chilean classrooms this segment is predominant. This is especially characteristic of Chilean public schools, which were by far the most group-oriented classrooms in the three country samples. However, the Chilean children rarely

TABLE 6.5
Group work segment in more detail

Variable	COUNTRY COMPARISON			URBAN ONLY			
	Brazil	Chile	Cuba	Brazil	Chile public	Chile private	Cuba
Total group work	29.6	34.4	11.3*	18.3	38.3*	28.9	13.8
By group work subsegment							
Individual solving (quiet)— teacher circulating	22.2	12.8	9.0	9.6	14.0	10.9	11.0
Individual solving (talking)— teacher circulating	0.1	1.0	0.0	0.2	1.7**	0.0	0.0
Individual solving (talking)— teacher on other task	0.3	12.9***	0.0	0.0	15.2**	9.5	0.0
Group solving/discussion	5.3	3.0	2.2	6.2	3.7	2.1	2.8

NOTE: Group work requires that students are sitting in groups. Segments refer to the predominant activity during each 15-minute period, and group work subsegments are measured as percentage of total time, not total group work. Due to rounding, these numbers do not always add up to the total for the segment. See text and Appendix B for more details on segment and subsegment definition. Statistical comparisons are between each group and the rest of the sample, either for all schools (country comparison) or urban schools only.

*Statistically significant at 0.10 level (two-tail)

**Statistically significant at 0.05 level (two-tail)

***Statistically significant at 0.01 level (two-tail)

worked collectively to solve problems. Students spent much of the group work segment in individual problem solving not interacting with other members of the group. This was also true of Brazilian schools. In Chile, individual students often solved problems while talking to each other—a difficult segment to define. This is not the same as working as a group toward a common solution, or handing in one assignment per group instead of identical individual worksheets. Only in the urban schools in Brazil was there a noticeable amount of "collective" group work. In one particular school, the groups were responsible for turning in one activity per group and students discussed (and argued about) how to complete the work. In all three countries this kind of group work was the exception to the rule.

Other Classroom Processes

The second part of the analysis focused on a series of indicators of the "quality" of classroom processes rather than the specific use of classroom

TABLE 6.6
Student engagement

Variable	COUNTRY COMPARISON			URBAN ONLY			
	Brazil	Chile	Cuba	Brazil	Chile public	Chile private	Cuba
Average engagement	2.4***	3.0	3.5***	2.5***	2.9	3.3	3.5***
By 10-minute periods							
At 10:00	2.6***	3.2	3.5***	2.7***	2.8	3.8*	3.7***
At 20:00	2.5***	3.2	3.5***	2.6***	3.2	3.3	3.4**
At 30:00	2.5**	2.8	3.4***	2.5*	2.7	3.0	3.4**
At 40:00	2.3***	3.1	3.4**	2.4**	3.0	3.3	3.5*
At 50:00	2.5**	2.9	3.4***	2.4**	2.5	3.3	3.5***

NOTE: Engagement is measured as both the degree of engagement in the lesson and the extent to which all students in the classroom are participating. Observations correspond to the entire 10-minute period (i.e., at 30:00 the observation is for the period from 20:00 to 30:00). See text and Appendix B for more details on engagement definition. Statistical comparisons are between entire samples and then between Chile Public and Chile Private in reference to Brazil urban only.

*Statistically significant at 0.10 level (two-tail)

**Statistically significant at 0.05 level (two-tail)

***Statistically significant at 0.01 level (two-tail)

time. These indicators include a measure of student engagement, whether the teacher checks student work, the kinds of questions the teacher asks pupils, class discipline, the use of manipulables, and the physical quality of the classroom space.

Table 6.6 presents the results for student engagement. This is a difficult concept to measure, as students may be fully involved without revealing it with their body language. Also, measuring the engagement of an entire class presents some problems. But the principal challenge is in interpreting the meaning of student engagement differences. Is greater engagement a product of the student's family background, including the quality of the breakfast the child ate that morning, or is it related to the teacher's successfully creating a learning environment that captures students' attention and maintains their interest? The results in Table 6.6 highlight this dilemma. The Brazilian sample is consistently less engaged, apparent to us when making the videos of the classrooms. Brazilian students were at times noticeably bored with the lesson or totally off task and engaged in an "activity" (talking, playing, spacing-out) that had nothing to do with the lesson. At the other extreme, Cuban students were consistently involved in the lessons and rarely exhibited body language or other signs indicating boredom or lack of

TABLE 6.7

Class structure and types of questions used

Variable	COUNTRY COMPARISON			URBAN ONLY			
	Brazil	Chile	Cuba	Brazil	Chile public	Chile private	Cuba
Class includes							
Checking some student work	66.7*	50.0	17.7**	66.7	82.9**	0.0**	21.9*
Checking all student work	24.6**	50.1	82.3**	22.0**	16.9*	100.0**	77.8**
Types of questions asked							
No questions asked	25.0**	0.0	0.0	11.1	0.0	0.0	0.0
Simple repetitive	75.0	80.0	90.9	88.9	83.3	75.0	88.9
Give example, short answer	25.0	40.0*	0.0**	22.2	33.3	50.0	0.0*
Conceptual, describe process	0.0***	40.0	54.5**	0.0***	33.3	50.0	66.7**

NOTE: Checking work refers to degree to which teacher would check work during or at the end of the lesson. For types of questions, the percentages do not sum to 100 because for each category the results only indicate if this kind of question was used, not whether or not it was the only type of question used. See text and Appendix B for more details on definitions. Statistical comparisons are between entire samples and then between Chile Public and Chile Private in reference to Brazil urban only.

*Statistically significant at 0.10 level (two-tail)

**Statistically significant at 0.05 level (two-tail)

***Statistically significant at 0.01 level (two-tail)

interest. Somewhere between are the Chilean students, although the results in Table 6.6 show again that engagement depends on the school sector in Chile. In the private schools, the level of student engagement rivaled the Cuban sample average, whereas in the Chilean public schools the averages were closer to the Brazilian sample. Interestingly, the level of engagement generally declined in almost all of the categories—except in Cuba—as the lesson progressed, and most of the significant differences were found in the first twenty minutes of class.

Table 6.7 details averages for other measures of class structure and incorporates teacher questions. Two significant differences stand out. First, Cuban teachers and Chilean private school teachers made an effort to check everyone's work. Given the differences in class size between these two categories of schools (see Table 6.2), this similarity is fascinating and indicates a high degree of alignment in the educational "mission" in each of these country/school types. The results highlight the probable effect of student composition on teacher behavior. In many of the Brazilian and Chilean public school classrooms, there is probably a good reason that teachers did not make an effort to check everyone's work: They knew what they would find. During the taping process we saw a lot of inequality in these classrooms. In some cases students had not even finished copying the instructions at the end of the lesson while other students had long since completed working the exercises. By not checking everyone's homework, these teachers may be simply avoiding having to embarrass their less prepared students. Instead, by checking the work of some students, they can focus more on the average student and move on to another task. Unfortunately, this is the reality of life in these lower-income classrooms.

The second important difference in Table 6.7 concerns the kinds of questions that teachers asked during the class. Cuban classrooms and, to a lesser extent, private Chilean classrooms, are very different from their counterparts in the public sectors in Brazil and Chile. Cuban teachers as well as teachers in some of the Chilean private schools at times asked students to explain their answers, or to correct the answers of other students, or even to provide explicitly conceptual explanations of mathematical concepts. An example of the latter is "explain why we cannot subtract the 9 from the 8 in the hundreds column for problem 1." This kind of questioning was virtually nonexistent in Brazilian schools and Chilean public schools, where teacher questions were usually much simpler or, in the case of Brazil, nonexistent.

The comparative analysis of the classroom activities in our sample of schools concludes with some final indicators in Table 6.8. Chilean private and Cuban classrooms have higher levels of discipline, as measured by the frequency of teacher requests for silence and the responsiveness of students to teacher instructions. In both the Chilean private schools and especially the Cuban schools, the level of discipline was extraordinary at times, as evidenced by the teacher rarely needing to request silence. The other classrooms in Chile and those in Brazil were less orderly, and the teachers sometimes appeared to be powerless to stop students from talking. Class size may have something to do with this. Chilean private school classrooms are large, so it is likely that students' socioeconomic composition and/or school management differences in public schools underlie these observed differences in student behavior. One compositional issue that we have not addressed is the average age of the students. In Brazil the students who took the Laboratorio tests were 1.5 years older than Cuban pupils, and Brazilian pupils ranged in

TABLE 6.8
Other comparisons

	COUNTRY COMPARISON			URBAN ONLY			
Variable	Brazil	Chile	Cuba	Brazil	Chile public	Chile private	Cuba
Degree of discipline	2.5***	3.	3.9***	2.3***	2.8	3.5	3.9***
Student-initiated activity	3.0***	2.2	0.6***	3.0***	2.3	2.0	0.7***
Sum of manipulables	0.5	1.0**	0.2**	0.2	1.0**	1.0*	0.2
Use of prepared activities/ homework	33.3*	60.0	72.7	44.4	66.6	50.0	66.7
Average physical condition of classroom	2.3	2.6	2.6	2.2	2.2	3.2**	2.5
Student-made things on walls	1.1	0.7	1.0	1.0	0.5	1.0	1.0

NOTE: See text and Appendix B for more details on variable definition. Statistical comparisons are for two countries and then comparing Chile Public and Chile Private with Brazil urban only.

*Statistically significant at 0.10 level (two-tail)

**Statistically significant at 0.05 level (two-tail)

***Statistically significant at 0.01 level (two-tail)

age from nine to seventeen years old. If older students are more difficult to control, we would expect to see less discipline in the Brazilian classrooms.

We also found an inverse correlation between discipline and "student-centeredness" (for lack of a better term). The Brazilian classrooms at times were fairly chaotic, especially in comparison with the private Chilean and Cuban classrooms. The Brazilian classrooms were also marked by a high degree of student freedom, as measured by the instances of students physically approaching the teacher to ask questions or even interrupting the teacher to ask questions. The Chilean private school classrooms were much more teacher-focused, where the only person with permission to talk was the teacher, students spoke only when called on, and they generally stayed in their seats. In the Cuban schools very few students approached the teacher during individual work or spoke when not addressed. The results in Table 6.8 confirm an earlier finding that Brazilian classrooms are significantly less likely to incorporate prepared activities or homework assignments than their Chilean and Cuban counterparts. Finally, physical conditions vary little by country, except in the case of the Chilean private schools. These had the best conditions by far.

Analyzing the Content of the Lesson

So far, we have discussed the methods teachers use in the classroom to teach the material. But what about the level of content of the material they are presenting? Mathematics educators have analyzed the cognitive difficulty of hundreds of mathematics lessons given in U.S. schools (Stein et al., 2000). They report the following two findings:

> (1) mathematical tasks with high level cognitive demands are most difficult to implement well, frequently being transformed into less-demanding tasks during instruction; and (2) student learning gains were greatest in class-rooms in which instructional tasks consistently encouraged high level student thinking and reasoning and least in classrooms in which instructional tasks were consistently procedural in nature. (Stein et al., 2000, p. 4)

Our videotapes of Chilean, Brazilian, and Cuban classrooms appear to confirm the first of these conclusions. Chilean and especially Brazilian activities were less demanding in terms of the cognitive skill content of the lessons. We cannot be sure whether this reflected teacher content knowledge or if on the day chosen for observation the teacher had decided to make things a bit easier so that the pupils would show better for their foreign visitors. However, because so many of the Brazilian lessons we videotaped were similarly less demanding, we think that teacher content knowledge is the more likely explanation. Our analysis supports this conclusion and by implication (especially given Stein et al.'s second conclusion) provides some support for the relatively low scores in the Laboratorio evaluation of Chilean and Brazilian pupils compared to Cubans.

Our assessment of classroom content centers on four main components: mathematical proficiency of the lesson, level of cognitive demand, format or goal of the lesson, and level of support. The first of these is derived from the National Research Council's definition of proficiency as five intertwined components necessary for any student to learn mathematics. As described earlier, these are conceptual understanding, procedural fluency, strategic competence, adaptive reasoning, and productive disposition. From the tapes we identified which of these five components was present in each of the classroom lessons (Table 6.9).

TABLE 6.9
Mathematical proficiency score

| Variable | COUNTRY COMPARISON | | | URBAN ONLY | | | |
	Brazil	Chile	Cuba	Brazil	Chile public	Chile private	Cuba
Number of classrooms	12	10	11	9	6	4	9
Mathematical proficiency score (max = 5)	2.17***	3.2	3.82**	2.11***	2.83	3.75	3.89***

*Statistically significant at 0.10 level (two-tail)
**Statistically significant at 0.05 level (two-tail)
***Statistically significant at 0.01 level (two-tail)

Classroom lessons in Brazil averaged 2.17 out of a possible 5 in mathematical proficiency. With the exception of one classroom, all lessons possessed the basic component of conceptual understanding, which indicates that both students and teachers understand the point of the lesson and the concepts behind it. The classroom that did not demonstrate this minimum level of proficiency was one characterized by rote memorization and copying with virtually no orientation from the teacher. Thus, it was impossible to determine whether conceptual understanding was present (classroom 4 in Brazil, which was given a score of 1 for procedural fluency only). Only one Brazilian lesson received the highest score of 5 on mathematical proficiency. Brazilian lessons scored significantly lower than Cuban and Chilean lessons in mathematical proficiency. Even when only urban classrooms were considered, the level of math proficiency in Brazilian lessons was lower than in urban schools in Chile and Cuba.

The average mathematical proficiency score in Chilean classrooms was 3.2 out of a possible 5. Only two Chilean classrooms scored two points on the mathematical proficiency score, and no Chilean classroom received a score of one. In general, adaptive reasoning was the most difficult characteristic to achieve in classroom lessons. This requires high levels of cognitive demand and linking of concepts throughout the lesson. Chilean lessons were not statistically different from lessons in the other two countries either in whole country or urban-only comparisons.

Cuban classrooms attained a mathematical proficiency score of 3.82 out of a possible 5 and had a lower standard deviation in performance from

TABLE 6.10
Cognitive demand level of tasks

Variable	COUNTRY COMPARISON			URBAN ONLY			
	Brazil	Chile	Cuba	Brazil	Chile public	Chile private	Cuba
Number of classrooms	12	10	11	9	6	4	9
Cognitive demand level (max = 4)	2.17***	2.80	2.91*	2.11***	2.67	3.00	2.89*

*Statistically significant at 0.10 level (two-tail)
**Statistically significant at 0.05 level (two-tail)
***Statistically significant at 0.01 level (two-tail)

classroom to classroom. Two classrooms attained a maximum score of 5 and no classrooms scored below 3 points. In general, the gap between Cuban classroom lessons and those of Chilean and Brazilian classrooms stemmed from the use of the proficiency strands of strategic competence and adaptive reasoning. That is, Cuban teachers engaged in continual dialogue with the students, asking them both how and why a given problem should be answered. Without fail, Cuban classroom teachers also maintained a productive disposition (demonstrating mathematics as a useful, worthwhile tool), in addition to demonstrating conceptual understanding and procedural fluency.

Table 6.10 presents the results for the cognitive demand of the lesson. The cognitive demand measure is derived from the work of Stein et al. (2000) in U.S. classrooms and is divided into four categories: memorization tasks and procedures without connections (both classified as lower-level demands) and procedures with connections and "doing mathematics" tasks (higher-level demands). A more detailed description of the type of each task is provided in Appendix B. In the analysis of all three countries' classrooms, only one (Cuban) classroom attained the highest score of 4 for "doing mathematics" that requires complex and non-algorithmic thinking, as well as exploring the nature of mathematical concepts, processes, and relationships. Thus, almost all the thirty-two classrooms we observed lacked a level of math teaching in which students explore problem solving independently from the teacher, with unpredictable solutions and considerable cognitive effort. Brazilian classrooms scored an average of 2.16 out of a possible 4 on the cognitive demand of the lesson. This average is just above "procedures without connections," as the lessons were focused on producing correct answers rather than developing understanding. Interestingly, when urban-only classrooms were considered, Brazil's score actually decreased as the rural teachers did better than their urban counterparts on cognitive demand. This may have been a result of the presence of a new curriculum and extensive training in two of the rural schools that are part of the *Escola Ativa* program (Brazil's answer to Colombia's *Escuela Nueva*). Brazilian lessons consisted mostly of a teacher writing on the board, students copying what the teacher wrote, and little interaction. In most cases, the teacher made almost no effort to link concepts to the procedure. Explanations, when they did occur, focused solely on describing the procedure that was used.

Chilean classrooms scored an average of 2.8 out of 4 on cognitive demand, approaching the level of "procedure with connections" category for all schools. That level stipulates that tasks be represented in multiple ways and require some degree of cognitive effort. The Chilean score mainly reflects the frequent use of "manipulables" by Chilean teachers. More than their Brazilian or Cuban counterparts, Chilean teachers frequently used blocks, string, paper cut-out shapes, and even food receptacles to represent and teach mathematical concepts, especially geometric shapes. Chilean classroom lessons, either urban only (including the comparison of private versus public) or all Chilean schools analyzed, were not statistically significantly different from the combined Cuban and Brazilian classrooms on the level of cognitive demand.

Cuban classrooms scored on average a 2.91 out of 4 on this measure. Both urban and rural Cuban classrooms scored significantly higher than the combined Brazilian and Chilean classrooms on this aspect of math teaching. The reason for this gap frequently turned on the use of procedures (and the explanation of those procedures by students). For example, if asked to indicate whether 430 is divisible by 10, Cuban students would be expected to explain that the zero in the units place is an indicator that 430 is a multiple of ten and is therefore divisible by 10. This description of procedures and connection to other mathematical concepts was not typically present in Brazilian (but *was* present, but to a lesser extent, in Chilean) classrooms.

The results of our analysis of the dominant mode of support used in the lesson are shown in Table 6.11. These results are consistent with the time-segment analysis presented earlier (see Table 6.4) and reveal a high level of

TABLE 6.11
Primary mode of support

Country	School code	Location	System	Primary mode of support
Brazil	1	Urban	State	All class recite with support from teacher
	2	Urban	State	All class recite with support from teacher
	3	Urban	State	All class recite with support from teacher
	4	Rural	State	Individual work with support from teacher
	5	Rural	Municipal	Individual and group work with support from teacher
	6	Rural	Municipal	Individual and group work with support from teacher
	7	Urban	State	Group work with support from teacher
	8	Urban	State	Individual work with support from teacher
	9	Urban	State	Group work with support from teacher
	10	Urban	State	Individual work with support from teacher
	11	Urban	Municipal	Individual work with support from teacher
	12	Urban	State	Individual work with support from teacher
Chile	1	Urban	Private voucher	Individual and group work with support from teacher
	2	Urban	Public	Individual and group work with support from teacher
	3	Urban	Public	Individual work with support from teacher
	4	Urban	Public	Individual and group work with support from teacher
	6	Urban	Public	Individual and group work with support from teacher
	7	Urban	Private voucher	Individual and group work with support from teacher
	8	Urban	Public	Individual and group work with support from teacher
	9	Urban	Public	Individual and group work with support from teacher
	11	Urban	Private voucher	Individual and group work with support from teacher
	12	Urban	Private	Individual and group work with support from teacher
Cuba	1	Urban	Public	Individual and group work with support from teacher
	2	Rural	Public	Individual and group work with support from teacher
	3	Rural	Public	Individual and group work with support from teacher
	4	Urban	Public	Individual and group work with support from teacher
	5	Urban	Public	Individual and group work with support from teacher
	6	Urban	Public	Individual and group work with support from teacher
	7	Urban	Public	Individual work with support from teacher
	8	Urban	Public	Individual and group work with support from teacher
	9	Urban	Public	Group work with support from teacher
	10	Urban	Public	Individual and group work with support from teacher
	11	Urban	Public	Individual and group work with support from teacher

TABLE 6.12
Primary lesson goal: Brazil

Country	School code	Primary lesson goal/format
Brazil	1	2-digit addition and multiplication
	2	Single-digit addition and subtraction with variables
	3	2-digit addition and subtraction
		Labeling numbers (ones, tens, hundreds)
	4	Copy from board
		2- and 3-digit multiplication
	5	Working from workbook with manipulables
		Basic geometry and shapes
	6	Working from workbook with manipulables
		Basic geometry and shapes
	7	Basic 2-digit addition and subtraction
	8	Working with large numbers
		Word problems
	9	Conceptual understanding and multiple mathematical representation of ideas
		Using data to make graphs
	10	Word problems using 3-digit operations
		Using decimals and money to "purchase" items/supermarket
	11	2-digit addition and subtraction
		Labeling numbers (ones, tens, hundreds)
	12	2-digit addition and multiplication

consistency among Chilean and Cuban classrooms. Chilean teachers tended to use both group and individual work, often at the same time. Brazilian teachers, with few exceptions, used either one mode or the other and did not transition into using multiple modes of interaction. The more static approach of Brazilian lessons may have been an exercise of control over students in order to maintain discipline. As stated above, Chilean teachers did not appear to need to discipline students as much as their Brazilian counterparts.

Cuban teachers, in contrast, tended to employ group and individual work in equal proportions throughout the lesson. Typically the Cuban lesson began with out-loud reciting by the entire class (accompanied by justification and explanation as mentioned above) and was followed by individual or group work with extensive support from the teacher. Continual teacher reinforcement and prodding regarding procedures and the underlying concepts characterized Cuban lessons.

Analysis of the focus or concept of the lesson is provided in Table 6.12. This analysis is derived from the National Council of Teachers of Mathematics' *Principles and Standards for School Mathematics* (NCTM, 2000). It is

TABLE 6.13
Primary lesson goal: Chile

Country	School code	Primary lesson goal/format
Chile	1	Basic addition, subtraction, division with three or four digits
		Multiplication with carrying
	2	Basic addition with two digits
		Grouping of numbers, conceptual understanding
	3	Memorization and practice
		Worksheet to identify geometric shapes
	4	Division with remainders
		Division using blocks and other manipulables
	6	Word problems with monetary transactions
		3- and four-digit multiplication/division and addition/subtraction
		Buy and sell interactions to simulate supermarket/ manipulables
	7	Memorization and practice, identify shapes
		Make shapes using string and pegboard/manipulables
	8	Fractions using blocks and shapes/manipulables
		Equivalent fractions
	9	Simple fractions and decimals
		Counting money, equating fractions
		Practice
	11	Equating simple fractions
	12	Categorizing and comparing shapes (sphere, cylinder, etc.) using household items/manipulables
		Conceptual understanding and connecting ideas

difficult to rank concepts taught in each of the classrooms for a number of reasons. First, expectations for what "should" be taught at the third grade vary according to the national curriculum in both countries. Fortunately, there is considerable overlap between the Brazilian National Curriculum Parameters and NCTM's *Principles and Standards*. Second, the analysis of a randomly selected day of teaching is not necessarily indicative of the teacher's average lesson. Although every effort was made to reduce any expectations that the videotaping represented any sort of evaluation of teacher performance, we cannot guarantee that teachers did not modify their behavior based on our presence.

Nonetheless, from Tables 6.12 to 6.14 it is possible to distinguish lower-level topics (2-digit addition) from higher-level topics (division with remainders). Both Brazilian and Chilean classroom lessons included geometric shapes, although Chilean lessons were more likely to use manipulables. Advanced or complex exercises included using "money," simulating market

TABLE 6.14
Primary lesson goal: Cuba

Country	School code	Primary lesson goal/format
Cuba	1	3- and four-digit division and multiplication
		Identification of units, tens, hundreds, thousands places
	2	3- and four-digit subtraction
		Conceptual explanation and procedural demonstration
	3	3- and four-digit subtraction
		Word problems and conceptual explanation
	4	2-, 3-, four-digit addition and subtraction
		Word problems with review of procedures and concepts
	5	2-digit subtraction and addition
		Review of procedures and concepts
	6	2-digit addition and subtraction
		Word problems with review of procedures and concepts
	7	2-digit addition and subtraction
		Word problems with review of procedures and concepts
	8	Adding and subtracting four-digit numbers
		Review of procedures and concepts
	9	Review of number places
		2- and three-digit subtraction and addition
		Review of procedures and concepts
	10	Review of number places
		Review of procedures and concepts
	11	2-digit addition and subtraction, four-digit addition
		Review of procedures and concepts

exchanges, and designing and identifying geometric shapes with string and pegboards. Less challenging lessons focused on practice and drill of multiplication tables and basic addition, even though these were sometimes presented in a "game" format. Finally, Cuban teachers did not necessarily demonstrate higher-order concepts, but they did go much deeper than classroom teachers in the other two countries into explaining concepts.

Again, the single lessons caught on videotape are not necessarily representative, but their consistency is surprising given the effort we made to sample different types of classrooms in each country. Most Brazilian classrooms spend a large amount of time copying problems from the board, a practice that is absent in Cuban and Chilean classrooms (mainly because of the use of worksheets). In one Brazilian classroom we observed a complete hour in which students copied basic math problems from the board into their notebooks. The teacher did not provide any orientation or explanation of the work, although she did circulate in the classroom responding to students who had questions.

Summing Up

Cuban classrooms are significantly different from classrooms in Chile and Brazil on a number of dimensions. It is difficult, however, to disentangle environmental (i.e., home and community) effects from actual teacher effects in classrooms. High levels of discipline and engagement and the use of conceptual questions in classrooms may be possible only with students who have better nutrition and better support at home. For example, it appears from the tapes that children studying in the average Brazilian school come from a less-advantaged background than do children in Cuban, private Chilean, and, to a lesser extent, Chilean public schools. This accords with the Laboratorio data, which also show Brazilian third and fourth graders with lower parents' education than Chileans and Cubans.

In analyzing the content and curriculum of the lesson in each classroom, we were able to differentiate the level of curriculum between a class devoted to basic adding and subtracting of 2–3 digit numbers and one devoted to, say, adding and dividing fractions. Our analysis also indicated differences in the analytical skills being developed. In some lessons the students are challenged more to think about the topic than in others, and they develop a different set of skills than just memorizing the lesson or the answers to problems. Finally, we analyzed teacher interaction and level of support for the lesson as a whole, giving us an indication of the teacher's overall approach to the lesson.

When we analyzed the third-grade math textbooks from Brazil, Chile, and Cuba, as described in the previous chapter, we found that two of the Brazilian textbooks covered more math than either the Chilean or Cuban textbooks. The third Brazilian textbook was on the same level as the Chilean textbook. In certain content areas, the Cuban textbook was more advanced than the others. From looking at the curriculum as reflected in textbooks, we would have concluded that Brazilian children learn more third-grade math than children in the other two countries. But that does not correspond to what happens in classrooms, at least not in the sample of classrooms we observed and videotaped. Whereas the lessons in Chilean and Cuban classrooms seem to coincide with the curriculum and the degree of difficulty of problems in the textbooks, there is a disconnect between the curriculum described in Brazilian textbooks and what we observed in Brazilian math lessons. The videotapes showed the level of math being taught in Brazil as significantly less challenging and less oriented to helping children learn higher-order skills than in Chile and Cuba, and especially compared to Cuba. Even in Chile, the lessons in the public school classrooms we observed were devoted to basic operations.

Further, Cuban teachers focus much more on working on individual skills through seat work than having students work grouped at tables either doing individual work (often talking to each other while working individually) or doing group work. When Cuban students are grouped at tables, they only do collective problem solving. Brazil was the only one of the three countries in which we observed teachers using traditional methods of having children copy off the blackboard.

The most dispiriting aspect of the comparison was to observe first-hand how differentiated the content level and task intensity was between lower- and higher-income students in Brazil and Chile. We found much less differentiation in Cuba. As noted, it is difficult to say whether teachers in lower-income classrooms in Chile and Brazil are less capable of teaching math at a higher level of conceptualization because of teacher sorting (less-capable teachers sort into lower-income schools) or because equally capable teachers have much lower expectations for lower-income children. Probably what we observed is a combination of these two factors.

CHAPTER SEVEN

Lessons Learned

In the beginning of this study we asked why Cuban elementary schoolers score so much higher in math and language tests than children in other Latin American countries. The answer turns out to be fairly straightforward: Cuban children attend schools that are intensely focused on instruction and are staffed by well-trained, regularly supervised teachers in a social environment that is dedicated to high academic achievement for all social groups. Combining high-quality teaching with high academic expectations and a tightly controlled school management hierarchy with well-defined goals is what makes the Cuban system tick. It distinguishes Cuban education from other systems in Latin America. In essence, Cuban education gives most Cuban pupils a primary education that only upper-middle-class children receive in other Latin American countries.

This result departs from what previous studies found. Typically, within a country, the single best correlate of higher test scores is a pupil's or student body's social-class background. On average, students who come from homes and neighborhoods where families are less educated and less well off economically come to school in first grade already less well-prepared academically. Particularly effective teachers and schools can make a dent in their academic disadvantage, but they are unlikely to overcome the effect of home and community environment on achievement (Rothstein, 2004).

Among countries and regions with differing economic conditions, students' average social-class background is also related to test scores for the same reasons. Students in Latin America score lower than students in Europe in part because Latin Americans have fewer family academic resources. Yet some countries' education systems seem to be characterized by higher student achievement levels than those in countries with considerably higher income per capita (PISA, 2004, Figure 2-19). For example, scores on the Third International Math and Science Survey (TIMSS) or the Program for International Student Assessment (PISA) in Korea or Hungary adjusted for income per capita are even higher than unadjusted scores when compared to achievement levels in richer European countries, including countries such as Finland where students do very well.

Cuba is one of those countries in which students achieve at a level much higher than their socioeconomic background or national income per capita would predict. When we account for the higher level of parents' education in Cuba than elsewhere in the region, Cuban pupils' adjusted scores are still much higher than the adjusted scores of students in six other Latin American countries.

Our findings are not surprising. Cuban children attend schools in a social context that supports children's health and learning. A government that guarantees employment to adults, provides reasonably good health care to all, and enforces child labor laws may not have an efficient economy, but it does assure that low-income children are well fed and do not have to work when they are not in school or instead of attending school. Strict government social controls are not good for individual *adult* liberties, but they do assure that lower-income children live in crime-free environments, are able to study in classrooms with few student-initiated disturbances, and attend schools that are more socially mixed. In an important sense, low-income children's rights are far better protected than in other Latin American countries, whereas adult rights and, to a much lesser extent, upper-middle-class children's rights are reduced. Cuban students can learn more in these conditions than similar low-income children who have to work for wages and who sit in frequently disrupted classrooms in schools that are highly socially stratified.

Children in Cuba also attend schools with generally high-quality teaching. On average, we observed that Cuban teachers seem to know more about the subject matter (mathematics) and appear to have a clearer idea of how to teach it effectively than most of their counterparts in Chile and Brazil. Children with more knowledgeable, pedagogically effective teachers are bound to learn more in school. However, it is not so obvious *why* some countries such as Cuba have teachers teaching primary school who know the subject matter well, teach a demanding curriculum, know how to deliver it effectively, and get to teach in peaceful classrooms to children who do not work and face little or no violence when they are not in school, whereas in other countries conditions are considerably less favorable to student learning.

From studying Brazil, Chile, and Cuba, we learn a number of important lessons that help answer this puzzle. Cuban students' high performance is not a fluke. True, it is partially a result of the higher average education of parents and more books in the homes of Cuban families, especially in comparison to Brazilian families. This is a standard explanation for higher test scores. Yet student performance is also the result of differing sociopolitical contexts in the three countries, particularly between Brazil and Cuba. And they are the result of just plain better preparation of teachers, a more demanding curriculum, and more instructional focus in schools, from top to bottom. This last finding is the most important because it is the most "transferable" to other countries. We must always keep in mind, however, that many of the organizational advantages in Cuba derive from the sociopolitical context in which Cuba's school system's organization developed.

Lesson 1: State-Generated Social Capital Matters

The most important indicator of state-generated social capital the way we defined it appears to be the degree of social inequality. Cuba is a low-middle-income country when measured by the material goods Cuban families consume. The average Chilean and southern Brazilian are probably better off than the average Cuban in those terms. But Cubans consume more health care and education than all but higher-income groups in Brazil and Chile. Poverty exists in Cuba, but even the very poor have access to food, shelter, health care, and education. The result is that almost no third and fourth graders work outside the home in Cuba, but in Brazil, a number report that they do. This affects performance in school. Children in all three countries reporting that they work even occasionally outside the home score much lower on the tests, especially in Brazil, where the difference is largest and statistically significant. Many more Brazilian and Chilean teachers report classroom disturbances than do interviewees in Cuba. Disturbances also have a negative effect on academic performance. Cuba may be a society with little material consumption, but it is a society that stresses education and a safe and healthy environment for children in and out of school. Chile and Brazil—especially Brazil—have much more political freedom for adults and much more inequality, poverty, crime, and greater numbers of street children. It is not difficult to imagine in which of these social contexts children come to school better prepared to learn.

Cuban students reap another advantage from their society's greater income equality. Cuban salary structures are fixed by the state—not a very efficient system for much of the rest of the economy (the most skilled labor is not necessarily allocated to the most profitable industries and firms)—and this enables education, where salaries are not very different from other sectors, to attract higher-skilled labor than in Brazil or Chile. Students are therefore better served in Cuba, perhaps at the cost of more efficient production in other sectors. Cuban leaders are quick to point out that this is a choice that they have made: provide high-quality public services at the cost of less consumption of material goods (and political freedom). It is questionable whether Cuban parents would make this choice. On the other hand, the mass of lower-income Brazilian and Chilean parents seem to want greater income equality and greatly improved teacher quality at the same cost per pupil. But they are not getting it, perhaps because it would require that more politically powerful middle- and upper-middle-class families pay higher taxes and consume fewer material goods.

It is unlikely that Chilean or Brazilian income distribution will change drastically to become more equal. Evidence for this is the existence of left of center governments in both countries for at least the past ten years (fifteen in Chile) with no perceptible change in income distribution in Chile and only a small degree of equalization in Brazil (Bourguignon, 2004). Both countries have extreme levels of income inequality. Many economists have argued that the persistence of unequal income distribution is the result of forces beyond governments' control, such as the increasing use of new technologies that favor highly skilled labor (for a review of this discussion, see Carnoy, 2001). There is certainly some truth to that claim. The new global economy and trade in increasingly more sophisticated and high-value goods puts a premium on high skills and higher levels of education, increasing the inequality of incomes between workers with more and less education. But we also observed that in some countries, such as Great Britain, the United States, and Australia, income distribution is becoming unequal much more rapidly than in other countries, such as Canada, France, or Sweden, even though the latter countries are involved just as much in the transformation into high-tech production (Carnoy, 2001). Societies apparently can choose greater income inequality without negative effects on economic growth or educational expansion and improvement.[1]

Achieving greater income equality in this day and age is not easy politically, but that does not mean it is not possible. One lesson for countries such as Brazil and Chile is that reducing poverty through a conscious effort to reduce income inequality, child labor, and the culture of poverty almost certainly means improving student performance in school.

The other part of improving state-generated social capital is reducing inequality in the distribution of students among schools. This is a surprising implication of our analysis. At least in primary and secondary school, healthy doses of parent choice and economic inequality—that is, market conditions in education—don't seem to produce more learning, society-wide. The negative aspects of inequality and markets, especially as they play out at the bottom of the social scale, seem to offset any positive effects of parents' "freedom" to pick and choose among schools.

The effect of concentration is most easily observed and measurable in Chile, where parents have the most choice. Apparently, one outcome of greater choice in Chile has been an increase in the concentration of students by social class. Chile's educational system has been remarkable in its experimentation with various incentive schemes aimed at improving student learning. The underlying theory for such social experiments is that market mechanisms, mainly tying teacher pay and employment to schools' ability to attract students and to increase test scores on a national test, will increase the effectiveness and efficiency of the educational process. The theory argues that parents will choose better-performing schools—those that are likely to teach children more in each grade—and that schools will organize themselves to be better performers in order to attract students and gain pay premiums.

These are interesting experiments, and it appears that, aside from a tendency toward greater inequality in the socioeconomic distribution of students among schools,[2] Chile's students, on average, have not become academically *worse* off as a result of market incentives. Educational attainment has increased rapidly in Chile since 1980, but average achievement in each year of schooling has remained flat. The Chilean government may be paying less for educational delivery than it would have otherwise, mainly by successfully shifting the costs of education directly to families and paying somewhat lower salaries to younger teachers (who work in private subsidized schools). Some would argue that this is preferable to increasing taxes, and, indeed, since collecting taxes is costly in a country such as Chile, it may be more efficient to fund education partially through direct tuition.

Nevertheless, it is evident now after twenty years that the educational market experiment has produced neither the achievement gains nor the cost savings envisaged by its supporters. It is difficult to say what Chilean primary and secondary education would be like had it continued to be 75 percent to 80 percent publicly run and had the compensatory policies of the 1990s also been implemented. The best guess is that it would have produced almost identical student outcomes and would have cost about the same. But it is also possible that a less unequal distribution of children among schools might have actually produced academic gains where educational markets and other incentives have failed. The impact of having more middle-class students in lower-income schools might have created an environment more conducive to greater achievement, particularly among lower-income students, without negatively influencing higher-income students.

Lesson 2: Curriculum Matters, but Its Implementation Depends on Teacher Capacity

In reviewing the third-grade math textbooks in Brazil, Cuba, and Chile, we found that all three cover similar material. The Cuban curriculum tends to teach math concepts in a more theoretical context, but two of the Brazilian textbooks cover more material—for example, fractions and certain kinds of measurements as well as division by two digits. Thus, if we had just looked at the textbooks, we might have concluded that pupils in Brazilian classrooms are getting a much greater opportunity to learn. Yet just the opposite seems to be true.

We can draw two possible conclusions from this paradox. The first is that curriculum writers in Brazil are much less interested in modifying their textbooks to fit the capacity of Brazilian teachers to teach the material in them. There is a major disconnect between the level of mathematics prescribed by the textbooks and the level of the material we observed being taught in Brazilian third-grade math lessons. The second possible conclusion is that there is great variation in what teachers cover during the third-grade year in Brazil, and the textbooks afford both lower-income and upper-middle-class schools a curriculum they can use for their own purposes.

In Chile, the single national textbook covers similar material but at a less advanced level than either the Cuban or the "best" two Brazilian textbooks. From extensive interviews of teachers and ministry officials in Chile about the process of the curriculum reform that began to be implemented in 1999 in the lower grades of primary school and then moved into secondary school by 2001, we concluded that curriculum writers must and do take into account teacher capacity in designing curriculum. If they had not, Chilean reformers correctly argue, the curriculum would not have been implemented or at best would have been only partially implemented. This was the case in the United States with the "new math" curriculum—a European-style, integrated math program that few teachers were able to teach effectively because of their mediocre preparation in math. Even fewer U.S. parents could understand new math, never having learned math in this way.

In Chile, the problem is similar. The reformed curriculum, even written with teacher capacity in mind, was already very challenging for most Chilean teachers, and, according to what they told us in interviews, it was difficult to implement. A recent report by the Chilean Ministry of Education using data from interviews conducted with fourth-grade teachers in 2001 shows that the lower the socioeconomic class of the school, the more likely the teacher is to feel uncomfortable with the math curriculum (Ministerio de Educación, 2002).

Most countries' educational systems are marked by a great diversity in how much of the curriculum is actually covered in schools and classrooms.

Teacher surveys in Chile indicate that in schools with lower socioeconomic students, less of the curriculum is implemented than in middle-class schools. We don't have similar studies for Brazil and Cuba, but it is evident from what we observed in classrooms in the two countries that children in Brazilian schools get a broad diversity of exposure to the contents of the recommended frameworks, perhaps an even greater variance than in Chile, whereas in Cuba, exposure is more equal.

One key to explaining the variation in applying curriculum among different classrooms is the variation in teacher capacity in each country. We hypothesize that, especially among primary teachers, the variance in teacher capacity depends largely on the quality of their secondary education. A "virtuous" circle occurs when there are high-quality math and language programs in secondary school. The subject knowledge of primary teachers is higher, curriculum can be more demanding, and students benefit. The circle can also be "vicious." If secondary school math and language programs are of low quality, the average subject knowledge of primary school teachers (who take little subject matter preparation after high school) is quite low, curriculum will necessarily be less challenging, or challenging curriculum will be only partially implemented, and students will suffer the consequences.

Lesson 3: Teacher Education Needs to Be Tightly Coordinated with Existing Curriculum: This Does Not Occur Spontaneously

We are not the first to identify poor teacher education as a major roadblock to improving student academic achievement, and we are not the first to suggest that the autonomy of teacher training colleges from direct state control is the most obvious part of the problem. These are well-known issues in the United States and Latin America, both with fairly similar systems of university-based teacher education only indirectly regulated by government educational authorities.

Comparing Brazilian and Chilean teacher education with the Cuban system underlines two parts of the autonomy problem: The first has to do with faculty incentive systems in Brazilian and Chilean universities, which stress the superiority of "theory" over teaching education students better practice; and the second has to do with the absence of any notion of "quality control" in certifying graduates of teachers' colleges or university faculties of education.

It is sensible to make even primary school teaching a university profession, as all three of our sample countries have done,[3] as this means that primary teachers would complete secondary school math and language requirements. But beyond that important advantage, preparing primary teachers in universities rather than in secondary-level teacher training colleges may have disadvantages if universities preparing young people to teach in a national education system focus on "ideologies" of teaching rather than turning out highly competent instructors of well-defined curriculum frameworks. Thus, each university should be made to focus the core of its teacher education on the notion that every teacher should be an expert at teaching to the pertinent national, state, or municipal curriculum standards. In many countries, this will require teaching education students more math and language courses even if they intend to teach only at the primary level. This is the case in Brazil and Chile, where many primary teachers—even the new crop graduating in the past few years—are under-prepared in math and language subject knowledge. Many schools of education in those two countries also underprepare secondary teachers.

The simplest solution in the short run to assuring minimum teacher competency in countries such as Brazil or Chile, where teachers are trained in autonomous educational institutions, is to test teacher subject knowledge and teaching skills once teachers graduate from university or teacher training college. This is a common way for a state to verify whether teachers meet the minimum levels of content and pedagogical standards required to deliver state-mandated curriculum. Many countries in Europe require teaching graduates to take an examination to compete for available jobs. More than forty U.S. states require education school graduates to take a minimum competency examination.

In the short run, absent the kind of instructional leadership and supervision provided by principals and vice principals in Cuban schools, Brazil and Chile need to provide a mechanism for evaluating teaching skills on the job. Testing teaching skills of young teachers is more complicated than testing their subject knowledge. Usually, teachers first undergo an apprenticeship as a student teacher, then go through an employment probationary period in which they are closely supervised and assisted to improve.

The problem in Brazil and Chile (and most countries of Latin America) is that there are no clear standards of what is considered good teaching, and there is very little evaluation of teaching even of student teachers and teachers in the first stages of their career. In most occupations, at least implicit measures of work output exist. Sales, customer satisfaction, low-error assembly, number of pieces produced per hour, creative capacity, writing ability, problem-solving skills, and caseload are all common measures of employee performance. It should also be possible to evaluate teaching quality, even in qualitative terms, if clear performance standards exist and managers are capable of applying such standards consistently.

Chile is in the throes of developing a teacher evaluation system in which all teachers would present a portfolio of lessons and a sample of teaching videotape to a panel of peers. In theory, this could at least provide an overall assessment of the state of teaching in Chilean classrooms. If peers do their job, it could also provide feedback to teachers with particularly poor pedagogical skills. Yet besides the logistical difficulty and cost of implementing an assessment on this scale, a "one-hit" peer evaluation falls far short of the ongoing, week-after-week supervision and feedback that young Cuban teachers are subjected to in the early years of their career. We will deal further with this below, in Lesson 4.

Such shorter-run efforts to make teacher training institutions conform to standards by measuring the quality of their output are useful but not sufficient. Governments in countries such as Brazil and Chile should also consider developing well-defined university curricula and course requirements for teacher training and adopt more stringent accreditation requirements, particularly regarding subject matter preparation and how such institutions prepare teachers to teach the national curriculum (Chile) or national frameworks (Brazil).

This suggestion flies in the face of analyses that argue for fewer teacher certification requirements. Many market advocates consider that certification requirements, required courses and degrees, and other state controls over who can teach create barriers to entry that impede many talented individuals from entering the profession, hence reducing the talent pool, especially in "shortage subjects" such as math and science. In one scenario, it would be possible for anyone to pass a certification test and a teaching evaluation such as those just discussed. If standards were high, this in itself would not be a bad idea. But if standards were high, few individuals would be able to walk off the street and pass the certification, especially the teaching part. It therefore makes good sense to provide for certification for walk-ons but also to assure that teacher training institutions are kept to desired standards in their teacher education programs through a stringent accreditation process. This implies that a clear vision exists of a high-quality, successful teacher education program. We think that there are such models—we saw one of them in Cuba, but there are others—and all of them revolve around real instruction rather than the ideology of instruction currently being taught in universities in Brazil and Chile.

Lesson 4: Instructional Leadership and Supervision Is Key to Improving Instruction: Market Incentives Are No Substitute for Good Management

The final lesson we learned from the comparison is that Cuban schools are much more likely to be organized around high-quality instruction than Brazilian and Chilean schools, and that this instructional focus is reflected largely in the greater emphasis that Cuban schools place on observing and improving classroom practice, particularly of young teachers.

It seems strange that Brazilian and Chilean school administrators, who are just as aware that good instruction is the foundation of high-quality education as the Cubans, do so much less to supervise and improve teaching in their schools. In part, this is the result of a system of supervision based on inspectors, imported from France and Spain—a system that dissociates the director of a school from responsibility for the quality of instruction or from assuring that the required curriculum is being implemented. In Chile, the inspector as supervisor disappeared during the military regime and tended to be replaced by the notion that market forces—schools competing for students—would suffice to promote high-quality teaching. In Brazil, the inspection system never worked well in any case, although it is still "on the books." School directors in both countries play largely administrative roles, overseeing the day-to-day functioning of the schools, public relations, and, in many schools in Chile, fund-raising. Schools in both countries also have assistant directors who supervise teachers' preparation of course plans to make sure that they conform to the national frameworks, but these technical-professional administrators, as they are known, rarely go further to check how well the course plans are being implemented.

The second explanation for lack of supervision is that school administrators in Brazil and Chile have no clear idea of what constitutes high-quality teaching of the required curriculum. Neither do they have the capacity to supervise teaching constructively. To do that, they would have needed considerable training and experience as, say, mentor teachers charged with assisting other teachers to improve.

A third explanation is that Brazil and Chile's teaching culture emphasizes teacher autonomy in the classroom. "The classroom is the teacher's sanctuary," a board member of the Chilean teachers' association (union) told us recently. School administrators are reluctant to observe teachers' practice with the intention of commenting on it, even constructively.

These explanations suggest why privatizing schools in Chile did not neatly lead to improved teaching and why private school administrators are not necessarily more likely to be instructional leaders than public school administrators. We met a few instructional leaders in both Chilean public and private schools, but they seem to appear serendipitously rather than as part of a systemic effort by the ministry to develop administrators who would play such a role. Our explanations also suggest that instructional leadership from school administration at any level is not going to develop spontaneously. Between the lack of capacity among school administrators to recognize poor teaching or know how to improve it and the cultural barriers to "interfering" in classroom teaching, school administrators in Brazil and Chile are not currently in a position to create the kind of instructional focus that exists in Cuban schools.

It is, however, possible to develop systems of instructional supervision and to create cultures of instructional improvement that would, when combined with better teacher education and with teacher certification, begin to raise standards of teaching and learning and to provide the assistance to teachers to meet those standards.

Chile is trying to develop a cadre of *supervisores* that would replace the inspectors and play the role we suggested for principals and vice principals in schools. The *supervisores* would cover a number of schools in the district, recommending professional courses to teachers to improve certain aspects of their teaching. This should help create standards of teaching excellence and possibly improve teaching across schools, but it may take longer and be less effective than developing teams at each school, including the principal, that become well versed in how to identify teachers with needs and how to make significant improvements in their classroom teaching.

Training a new generation of educational managers *qua* instructional leaders is not simple. It requires a sizable investment in management courses for school principals (or external supervisors) preceded by a redefinition of the principal's role as an instructional leader with skills in assessing student performance and teacher practice. Instructional leaders or external supervisors also have to have good human resource management and communication skills to help their teaching staff adopt more effective techniques.

Brazil and Chile could also adopt the Cuban practice of maintaining a single teacher for a cohort of students over a number of school years, say, from first to fourth grades. Montessori schools use such a cohort approach to teaching, and so do many schools in Italy. When teachers are with students for several years, teachers can become familiar with the strengths and idiosyncrasies of each child in the class. The class becomes more a family than a temporary relationship over a single year. The effectiveness of this practice depends on having a cohort of teachers in schools that vary relatively little in quality. This is the case in Cuba, and in some schools in Chile, but is much less likely in Brazil. If schools have really "good" teachers and also quite "bad" teachers, a teaching system that assigns children to the same teacher for several years would be lucky for some pupils and a disaster for others.[4] Thus, a potential improvement in the way children are processed through the education system cannot be implemented in many countries because the system cannot guarantee that all teachers meet a reasonably high standard of excellence.

Conclusions

Cuban students' higher performance is the result of a number of factors. We were able to measure the effect of some of these factors through standard production function estimates. Yet these estimates could not explain a significant portion of Cubans' superior math skills, particularly those resulting from differences in the quality of teaching in classrooms and a management system that assures that a fairly demanding national curriculum is applied universally regardless of students' social class. To understand the existence and potential impact of those effects, we turned to a combination of qualitative analysis—interviews in schools, analysis of textbooks, and videotapes of third-grade math lessons in individual classrooms. The qualitative analysis suggested that Cuban children are getting a fairly demanding math curriculum delivered more effectively by better-trained, more frequently supervised and guided teachers, in schools that are, on average, more directly focused on instruction than Brazilian or Chilean schools.

In our production function estimates, we included student family background variables, school resource variables, and a more controversial set of variables we called "social context," or state-driven social capital. These sociopolitical context variables, mainly related to children's social condition outside primary school and the social-class distribution of children among schools, are important in explaining at least part of Cuban's higher test performance. This is an interesting finding with important implications for educational policy. Countries, regions, or school districts can expect to continue to have difficulty achieving high levels of student learning in school if the children live in a sociopolitical context outside school that does not provide the safety, health, and moral support needed to function well in a classroom environment.

Similarly, unequal learning, characterized by much lower expectations and results for low-income children, is reinforced by school systems that tend to concentrate children with similar social-class backgrounds in schools that are identified as low-income schools. A recent Chilean study suggests that a higher fraction of teachers in low socioeconomic schools feel less well prepared to teach the Chilean mathematics curriculum, suggesting that the least "able" teachers eventually end up teaching in such schools. Thus, the greater the concentration of students by socioeconomic status in different schools, the more likely school resources are to be distributed more unequally, and the more likely the system will be to produce more unequal results.

In our qualitative analysis, we identified other effects of state-generated social capital that are important in explaining Cubans' higher test scores. Because of wage setting by the state, Cuban teachers are more likely to be drawn from a pool of high school graduates who performed better academically than the teacher candidate pool in either Brazil or Chile. With access to young people who have higher levels of subject matter knowledge, Cuban curriculum writers have been able to bring a reasonably demanding curriculum into all levels of schooling, especially primary school.

State-driven social capital is an important construct for understanding why children in some countries do better in school, but it is difficult to transport higher social capital from one country to another. State-generated social capital is usually the result of historical forces that are rather country specific and is both the product and shaper of specific cultural values. Nevertheless, nation-states can improve children's welfare substantially by providing free early childhood education beginning with very young children, providing family subsidies to low-income families contingent on sending children to school and prohibiting child labor, and providing access to early childhood education and school-based nutrition and health care.

Many of our findings concerning Cuban school success, however, can be attributed directly to what takes place within the Cuban education system. Three of the four main lessons we learned from our study could be incorporated into the Brazilian and Chilean education system, beginning with much better initial training of teachers, with more emphasis on subject matter preparation (in part to compensate for low levels of subject matter learning—especially math—in Brazilian and Chilean secondary schools) and learning to teach the required curriculum frameworks.

Beyond getting tighter control of teacher education in universities and teacher training colleges, Brazilian and Chilean education authorities can learn a lot from the way Cuban school principals are charged with supervising new teachers and assuring a high standard of curriculum delivery in Cuban classrooms. Brazil and Chile could also shift to a system of keeping the same cohort of pupils with one teacher from first to fourth grade. When Chilean students take their fourth-grade SIMCE test, the result would be the cumulative effect of one teacher's work, increasing the responsibility of the teacher and the school (as in Cuba) to assure that each teacher is providing a high quality of instruction.

As a final thought, we would like to remind the reader of the possible conflict in democratic societies between individual freedom in most other aspects of human life and in schooling, which is hardly democratic. Few children beyond third grade would voluntarily choose to spend thirty or more hours a week for forty weeks per year sitting in classes, but they are compelled to do so. As part of the individual freedoms guaranteed by democratic societies, parents often demand the right to choose schools for their children or to choose to send their children to work, and teachers demand many "rights," including the right to professional autonomy in their classrooms. Such autonomy is meant to protect teachers from uncalled-for interference by administrators in the way teachers conduct their teaching and to protect teachers from ideologically based judgments of what constitutes good teaching.

The Cuban educational system is not faced by these contradictions, and because the Cuban state is genuinely interested in delivering high-quality basic academic skills, the system is able to invoke collective interests in pressuring families and teachers to conform to its standards for student learning. In doing so, the state takes ultimate responsibility for children's education, including the responsibility for assuring that parents, who, coincidently are also state employees, do their share in guaranteeing that children reach high levels of academic performance. This is possible only in democratic societies when the public sector—the state—has the implicit confidence of civil society. Parents have to have full confidence that the state is capable of delivering high-quality services and that state employees (such as teachers) are totally committed to that task.

We did not find these conditions prevailing in either Brazil or Chile, with good reason. In Brazil, the state has historically not been committed to delivering high-quality education to most of the Brazilian population. In Chile, as in Brazil, good public education existed in the past for an upper-middle-class elite, but not for the masses. As a result, once vouchers were made available in Chile, there was a rapid flight to private education. Even low-quality private education was preferable to public. Under such circumstances, the central role of the state as the guarantor of high-quality services loses its meaning, and the competitive individual, struggling to gain advantage over others, reigns supreme. The notion of pulling together—teachers, administrators, parents, and students—to improve children's learning degenerates into placing the highest value on parents' and teachers' individual choices and individual rights, in the premise that if adults use those rights wisely, children will come out ahead.

The Cuban system has obvious severe drawbacks, especially in the lack of political freedom and limits on individual choice. The high level of self-discipline and cooperative behavior that make Cuban classrooms function so smoothly at the primary level are important to developing basic skills and proficiency in problem solving. But at higher levels of education, in middle and high school, creative rebellion and dissent—traits that flourish to the extreme in societies such as the United States—are largely suppressed in Cuba.

The path to better education in democratic societies need not be a turn to authoritarianism. The lessons we have drawn from the Cuban experience do suggest, however, that the state has be much more of a *guarantor* of quality education for all—the state needs to take public responsibility for children's success. The state has to be an effective activist in transforming educational management toward greater control over what happens at the school. It has to take full responsibility for improving instruction, even at the cost of decreasing faculty and administrative autonomy of universities' schools of education in their initial formation of teachers, and of decreasing the autonomy of classroom teachers who do not show the creativity and competence to function at a high level when given autonomy. The state needs to guarantee that all teachers are effective in producing student learning by regularly evaluating them, from initial certification to evaluative supervision of their work in classrooms. By setting high standards for schools and teachers and enforcing them, the state reduces the need for parents to agonize over where they should send their children to school, as almost all schools would be delivering similarly and reasonably high-quality education. This is what the public wants in a democratic state, and this is what the public should get.

Reference Matter

Production Function Estimates of Student Achievement in Latin America, by Country

Estimating Production Functions

The definition of the variables used in the regression analysis are shown in Appendix Table A.1.

The results shown in Tables A.2 and A.3 represent the estimated (cluster adjusted) ordinary least-squares (OLS) relationships for the entire sample of third and fourth graders between pupil achievement scores (math in Table A.2 and language in Table A.3) and student/family characteristics, teacher/school characteristics, and social context variables as expressed in the equation in Chapter 4. The relationships were estimated separately for each country as well as for all countries together (column 9), with dummy variables added for each country (Cuba is omitted to serve as the reference variable). The sample size varies from country to country, mainly because of variation in the number of missing values for independent variables. We included a dummy for fourth graders to control for grade differences on

Definitions for all variables included in analysis

Variable	Definition
Student and Family Characteristics	
Female	1 = Female; 0 = Male
Student self-confidence	Compared to other students in class/section: 1 = "I understand less"; 2 = "I understand the same"; 3 = "I understand more"
Parental education	Average for both parents' education in levels 0 to 6
Read to child	Parents read to student when he/she was young: 0 = "Never"; 1 = "2–3 times a year"; 2 = "Once a month"; 3 = "More than once a month"; 4 = "Almost every day"
Expected level of study	Parental expectations for years of education student will complete, in levels 0 to 6
Books in household	Ordinal measure of number of books in household: 1 = "No books"; 2 = "Less than 10 books"; 3 = "10–50 books"; 4 = "More than 50 books"
Teacher/School Characteristics	
Fourth grade	1 = Student in fourth grade; 0 = Student in third grade
Student average grade 3	School/classroom average of third-grade test score
Student has math/Spanish textbook	1 = Student indicated in interview he/she has a textbook; 0 = No
Teacher education	Three categories: "High School" (*Normalista*), "University," and "Other"
Teacher training sessions	Number of training courses taken by teacher in last three years
Classroom condition	Average condition of classroom (according to teacher) for lighting, temperature, hygiene, safety and acoustics. 0 = "Inadequate"; 1 = "Adequate"

Classroom materials — Sum of materials available in classroom (according to teacher): blackboard, classroom library, calculators, games, maps/globes, overhead projector, slide projector, geometry materials, textbooks, computer, television, and VCR. Index from 0 to 12

Principal autonomy — Average degree of autonomy (according to principal) for hiring/firing teachers, budget allocation, textbook/material selection, student admissions/suspensions, student promotion, rules, pedagogical prioritizing, planning extracurricular activities. Response range: 1 = "No autonomy"; 2 = "Partial autonomy"; 3 = "Full autonomy"

Rural school — 1 = Rural school (excluded category is urban public school)

Private school — 1 = Private school (excluded category is urban public school)

Social Context

Student attended preschool — 1 = Yes; 0 = No

SES factor (school) — Classroom average for principal component factor analysis using parental education, books in household, and work outside the home as factor loadings

Classroom fights — Classroom averages for percentage of children reporting fights with other students: 1 = "Hardly ever"; 2 = "Sometimes"; 3 = "Almost always"

Works outside the home — Class averages of frequency students report working outside of home: 1 = "Hardly ever"; 2 = "Sometimes"; 3 = "Almost always"

Works in the home — Class averages of frequency students report working in the home: 1 = "Hardly ever"; 2 = "Sometimes"; 3 = "Almost always"

Children free from work — Class averages of frequency students report being free to do what they want outside of school: 1 = "Hardly ever"; 2 = "Sometimes"; 3 = "Almost always"

Ordinary least squares (OLS) cluster-adjusted estimates of the determinants of academic achievement in mathematics (T-statistics in parentheses), third and fourth graders combined, seven Latin American countries

Variables	COUNTRY								
	Argentina (1)	Bolivia (2)	Brazil (3)	Chile (4)	Colombia (5)	Cuba (6)	Mexico (7)	All 7 (8)	All 7 (9)
Student/Family Characteristics									
Female	-8.62 (-4.17)	-5.08 (-2.19)	-7.26 (-4.56)	-4.38 (-2.08)	-4.67 (-2.89)	2.03 (0.83)	-1.80 (-1.17)	-4.45 (-4.02)	-3.38 (-3.76)
Student self-confidence	9.28 (4.02)	6.09 (1.98)	11.27 (5.20)	16.19 (6.01)	3.45 (1.66)	31.34 (5.75)	8.36 (3.59)	12.37 (9.46)	11.99 (9.63)
Parental education	2.04 (2.48)	2.43 (3.05)	1.98 (2.26)	1.79 (2.02)	1.50 (2.46)	3.82 (3.00)	3.73 (4.82)	3.20 (7.11)	2.47 (5.92)
Read to child	0.37 (0.55)	1.01 (2.24)	1.68 (3.15)	1.45 (2.13)	1.19 (1.97)	1.98 (1.43)	0.87 (1.56)	2.44 (7.50)	1.22 (4.45)
Expected level of study	2.24 (2.59)	1.02 (1.44)	2.00 (2.98)	3.07 (3.79)	1.11 (1.43)	9.83 (6.31)	2.11 (2.54)	2.60 (5.89)	2.45 (5.96)
Books in household	1.56 (1.04)	2.06 (2.32)	1.79 (1.66)	2.13 (1.63)	2.34 (2.61)	6.96 (3.95)	2.12 (1.91)	2.00 (3.25)	3.78 (6.79)
Teacher/School Characteristics									
Fourth grade	22.22 (7.92)	2.90 (0.70)	23.22 (10.08)	22.55 (10.91)	15.44 (8.51)	5.17 (1.22)	18.89 (9.52)	13.09 (9.33)	13.46 (9.88)
Classroom materials	0.64 (0.10)	1.30 (1.53)	1.39 (2.19)	0.79 (1.66)	0.93 (1.57)	5.83 (2.05)	1.09 (1.74)	0.73 (1.63)	1.36 (3.32)
Student has math textbook	-1.35 (-0.59)	-10.06 (-2.89)	1.94 (0.84)	2.78 (0.79)	0.30 (0.12)	-5.20 (-0.81)	5.25 (1.15)	0.34 (0.18)	-3.21 (-1.92)

Teacher education:[a]								
University								
−2.42	−8.46	6.56	6.02	0.59	12.60	0.68	10.59	3.17
(−0.80)	(−1.51)	(2.08)	(2.32)	(0.20)	(1.49)	(0.23)	(5.07)	(1.82)
Other								
5.79	20.43	—	—	21.45	—	—	24.96	21.25
(0.93)	(2.08)			(1.17)			(3.22)	(3.45)
Teacher training sessions								
0.38	−0.10	1.15	−0.02	−0.032	1.76	−0.15	0.76	0.91
(1.29)	(−0.21)	(6.87)	(−0.05)	(−0.11)	(3.77)	(−0.74)	(2.63)	(3.76)
Classroom condition								
0.88	11.14	−8.48	2.81	−4.59	−12.74	3.76	8.18	2.06
(0.13)	(1.41)	(−1.84)	(0.56)	(−0.85)	(−0.99)	(0.72)	(1.94)	(0.52)
Principal autonomy								
−5.40	6.26	8.77	7.23	4.98	0.69	−2.01	7.71	6.44
(−0.75)	(0.77)	(1.79)	(1.15)	(1.11)	(0.01)	(−0.47)	(2.25)	(2.08)
Rural school								
−13.88	5.62	3.32	1.12	15.62	6.18	−0.06	10.84	4.79
(−2.68)	(0.73)	(0.76)	(0.22)	(3.94)	(0.67)	(−0.02)	(3.42)	(1.52)
Private school								
−0.38	1.40	−6.45	−15.81	0.32	0	4.17	−18.43	−3.96
(−0.07)	(0.15)	(−1.57)	(−2.58)	(0.07)	—	(0.47)	(−4.63)	(−1.04)
Social Context								
Student attended preschool								
5.07	2.97	−0.16	1.98	4.03	−13.32	7.10	0.17	−0.83
(1.73)	(1.40)	(−0.07)	(0.79)	(−2.16)	(−1.42)	(2.84)	(0.12)	(−0.62)
Work outside the home								
−24.65	−14.05	−42.63	7.25	−10.39	7.76	−26.47	−48.20	−13.32
(−2.17)	(−0.91)	(−4.85)	(0.81)	(−1.60)	(0.25)	(−3.05)	(9.55)	(−2.36)
Work in the home								
−18.57	−30.72	12.08	−38.72	−9.28	46.45	−1.66	41.62	3.67
(−1.23)	(−1.53)	(1.22)	(−2.82)	(−0.93)	(1.79)	(−0.13)	(5.40)	(0.46)
Children free from work								
18.41	−26.65	−13.20	2.59	−2.41	−14.11	6.29	−6.07	−2.35
(1.72)	(−1.50)	(−1.52)	(0.25)	(−0.35)	(1.05)	(0.74)	(0.94)	(−0.38)
Classroom fights								
−45.65	−64.94	−8.19	−23.97	−31.20	−130.13	−8.26	−53.43	−39.92
(−3.02)	(−3.50)	(−0.87)	(−1.53)	(−3.15)	(−2.92)	(−0.76)	(−7.13)	(−5.77)
SES factor (school)								
8.35	5.33	11.17	12.20	2.48	3.66	2.16	8.01	4.52
(2.01)	(−0.72)	(3.57)	(3.93)	(0.73)	(0.40)	(0.45)	(3.30)	(1.64)

(continued)

TABLE A.2
(*continued*)

	COUNTRY								
Variables	Argentina (1)	Bolivia (2)	Brazil (3)	Chile (4)	Colombia (5)	Cuba (6)	Mexico (7)	All 7 (8)	All 7 (9)
Country Dummies									
Argentina dummy	—	—	—	—	—	—	—	—	−60.59 (−9.99)
Bolivia dummy	—	—	—	—	—	—	—	—	−67.32 (−9.35)
Brazil dummy	—	—	—	—	—	—	—	—	−55.26 (−8.46)
Chile dummy	—	—	—	—	—	—	—	—	−66.45 (−10.43)
Colombia dummy	—	—	—	—	—	—	—	—	−65.37 (−10.57)
Mexico dummy[b]	—	—	—	—	—	—	—	—	−62.12 (−9.90)
Constant	275.19	369.50	240.57	236.47	249.61	46.58	214.88	160.44	256.04
Number of classroom clusters	83	62	112	99	160	98	105	719	719
N	1,413	2,679	2,109	1,331	2,477	3,409	2,411	15,829	15,829
R^2	0.371	0.235	0.393	0.273	0.152	0.177	0.244	0.457	0.494

NOTE: Due to clustered nature of sample, robust standard errors are used.

[a]Excluded category for teacher education is high school.

[b]Excluded category for country is Cuba.

TABLE A·3
Ordinary least squares (OLS) cluster-adjusted estimates of the determinants of academic achievement in language (T-statistics in parentheses), seven Latin American countries

Variables	COUNTRY								
	Argentina (1)	Bolivia (2)	Brazil (3)	Chile (4)	Colombia (5)	Cuba (6)	Mexico (7)	All 7 (8)	All 7 (9)
Student/Family Characteristics									
Female	6.54	2.32	8.00	7.91	5.84	6.28	8.01	5.42	6.22
	(2.54)	(1.27)	(4.69)	(3.92)	(3.53)	(3.31)	(3.95)	(5.92)	(7.83)
Student self-confidence	10.54	5.68	4.48	17.63	3.68	8.80	6.53	8.12	8.31
	(3.03)	(2.19)	(2.05)	(6.96)	(1.58)	(2.22)	(2.36)	(7.11)	(7.35)
Parental education	2.81	2.15	2.90	1.73	2.43	0.61	5.12	2.11	2.22
	(2.80)	(2.46)	(3.48)	(1.57)	(2.75)	(0.67)	(4.66)	(5.23)	(5.61)
Read to child	1.95	0.85	1.20	2.32	0.56	1.28	2.33	2.66	1.58
	(2.26)	(1.36)	(2.05)	(3.16)	(0.74)	(1.17)	(2.94)	(8.25)	(5.44)
Expected level of study	2.54	1.91	2.28	5.55	1.82	5.16	1.43	2.96	2.80
	(2.35)	(1.90)	(3.59)	(5.61)	(1.96)	(3.34)	(1.71)	(7.04)	(6.80)
Books in household	−0.66	2.81	1.39	2.80	3.38	2.57	2.86	2.32	2.75
	(−0.46)	(2.12)	(1.22)	(1.95)	(2.68)	(2.07)	(2.21)	(4.14)	(5.05)
Teacher/School Characteristics									
Fourth grade	25.75	4.82	22.42	26.95	23.40	4.93	25.10	16.80	16.86
	(9.38)	(1.06)	(10.35)	(10.92)	(10.87)	(1.58)	(10.71)	(13.89)	(14.02)
Classroom materials	−0.32	0.98	0.78	0.46	1.68	1.69	2.73	1.32	1.11
	(−0.54)	(1.33)	(1.26)	(1.00)	(2.47)	(1.01)	(2.75)	(3.62)	(3.50)
Student has language textbook	3.37	−5.48	−1.00	15.85	1.15	11.93	17.18	1.69	0.81
	(1.33)	(−1.53)	(−0.40)	(3.97)	(0.42)	(1.67)	(4.53)	(1.05)	(0.51)

(continued)

TABLE A.3
(continued)

Variables	COUNTRY								
	Argentina (1)	Bolivia (2)	Brazil (3)	Chile (4)	Colombia (5)	Cuba (6)	Mexico (7)	All 7 (8)	All 7 (9)
Teacher education[a]									
University	1.82	-12.42	2.89	2.92	3.80	0.99	0.52	10.11	1.93
	(0.54)	(-2.35)	(1.04)	(0.99)	(1.19)	(0.16)	(0.15)	(5.68)	(1.21)
Other	10.61	15.73	—	—	-9.36	—	—	12.34	9.89
	(1.94)	(1.91)			(-0.66)			(1.99)	(1.56)
Teacher training sessions	0.84	-0.32	0.93	-0.58	0.11	0.68	-0.64	0.11	0.27
	(3.79)	(-0.65)	(6.59)	(-2.25)	(0.29)	(2.06)	(-2.26)	(0.59)	(1.85)
Classroom condition	2.48	6.98	-3.18	-0.67	-1.68	15.15	2.77	7.82	4.88
	(0.42)	(0.83)	(-0.59)	(-0.12)	(-0.26)	(1.78)	(0.35)	(2.53)	(1.61)
Principal autonomy	-3.65	10.36	11.70	11.03	1.04	-4.98	3.39	7.96	6.63
	(-0.59)	(6.11)	(2.69)	(1.91)	(0.20)	(-0.59)	(0.70)	(2.77)	(2.39)
Rural school	-29.06	-4.83	-4.21	6.29	7.59	-9.53	-6.45	1.94	-2.29
	(-5.13)	(-0.64)	(-1.08)	(1.11)	(1.78)	(-1.30)	(-1.56)	(0.79)	(-0.93)
Private school	4.14	-17.22	-5.30	-10.54	0.43	—	7.94	-13.64	-4.44
	(0.77)	(-2.01)	(-1.34)	(-2.38)	(0.09)		(0.93)	(-5.22)	(-1.64)
Social Context									
Student attended preschool	5.97	5.39	1.84	0.23	-5.17	-5.05	6.91	1.02	1.17
	(1.67)	(1.96)	(0.85)	(0.10)	(-2.35)	(-0.79)	(2.53)	(0.80)	(0.98)
Work outside the home	-12.08	3.24	-35.96	1.55	-14.06	-2.86	-28.06	-44.10	-14.49
	(-1.07)	(0.18)	(-4.36)	(0.17)	(-2.02)	(-0.19)	(-2.86)	(-9.75)	(-3.31)
Work in the home	-18.60	-24.29	12.83	-36.68	-3.44	35.40	16.40	22.65	1.01
	(-1.49)	(-1.43)	(1.47)	(-2.75)	(-0.35)	(1.92)	(1.02)	(4.07)	(0.17)
Children free from work	11.15	-30.68	1.85	-6.14	1.08	-2.05	9.32	6.34	2.93
	(1.02)	(-1.96)	(0.19)	(-0.55)	(0.14)	(-0.21)	(0.97)	(1.43)	(0.63)

	(1)	(2)	(3)	(4)	(5)	(6)	(7)	(8)	(9)
Classroom fights	-30.38	-70.93	-11.37	-40.77	-28.61	-76.98	-11.31	-38.80	-34.25
	(-2.50)	(-4.48)	(-1.21)	(-3.37)	(-3.36)	(-2.40)	(-0.90)	(-6.43)	(-6.04)
SES factor (school)	9.57	5.97	8.30	11.99	7.35	4.64	1.42	8.52	7.55
	(2.92)	(1.04)	(2.39)	(3.37)	(2.06)	(0.70)	(0.29)	(5.26)	(4.25)
Country Dummies									
Argentina dummy	—	—	—	—	—	—	—	—	-28.83
									(-6.61)
Bolivia dummy	—	—	—	—	—	—	—	—	-53.25
									(-9.60)
Brazil dummy	—	—	—	—	—	—	—	—	-31.96
									(-6.56)
Chile dummy	—	—	—	—	—	—	—	—	-31.93
									(-6.88)
Colombia dummy	—	—	—	—	—	—	—	—	-44.08
									(-9.45)
Mexico dummy[b]	—	—	—	—	—	—	—	—	-48.59
									(-10.35)
Constant	264.09	314.32	196.95	237.96	217.53	170.28	121.53	171.37	232.85
Number of classroom clusters	83	62	112	99	160	97	104	717	717
N	1,402	2,825	2,065	2,127	2,451	3,063	2,378	16,311	16,311
R^2	0.296	0.188	0.344	0.261	0.207	0.106	0.270	0.386	0.411

NOTE: Due to clustered nature of sample, robust standard errors are used.

[a]Excluded category for teacher education is high school.

[b]Excluded category for country is Cuba.

169

the test. Because the estimates were "two level" (individual students and classrooms/schools), we corrected standard errors of the OLS coefficients for "cluster effects" to eliminate bias.

The general equation in column 9 (in both tables) indicates that Cuban students score higher than students in all other countries, even when family human and social capital characteristics, school conditions, and social context differences are accounted for.[1] Each of the country coefficients for school variables can be regarded as an approximation of the relative "achievement score effectiveness" of each country's educational system compared with Cuba's education system. When taking account of family, school resources, and our proxies for social context, the smallest differences compared to Cuba for mathematics were found in Brazil, Argentina, and Mexico, although the differences between the six non-Cuban countries are not great (Table A.2). For example, the difference between the Argentine and Chilean coefficients in mathematics (compared to Cuba) is about seven points, which corresponds to about one-tenth of a standard deviation for mathematics. The biggest difference is between the Brazilian and Chilean coefficients (about 11 points). This represents almost 15 percent of one standard deviation. The "achievement score efficiency" differences between the six non-Cuban countries in language performance are greater than in math. Controlling for socioeconomic and school differences within and between countries, students in Brazil, Argentina, and Chile score between 20 percent and 40 percent of a standard deviation higher than students in Colombia, Mexico, and Bolivia, when controlling for family, school, and social context characteristics.

The general equation with all countries included also shows that a student's home characteristics and the social context of his or her classroom and school are highly significant in explaining student achievement scores, but the school resources are much less so. Several variables that were expected to be significant determinants of achievement, including preschool attendance (as measured in this survey), private and rural school enrollment, and whether the student has a language textbook (significantly negative for math textbook), are not significant in the pooled models that include the country dummies.

Tables A.4 and A.5 present the estimates using fourth-grade scores. The difference between this "gain" in student performance in Cuba and in the other six countries is much smaller than the overall score differences shown

TABLE A.4

Ordinary least squares (OLS) cluster-adjusted estimates of the determinants of fourth-grade academic achievement in mathematics (T-statistics in parentheses), seven Latin American countries

| | | | | | COUNTRY | | | | |
Variables	Argentina (1)	Bolivia (2)	Brazil (3)	Chile (4)	Colombia (5)	Cuba (6)	Mexico (7)	All 7 (8)	All 7 (9)
School average grade 3	0.60	0.32	0.32	0.58	0.60	0.44	0.32	0.52	0.48
	(3.70)	(2.24)	(2.09)	(8.84)	(10.72)	(7.02)	(2.46)	(11.36)	(9.50)
Student/Family Characteristics									
Female	−8.59	−2.49	−6.58	−5.91	−6.10	2.97	1.01	−2.96	−2.54
	(−3.15)	(−1.06)	(−2.98)	(−2.26)	(−3.00)	(1.00)	(0.41)	(−2.72)	(−0.04)
Student self-confidence	14.50	3.84	18.53	16.56	7.10	30.04	8.44	13.58	13.42
	(4.39)	(0.92)	(6.15)	(4.72)	(2.62)	(5.45)	(2.54)	(8.45)	(8.43)
Parental education	2.35	1.40	2.02	2.23	0.33	5.90	4.45	2.99	2.98
	(2.16)	(1.79)	(1.52)	(1.70)	(0.40)	(4.97)	(4.23)	(6.38)	(6.55)
Read to child	0.50	0.04	1.84	2.66	0.45	0.50	−0.22	1.06	0.61
	(0.53)	(0.07)	(2.38)	(2.79)	(0.74)	(0.28)	(−0.25)	(2.90)	(1.75)
Expected level of study	1.25	0.76	1.94	2.61	0.58	7.46	1.55	1.46	1.77
	(1.10)	(0.81)	(2.16)	(2.12)	(0.69)	(4.14)	(1.61)	(3.00)	(3.72)
Books in household	2.30	1.48	2.20	1.69	3.47	6.68	3.23	3.85	3.97
	(1.17)	(1.14)	(1.40)	(0.95)	(2.91)	(3.79)	(2.31)	(5.61)	(6.08)
Teacher/School Characteristics									
Classroom materials	−1.19	1.79	1.78	0.22	1.40	3.58	0.70	1.47	1.16
	(−1.42)	(1.97)	(1.77)	(0.47)	(2.69)	(1.62)	(0.92)	(4.06)	(3.14)
Student has math textbook	−0.39	−9.14	5.93	2.51	−3.58	−2.16	4.55	0.15	−2.29
	(−0.13)	(−4.09)	(1.82)	(0.44)	(−1.42)	(−0.26)	(0.82)	(0.09)	(−1.39)

(continued)

TABLE A.4
(continued)

					COUNTRY				
Variables	Argentina (1)	Bolivia (2)	Brazil (3)	Chile (4)	Colombia (5)	Cuba (6)	Mexico (7)	All 7 (8)	All 7 (9)
Teacher education[a]									
University	-1.63	4.29	6.43	0.39	1.26	21.72	-1.10	5.87	2.79
	(-0.40)	(0.55)	(1.57)	(0.12)	(0.47)	(2.43)	(-0.27)	(3.01)	(1.35)
Other	-22.67	22.79	—	—	-14.69	—	—	9.19	11.13
	(2.33)	(1.36)			(-1.52)			(0.89)	(1.09)
Teacher training sessions	0.11	-0.62	0.60	0.09	-0.88	0.90	-0.08	0.22	0.38
	(0.38)	(-1.45)	(1.72)	(0.40)	(-0.28)	(2.92)	(-0.38)	(0.98)	(1.91)
Classroom condition	-9.16	14.39	-7.58	2.10	-4.67	-9.82	1.17	2.82	0.76
	(-1.08)	(1.69)	(-1.19)	(0.44)	(-1.03)	(-0.91)	(0.19)	(0.71)	(0.21)
Principal autonomy	-17.55	7.07	5.55	13.42	2.66	3.08	-4.37	3.86	4.03
	(-1.78)	(0.94)	(0.82)	(2.53)	(0.70)	(0.35)	(-0.86)	(1.07)	(1.14)
Rural school	-3.46	7.01	3.19	10.30	7.49	0.90	-0.16	3.30	2.48
	(-0.50)	(0.93)	(0.47)	(2.23)	(2.09)	(0.09)	(-0.03)	(1.04)	(0.77)
Private school	15.68	2.96	-9.87	-9.42	-2.28	—	2.38	-7.68	-2.76
	(1.66)	(0.37)	(-1.40)	(-1.76)	(-0.52)		(0.25)	(-2.27)	(-0.80)
Social Context									
Student attended preschool	1.76	1.24	-3.59	3.11	-3.36	-14.54	6.29	-0.59	-1.87
	(0.42)	(0.53)	(-1.02)	(1.01)	(-1.49)	(-1.43)	(1.83)	(-0.44)	(-1.39)
Work outside the home	-23.63	-11.73	-35.42	-0.53	4.41	-13.60	-28.00	-24.46	-9.88
	(-1.52)	(-0.58)	(-2.30)	(-0.05)	(0.64)	(-0.39)	(-2.65)	(-4.77)	(-1.84)
Work in the home	18.39	-15.48	19.27	18.64	-3.42	-10.73	-4.82	9.54	6.18
	(1.08)	(-0.58)	(1.32)	(1.60)	(-0.41)	(-0.52)	(-0.33)	(1.43)	(0.87)

172

	(1)	(2)	(3)	(4)	(5)	(6)	(7)	(8)	(9)
Children free from work	20.37 (1.68)	−2.33 (−0.12)	−9.78 (−0.62)	−2.24 (−0.24)	0.66 (0.11)	21.80 (1.90)	−1.18 (−0.13)	11.25 (2.23)	9.24 (1.73)
Classroom fights	−19.09 (−1.17)	−69.44 (−3.98)	−7.63 (−0.55)	−19.14 (−1.64)	−15.51 (−2.24)	−92.60 (−2.22)	−5.78 (−0.47)	−28.42 (−4.29)	−28.85 (−4.40)
SES factor (school)	−3.32 (−0.54)	−5.22 (−0.82)	8.67 (1.71)	6.34 (1.57)	−0.46 (−0.14)	1.35 (0.15)	−3.52 (−0.66)	−3.45 (−1.66)	−1.57 (−0.62)
Country Dummies									
Argentina dummy	—	—	—	—	—	—	—	—	−15.37 (−2.80)
Bolivia dummy	—	—	—	—	—	—	—	—	−29.45 (−4.65)
Brazil dummy	—	—	—	—	—	—	—	—	−10.83 (−1.82)
Chile dummy	—	—	—	—	—	—	—	—	−17.74 (−2.93)
Colombia dummy	—	—	—	—	—	—	—	—	−21.10 (−3.67)
Mexico dummy[b]	—	—	—	—	—	—	—	—	−15.49 (−2.66)
Constant	80.33	206.90	137.66	−10.58	76.15	19.14	190.59	55.60	79.25
Number of classroom clusters	77	61	101	96	149	95	104	683	683
N	733	1373	962	705	1,304	1,688	1,216	7,981	7,981
R^2	0.374	0.332	0.391	0.301	0.236	0.317	0.227	0.534	0.540

NOTE: Due to clustered nature of sample, robust standard errors are used.

[a]Excluded category for teacher education is high school.

[b]Excluded category for country is Cuba.

173

TABLE A.5

Ordinary least squares (OLS) cluster-adjusted estimates of the determinants of fourth-grade academic achievement in language (T-statistics in parentheses), seven Latin American countries

Variables	COUNTRY								
	Argentina (1)	Bolivia (2)	Brazil (3)	Chile (4)	Colombia (5)	Cuba (6)	Mexico (7)	All 7 (8)	All 7 (9)
School average grade 3	0.12 (1.17)	0.09 (1.39)	0.28 (2.00)	0.35 (2.98)	0.49 (6.65)	0.41 (5.58)	0.52 (4.74)	0.41 (10.08)	0.36 (9.00)
Student/Family Characteristics									
Female	8.25 (2.45)	5.33 (2.62)	7.90 (2.82)	8.48 (3.15)	7.90 (3.17)	10.76 (4.60)	12.87 (4.49)	8.44 (8.01)	8.90 (8.27)
Student self-confidence	9.84 (2.41)	2.57 (0.55)	6.63 (2.08)	15.51 (4.13)	7.53 (2.43)	14.15 (3.14)	8.24 (2.13)	8.96 (5.61)	9.03 (5.71)
Parental education	2.24 (1.46)	2.34 (2.10)	2.58 (2.01)	1.94 (1.34)	2.03 (1.61)	0.48 (0.37)	6.10 (3.95)	2.23 (4.20)	2.48 (4.70)
Read to child	0.84 (0.80)	0.44 (0.57)	1.39 (1.52)	1.47 (1.18)	-0.09 (-0.10)	0.53 (0.36)	1.73 (1.66)	1.31 (3.35)	0.81 (2.08)
Expected level of study	3.90 (2.91)	1.44 (1.18)	2.47 (2.44)	6.58 (3.99)	1.15 (1.04)	6.97 (3.70)	1.63 (1.45)	2.71 (5.47)	2.93 (5.81)
Books in household	0.19 (0.10)	3.84 (2.34)	2.97 (1.56)	2.87 (1.45)	4.62 (2.49)	2.20 (1.37)	3.56 (1.62)	3.86 (5.12)	3.51 (4.68)
Teacher/School Characteristics									
Classroom materials	-0.69 (-0.92)	1.13 (1.48)	1.96 (1.85)	-0.38 (-0.62)	0.34 (0.46)	4.29 (2.75)	1.63 (1.93)	1.73 (4.81)	1.05 (3.03)
Student has language Textbook	2.06 (0.63)	-3.12 (-0.95)	6.31 (1.48)	16.68 (2.47)	0.71 (0.20)	7.28 (0.65)	15.99 (2.13)	4.00 (2.01)	2.65 (1.43)
Teacher education[a] University	-0.02 (-0.01)	-11.29 (-1.81)	0.05 (0.01)	2.35 (0.47)	0.60 (0.17)	10.15 (1.42)	1.96 (0.45)	7.16 (3.88)	1.70 (0.89)

Other	17.04	22.38	0	0	-1.51	0	0	12.33	14.68
	(2.32)	(3.74)	—	—	(-0.14)	—	—	(2.55)	(2.54)
Teacher training sessions	0.91	-0.59	0.40	-0.26	-0.30	0.17	-0.70	-0.10	0.87
	(3.30)	(-1.94)	(1.11)	(-1.56)	(-0.71)	(0.67)	(-2.45)	(-0.70)	(0.70)
Classroom condition	-0.18	12.93	-6.40	9.13	0.15	4.29	1.13	7.42	6.66
	(-0.02)	(1.75)	(-0.88)	(1.23)	(0.02)	(2.75)	(0.16)	(2.04)	(2.01)
Principal autonomy	-3.62	1.47	0.98	9.27	6.86	-11.84	-1.43	2.67	2.55
	(-0.47)	(0.27)	(0.15)	(1.27)	(1.49)	(-1.72)	(-0.28)	(0.95)	(0.95)
Rural school	-23.57	-1.74	0.05	10.96	-2.04	-7.54	-7.34	-2.94	-3.84
	(-3.73)	(-0.22)	(0.01)	(1.65)	(-0.40)	(-1.20)	(-1.46)	(-1.15)	(-1.51)
Private school	9.27	0.34	-7.98	-5.52	-4.62	0	7.54	-3.85	-0.27
	(1.34)	(0.05)	(-1.44)	(-0.91)	(-0.90)	—	(0.94)	(-1.54)	(-0.11)
Social Context									
Student attended preschool	0.20	0.46	1.96	3.21	-4.52	0.27	7.04	0.23	-0.22
	(0.04)	(0.17)	(0.54)	(1.13)	(-1.56)	(0.03)	(1.51)	(0.16)	(0.15)
Work outside the home	-26.17	-26.63	-29.59	-0.76	-9.09	21.22	-14.40	-26.71	-12.69
	(-1.82)	(-1.73)	(-2.27)	(-0.06)	(-1.16)	(0.78)	(-1.30)	(-5.39)	(-2.73)
Work in the home	-5.66	-22.06	24.34	-5.40	-8.47	19.37	-4.26	-1.53	1.54
	(-0.40)	(-1.04)	(1.90)	(-0.30)	(-0.82)	(1.22)	(-0.29)	(-0.29)	(0.27)
Children free from work	16.75	-12.82	19.96	-10.10	1.34	6.06	-14.07	7.24	2.38
	(1.18)	(-0.81)	(1.36)	(-0.68)	(0.17)	(0.64)	(-1.45)	(1.60)	(0.48)
Classroom fights	-39.23	-56.74	7.22	-14.98	-24.12	-73.90	3.56	-17.68	-22.38
	(-2.84)	(-3.70)	(0.47)	(-0.66)	(-2.80)	(-2.50)	(0.26)	(-2.97)	(-3.93)
SES factor (school)	4.32	-0.65	6.45	5.18	0.22	6.52	-9.76	-2.67	0.30
	(0.78)	(-0.14)	(1.24)	(0.85)	(0.06)	(0.97)	(-1.74)	(-1.43)	(0.15)
Country Dummies									
Argentina dummy	—	—	—	—	—	—	—	—	-3.25
									(-0.73)
Bolivia dummy	—	—	—	—	—	—	—	—	-29.79
									(-5.40)
Brazil dummy	—	—	—	—	—	—	—	—	-5.91
									(-1.23)

(continued)

TABLE A.5
(continued)

Variables	COUNTRY								
	Argentina (1)	Bolivia (2)	Brazil (3)	Chile (4)	Colombia (5)	Cuba (6)	Mexico (7)	All 7 (8)	All 7 (9)
Chile dummy	—	—	—	—	—	—	—	—	−2.38
									(−0.50)
Colombia dummy	—	—	—	—	—	—	—	—	−12.33
									(−2.52)
Mexico dummy[b]	—	—	—	—	—	—	—	—	−14.30
									(−2.85)
Constant	243.27	327.31	77.75	100.00	112.93	9.17	101.61	115.72	129.43
Number of classroom clusters	77	61	100	97	149	95	103	682	682
N	691	1298	933	1072	1242	1549	1162	7947	7947
R^2	0.282	0.294	0.296	0.237	0.221	0.231	0.255	0.410	0.422

NOTE: Due to clustered nature of sample, robust standard errors are used.

[a]Excluded category for teacher education is high school.

[b]Excluded category for country is Cuba.

in Tables A.2 and A.3. For example, in math, Brazilian fourth graders scored one-sixth of a standard deviation less than Cuban students, controlling for other variables, including third-grade test score. Argentine, Chilean, and Mexican fourth graders made about one-fourth of a standard deviation gain less than Cuban students. On the language test, fourth graders in Argentina, Brazil, Chile, and Cuba scored about the same, controlling for other variables and third-grade test scores.

Simulating Student Achievement

We simulated student scores in each country using the estimated equation for each country, but assuming that means of the student/family characteristics, school characteristics, and social context were those of the Cuban students. This entailed predicting pupil performance in each country assuming that institutional conditions were specific to each country but the characteristics of students and schools were similar to those in Cuba.[2]

When we used the entire sample of third and fourth graders, the predicted achievement scores of each country's students, when actual student and family characteristics in each country were replaced with the means for Cuban students, show that the raw differences between the Cuban averages for achievement and those for each of the other six countries were reduced surprisingly little. A relatively small portion of the difference in student achievement is due to student family characteristics, such as parent education or parent social capital for their children. Of the equalizing impact of student and family characteristics on student achievement differences, *consistently one-third to one-half is associated with family social capital differences between Cuba and other Latin American countries.*

Equalizing the means of *school variables* to Cuban levels had an even smaller effect on equalizing student achievement. The teacher education and classroom materials variables were the most important, but their effects on equalizing scores were relatively small.

Except for Chile, by far the largest impact on students' achievement occurred when state-generated social capital variables were made equal to Cuban levels. This supports our claim that Cuba's social context goes far in explaining why Cuban pupils scored so much higher on the LLECE test than pupils in other countries. The biggest social context effects generally come from the "work outside the home" and the "classroom fights" variables. Cuban students are highly unlikely to work, and working has a relatively large and significant effect on student achievement in every country but Chile. If students elsewhere worked outside the home at the same low rate as students in Cuba, their achievement should rise appreciably. The positive, potentially large, effect on pupil performance of a low rate of children working outside the home needs to be underlined, especially since Cuba is not a rich country in terms of income per capita.

The classroom fights variable also had a large impact—it was largest in Argentina, Bolivia, and Mexico. This variable may reflect the quality of classroom management, but we think it is more likely to reflect underlying social problems in the lives of the children who come to school, including poor nutrition, that make them less able to stay quiet and increases the likelihood of conflicts among pupils. The relatively large effects on student performance of reducing children's work and classroom disturbances suggest that when a high fraction of children come from low-income families, social policies connected to reducing abject poverty may have a significant effect on average pupil performance in school.

In Brazil, raising average school (classroom) socioeconomic status (SES) to Cuban levels would also equalize both math and Spanish achievement substantially, in part because the Cuban SES factor is much higher than the Brazilian one. As important, the Brazilian coefficient for the SES factor is large. This suggests that the average SES of a school's pupils in Brazil is strongly related to the school's average achievement. We are aware that only part of the average SES variable's effect can be attributed to social capital, so we also show the collective social capital effect without including the effect of equalizing school SES to Cuban means. Even excluding it, however, leaves social context variables much more important than family background and school variables in explaining country/Cuban difference, except in the Chilean case.

Does Principal Autonomy Represent a Private School Effect?

Although a relatively large percentage of sampled pupils in every country except Cuba attended private schools, the only somewhat positive private school effects were found in the fourth-grade achievement estimates for Argentina (Table A.2).[3] However, there are very large and significant principal autonomy coefficients in Brazil, Chile, and the Bolivian total sample math estimates (the Chilean coefficient is also significant in the fourth-grade estimates—Table A.4). It is possible, therefore, that the principal autonomy variable is mainly a private school effect. This would support the argument that schools operating in a market give their directors more autonomy and that this autonomy, in turn, produces higher pupil achievement. It is also possible that other social context effects are private school effects as well, in the sense that the social context effect as a whole is picking up the social context differences that obtain mainly between private and public schools. Together with principal autonomy, this would support the argument that societies that opt for choice and greater social differentiation (a less regulated economy and society) are likely to have a much higher percentage of pupils in private schools and a large and significant difference in performance between pupils in private and public schools even when individual SES or third-grade test score is accounted for.

To test this hypothesis, we estimated the math and language equations for fourth grade with the private school variable (controlling for student/family characteristics and third-grade average score) and then included sequentially principal autonomy, other school variables, and then social context variables. We found that when only family characteristics were included, the private school effect was generally large, positive, and significant in Argentina and Bolivia. This value added for private schools was negative in the other countries. When principal autonomy was added, not much changes, except in the Chile mathematics equation—the private coefficient became highly negative. When school and social context variables were added, the general effect was to reduce the size and significance of the positive coefficients (especially in Bolivia) and to make the negative coefficients in the other countries more negative. Thus, principal autonomy had little impact on the private school coefficient. For details, see the electronic version of Carnoy and Marshall 2005 posted at http://www.journals.uchicago.edu/CER/journal/issues/v49n2/490205/490205.html.

Definitions of Terms Used in Chapter 6
and Task Analysis Guide

Definition of Terms Used in Chapter 6

Segment type	Definition
1. Seat work	Students are seated individually and working.
1a. Copying instructions/problems	Students are copying off the blackboard.
1b. Solving problems individually— teacher circulating	Teacher is moving around room observing and occasionally commenting on individual work.
1c. Solving problems individually— teacher on other task	Teacher is at desk or chalkboard while students work individually.
1d. Checking work individually (working)	Teacher is moving about room checking work while other students continue to work.
1e. Checking work individually (stopped)	Teacher is moving about room checking work while other students wait their turn.
2. Recitation	Students responding and interacting with teacher in various forms.
2a. Q-A whole class individual	Students respond to teacher individually but are chosen from entire class who listen to each answer.

2b. Q-A demonstration/review/working whole class chorus	Students respond to questions in a chorus.
2c. Q-A whole class groups reporting	Individual groups report their answers/results while the other groups listen to them.
2d. Individual/whole class read orally	An individual student or whole class (in chorus) reads a written passage out loud.
2e. Solve at blackboard	Individual student(s) works at blackboard while others watch.
3. Group work	Students are arranged in groups.
3a. Individual solving (quiet)—teacher circulating	Students are in groups but are working individually with no interaction (quiet) while teacher circulates. Same as 1b.
3b. Individual solving (quiet)—teacher on other task	Same as 1c, only students are seated in groups.
3c. Individual solving (talking)—teacher circulating	Students are working on problems or activities individually and talking with each other, asking questions, or giving examples. But they are not working on the same problems together or preparing a common response.
3d. Individual solving (talking)—teacher on other task	Same as 3c only teacher is not circulating.
3e. Group discussion	Group is having general discussion about the problem, such as dividing up the work to be done or reading it out loud to better understand.
3f. Group solving	Students are working together to solve the problem and are actually working through problem or debating what is the correct method and/or answer.
3g. Checking work group (working)	Groups working while teacher circulates checking work.
3h. Checking work group (stopped)	Same as 3g only groups are stopped and waiting to have work checked.
4. Whole class instruction, demonstrations, lecture, review (teacher only)	Teacher-dominated segment where students are stopped and teacher is giving instructions, a demonstration, lecturing, reading out loud, etc.
5. Transition	Time in between segments when students put away books rearrange desks, move back to their seats, etc.
6. Interruption/discipline	Segment stops due to interruption from without (such as another teacher poking head in to ask for something) or a disciplinary action.

7. Engagement (degree to which whole class is on task at different periods of class)
   Not engaged: Numerous instances of side conversations, horsing around, spacing out; general sense of nonengagement.
   Moderately engaged: Some students are on task, some are nonengaged; hard to tell with others.
   Engaged: Almost all students are on task, or at least paying attention to goings-on with out necessarily actively participating.

Very engaged: Almost all are very engaged and working and/or discussing with group members. If in whole group actively participating in recitation, raising hands, watching others.

Minutes

10	____ Not engaged ____ Moderately engaged	____ Engaged	____ Very engaged
20	____ Not engaged ____ Moderately engaged	____ Engaged	____ Very engaged
30	____ Not engaged ____ Moderately engaged	____ Engaged	____ Very engaged
40	____ Not engaged ____ Moderately engaged	____ Engaged	____ Very engaged
50	____ Not engaged ____ Moderately engaged	____ Engaged	____ Very engaged
60	____ Not engaged ____ Moderately engaged	____ Engaged	____ Very engaged

8. Does class include?
   ____ Review of work completed today   ____ Checking some work
   ____ Checking everyone's work   ____ Homework   ____ Cannot tell about homework

9. Kinds of questions used in recitation (if multiple rank in order of most frequent to least frequent):
   ____ Very few/no questions asked of students
   ____ Simple, repetitive questions to individuals or class chorus (basic operations, yes/no, etc.)
   ____ Give examples, short answer
   ____ Conceptual (describe process, explain your answer)

10. Overall degree of discipline:
    ____ Low (many instances of students talking out of turn, not being quiet when asked by teacher, getting up and moving about the class, fooling around, teacher repeatedly telling students to sit down, stop talking, etc.)
    ____ Adequate (some instances of talking out of turn or moving about room, teacher not always obeyed immediately)
    ____ Good (few instances of talking, fooling around, moving about room, but respond quickly to teacher requests to stop)
    ____ High (students are very quiet or discussions are orderly; teacher doesn't have to ask to be quiet, etc.)

11. Student-initiated activity
    ____ None (teacher-directed class, students watch teacher and very little [engaged] interaction between students, teacher-student interaction is form of simple questions put to individuals or whole class chorus)
    ____ Students ask some questions for clarification, raise hands, but generally teacher-centered class
    ____ Students freely ask questions, approach teacher physically, ask/respond to each other
    ____ Student-centered class marked by high degree of student control of discussion, asking and responding to each other, teacher mainly supervising discussion, not leading it

12. Handouts/manipulables

1. Prepared activities	____ No	____ Yes	
2. Prepared homework	____ No	____ Yes	____ Cannot tell
3. Written materials used			
3.1. Textbook	____ No	____ Yes	
3.2. Workbook	____ No	____ Yes	
3.3. Other	____ No	____ Yes	
4. Manipulables used			
4.1. Counting materials	____ No	____ Yes	
4.2. Shapes	____ No	____ Yes	
4.3. Learning games/ activities	____ No	____ Yes	

   Describe: _____
   4.4. Other _____

13. Physical
    1. Space (room is big enough)
       ____ Poor ____ Adequate ____ Good ____ Excellent
    2. Lighting
       ____ Poor ____ Adequate ____ Good ____ Excellent
    3. Desks (sufficient number, space)
       ____ Poor ____ Adequate ____ Good ____ Excellent
    4. Sound (noise from without, resonance)
       ____ Poor ____ Adequate ____ Good ____ Excellent
14. Are there student-made things on walls?
    ____ None
    ____ Few
    ____ Many
    ____ Cannot tell

Task Analysis Guide[1]

LOWER-LEVEL DEMANDS

Memorization Tasks

- involve either reproducing previously learned facts, rules, formulae, or definitions OR committing facts, rules formulae, or definitions to memory.
- cannot be solved using procedures because a procedure does not exist or because the time frame in which the task is being completed is too short to use a procedure.
- are not ambiguous—such tasks involve exact reproduction of previously seen material and what is to be reproduced is clearly and directly stated.
- have no connection to the concepts or meaning that underlie the facts, rules, formulae, or definitions being learned or reproduced.

Procedures without Connections Tasks

- are algorithmic. Use of the procedure is either specifically called for or its use is evident based on prior instruction, experience, or placement of the task.
- require limited cognitive demand for successful completion. There is little ambiguity about what needs to be done and how to do it.
- have no connection to the concepts or meaning that underlie the procedure being used.
- are focused on producing correct answers rather than developing mathematical understanding.

- require no explanations, or explanations that focus solely on describing the procedure that was used.

Procedures with Connections Tasks

- focus students' attention on the use of procedures for the purpose of developing deeper levels of understanding of mathematical concepts and ideas.
- suggest pathways to follow (explicitly or implicitly) that are broad general procedures that have close connections to the underlying conceptual ideas as opposed to narrow algorithms that are opaque with respect to underlying concepts.
- usually are represented in multiple ways (e.g., visual diagrams, manipulables, symbols, problem situations). Making connections among multiple representations helps to develop meaning.
- require some degree of cognitive effort. Although general procedures may be followed, they cannot be followed mindlessly. Students need to engage with the conceptual ideas that underlie the procedures in order to successfully complete the task and develop understanding.

Doing Mathematics Tasks

- require complex and nonalgorithmic thinking (i.e., there is not a predictable, well-rehearsed approach or pathway explicitly suggested by the task, task instructions, or a worked-out example).
- require students to explore and understand the nature of mathematical concepts, processes, or relationships.
- demand self-monitoring or self-regulation of one's own cognitive processes.
- require students to access relevant knowledge and experiences and make appropriate use of them in working through the task.
- require students to analyze the task and actively examine task constraints that may limit possible solution strategies and solutions.
- require considerable cognitive effort and may involve some level of anxiety for the student due to the unpredictable nature of the solution process required.

Notes

1. In practice, the division between these two types of pedagogy is often artificial. Good teaching is a combination of styles and methods. Obviously, students need to learn basic skills to become good at problem solving and good readers. How best to teach basic skills varies from child to child, and good teachers incorporate many different teaching methods. A good curriculum framework is important to teaching in any method, and the more a teacher knows about the subject, the more likely she or he will be able to use multiple methods. For these reasons, later in the book, when we analyze classroom teaching in three countries, we do *not* use the constructivist/teacher-centered division in our analysis.

2. For example, Bruce Fuller et al. (1999).

3. Researchers in the Third International Mathematics and Science Survey (TIMSS) have done macro-analysis using survey data (Schmidt et al., 2001), and other researchers have videotaped eighth-grade math classrooms in several countries and compared teaching methods from these videotapes (Stigler et al., 1999). But the focus of both studies is limited mainly to the impact of curriculum and its application in the classroom. Our analysis is much broader, linking social context to school system organization to classroom applications.

CHAPTER TWO

1. In a study that compares student testing in Argentina, Chile, and Uruguay, Benveniste shows that the use of student testing in a country is heavily influenced by the underlying politics of state delivery of education (Benveniste, 2003).

2. Evidence on academic performance is mixed, but there is increasing evidence that the economic payoffs to society from high-quality preschooling are enormous. Research in the United States has used data from field trials in which low-income children randomly assigned to preschool were compared over time

to a control group without preschool; the findings suggest only small differences in later academic performance but very high payoffs in greater likelihood of high school graduation, lower incarceration rates, and lower likelihood to be on welfare (Karoly, Kilburn, and Cannon, 2005).

3. The black-white test score gap in department of defense schools is half that of non-DOD schools nationwide.

4. For a brilliant discussion of the eighteenth-century debate on this issue, see Hirschman (1977).

CHAPTER THREE

1. See, for example, an early study by Heyneman and Loxley (1982) on the 1970s IEA science test results, which argued that socioeconomic background variables are key to explaining student outcomes in developed countries, whereas school variables are more important in explaining student outcomes in developing countries. See also recent work by the OECD on the PISA test (OECD, 2003), and Willms and Somers (1999, 2001), analyzing the Latin American data that are the subject of our study. Willms and Somers do analyses similar to what we do here. The main difference is that they tend to compare the impact of various variables across countries rather than to focus on which sets of variables are likely to account for the differences between Cuban and other countries' student performance. The interested reader should also refer to Willms and Somers's work for additional insights into inter-Latin American educational performance comparisons.

2. The best analysis of this problem is by Henry Levin (1980).

3. We are fully aware that the term *socioeconomic background/status* (SES) rather than *social class* emerged in the literature as a social functionalist terminology to supersede the historical discussion of the term *class* (see, for example, Parsons, 1977). Social class in Marxian theory is rooted in the social relations of production, so that class in capitalist societies is identified with the individual's or family's relationship to ownership of the means of production (Wright, 1977). However, as workers in capitalist societies gained more political power, the argument goes, the Marxian definition of class became less relevant—in particular, it missed meaningful socioeconomic differences within the working class, differences that went beyond Marx and Engels's notion of proletariat and lumpen-proletariat. Because, in Marxist theory, socialism eliminates social classes, this definition also missed socioeconomic differences in state socialist societies (see, for example, Bahro, 1990). In our study, however, we do not abandon the idea that socioeconomic background, or SES, has different meaning in societies with different social/economic organization.

4. In a recent Ph.D. dissertation, Uruguayan sociologist Tabaré Fernández develops a similar argument in the context of the relative reproduction of the class structure by the educational system in four Latin American countries: Argentina, Chile, Mexico, and Uruguay (Fernández, 2004).

5. For example, families that move often would, in this conception, have less social capital outside the family than those staying put. Other researchers have called these "neighborhood effects" (Jencks and Mayer, 1990).

6. We note that they were/are aided by (relatively authoritarian) family structures that place high value on academic success.

7. This raises the important question of whether democratic capitalist societies that are highly regulative and stress socialist or communal values, such as the Scandinavian countries, have higher-quality education because of the relative social equality and emphasis on collective responsibility that characterizes them (see, for example, Castells and Himanen, 2002). The voters in those societies have voluntarily opted for a highly regulated social context. The OECD seems to take the position that greater equality in educational provision is an important explainer of higher performance on the PISA test (OECD, 2003). There is evidence that schooling in mini-state socialist conditions, such as those represented by military bases in the United States, seems to be much more effective for minority students than schools in civilian U.S. society (Smrekar et al., 2001).

8. Researchers generally find significant negative effects on student performance when pupils have changed schools during, say, primary schooling, especially for children of lower-income families (Coleman, 1988; see also Rumberger, 2003).

CHAPTER FOUR

The material in this chapter first appeared in the Comparative Education Review in 2005. That material is reprinted here by permission of the Comparative and International Education Society. *Comparative Education Review*, vol. 49, no. 2. © 2005 by the Comparative and International Education Society. All rights reserved.

1. For earlier, qualitative research that focuses on Cuban education, see Carnoy and Werthein (1980) and Gasperini (2000).

2. Cross-state or cross-province comparisons within the same country could capture such differences if there is sufficient within-country variation and the educational and social service system is sufficiently decentralized. The United States, Brazil, and Germany are examples of countries with relatively decentralized education systems and some variation in the way states deal with social inequality.

3. A major study of rural schools in Brazil collected longitudinal data on students, schools, and teachers between 1982 and 1986, and identified a number of policy-relevant variables (such as learning materials and school "hardware") that were not only significant determinants of achievement but also appeared to be cost-effective educational interventions (Harbison and Hanushek, 1992). In another ambitious study using Brazilian data, Bruce Fuller and a team of Brazilians measured test scores and conventional input variables, and also observed classrooms, videotaped teachers teaching, and conducted extensive teacher interviews (Fuller

et al., 1999). Their findings showed that accounting for teaching methodology is important when considering the determinants of academic achievement.

4. We estimate the following equations for each country:

$$A = \alpha + \beta X + \delta P + \varphi S + \gamma G + \mu, \tag{1}$$

where A is the student's measured achievement in third or fourth grade, X is a vector of school inputs, P is a vector of student and student's family characteristics, S is a vector of variables that proxy social context conditions as reflected at the level of the school, G is a dummy variable for the grade in which the student was tested (third or fourth), and μ is the error term. Alternatively, we estimated fourth-grade achievement (A') as the dependent variable, taking average third-grade achievement (M) in the school as an independent variable.

$$A' = \alpha' + \beta' X + \delta' P + \varphi' S + \eta M + \mu' \tag{2}$$

Our estimation method is subject to the critique that with multilevel observations (clusters of students nested within schools) we should be using multilevel modeling, and that our ordinary least squares (OLS) estimates will necessarily bias error terms (although not the regression coefficients themselves). By using robust standard errors that account for intra-cluster correlation we can deal with the standard error issue. Multilevel models are especially useful for studying interaction because they allow slopes to vary by school. But for the second phase of our analysis—the simulation of student achievement—we are primarily interested in the mean effect of each variable on achievement and are less concerned about variation in parameters within each country. For comparison's sake we estimated these models using the hierarchical linear model (HLM) program, and the results are not much different (see also Willms and Somers, 2001).

5. There is increasing evidence that primary school teachers in Latin America receive very little, if any, additional courses in mathematics and language in their preservice higher education (see OECD, 2003). Thus, if subject content knowledge is key to increasing student learning, a higher fraction of teachers with teacher education at university may not have the expected impact on how much students learn.

6. The factor analysis was conducted using school averages for parental education and job prestige, and identified one factor that accounted for 61 percent of the variance. The loadings were 0.83 for parental education and 0.81 for job prestige.

7. Of course, working on the family farm is a common activity for rural young children even in the developed countries, but it still expresses family economic needs and a continuing culture of using child labor.

8. The LLECE survey asks students whether they work rarely, sometimes, or frequently. The "free from work" variable asks them if they do what they choose to do when not in school. In order to maintain the number of cases in each country, we

recoded missing values to 1 (rarely work) for everyone. This makes the unrealistic argument that those who did not answer the question worked rarely. When we compare the characteristics of children who were missing these data in countries other than Cuba, they generally appeared to be from lower-SES families. Thus, in non-Cuba countries, those who did not answer are probably working more, not less. But missing values constitute a very small proportion of the total sample. In contrast, a relatively high percentage of Cuban children did not respond to the question about work outside the home, yet their SES characteristics are very similar to the mean of the sample. In Cuba, a tiny percentage of children reported working outside the home. We are therefore almost certainly on solid ground in recoding the missing values as "rarely."

9. It is also possible that teachers and students in more violence-ridden societies are more likely to be violent with each other. We have no measure of teacher-student violence, but anecdotal evidence suggests that violence in schools is not limited to students.

10. We sum the ordinal values of the individual responses to child labor outside the home (a proxy for family income), parental education, and books in home, then average this index across students in each sampled school to get a school average factor.

11. As in all our variables, the greater the variance in a particular variable, the larger we would expect the estimated coefficient of the variable to be, other factors equal. For example, we would expect a larger peer effect on individual student achievement when students are more divided up among different "quality" schools by student socioeconomic background characteristics. Consider the situation in which students of different SES are distributed randomly among schools and classrooms. The peer coefficient would be zero. The greater the SES segregation across schools, the greater the peer effect, provided that students learn more when surrounded by higher-SES (and presumably more academically able) peers. If the coefficient of average SES is large and positive, a small increase in average school SES could have a large impact on average student performance. But if the coefficient is small, this means that how students are grouped in school has little effect on how much they learn. This may be the result of fairly equal social-class distribution of pupils across schools, once rural/urban and private/public school differences in test scores are accounted for, or it may result from homogeneously high or low academic standards across schools, independent of average student social class.

12. For this methodology, see Oaxaca (1973) and Carnoy (1994). Although both these studies simulate earnings, the methodology is applicable to other types of dependent variables, such as student achievement.

13. It is also possible to simulate the contribution of "effectiveness" of schooling across countries by comparing achievement results when the Cuban coefficients are applied to the average "resources" of each of the other countries. We did these estimates and can make them available to interested readers.

14. The estimated equations and the technical discussion of the results are shown in Appendix A (Tables A.2 and A.3).

15. Readers interested in the estimates behind Figures 4.1, 4.2, 4.3, and 4.4 should refer to the electronic version of Carnoy and Marshall, 2005, posted at http://www.journals.uchicago.edu/CER/journal/issues/v49n2/490205/490205.html

16. It is important to note, however, that all of these results may be subject to omitted variable bias. That is, Cuba may have made successful efforts to reduce child labor and may have also developed very good teachers, a variable that is poorly measured by the LLECE survey. The observed correlation between low child labor and test scores may imply that this is a good policy (reducing child labor) when in reality this relation is largely spurious and instead driven by the good teacher effect that is also correlated with low levels of child labor. It may not be a lack of child labor per se that is driving higher test scores but instead a menu of things that we are not measuring well (especially those variables dealing with teacher quality) that are also correlated (especially in Cuba but in other countries as well) with lower levels of child labor. In a structural sense, our argument about Cuban social capital would remain correct: Cuba does a number of things that improve student achievement. Yet as we move on to specific components, there is the question about whether these are the actual causal policy variables.

CHAPTER FIVE

1. This is a schematic of educational delivery by the state and it consciously does not include the influence of parents, which, to various degrees, affects ministry policies, school practice, and student outcomes. The figure is meant to represent the main variables affecting outcomes *controlling for* parent socioeconomic background. Student outcomes include achievement scores, and also student attendance, student promotion, and student attainment.

2. In an analysis of the *Carrera Magisterial* data in Mexico's Federal District, Lucrecia Santibañez found that subject content knowledge was the only part of the teacher evaluation that had a significant effect on student test score gains (Santibañez, 2002). These results were confirmed in another study by Thomas Luschei in the states of Aguas Calientes and Sonora (Luschei, 2005).

3. According to a ministry of education document, entrance scores of those studying to be preschool teachers rose 6 percent in the four years; of those studying to be elementary teachers, 8 percent; and of secondary teachers, 10 percent (OECD, 2003).

4. The ministry selected *emergentes* from among the best secondary graduates in a number of provinces, offering them entrance into a humanities degree program in the university, to be completed while they taught in lower secondary school. Their teaching contracts are five years. Students were selected on the basis of their academic performance in secondary school plus their social leadership.

5. On the other hand, there is evidence in Brazil that average test scores are increasing in the lowest-performing regions, but this is associated with the FUNDEF reform rather than response to testing or parent participation (World Bank, 2001).

6. This is the general case, but there are several efforts to correct this problem. In the Brazilian state of Paraná, for example, there is a strong policy of inservice training and supervising new teachers. So sweeping conclusions are not always justified.

CHAPTER SIX

1. For a definition of constructivism, see the URL: http://www.cdli.ca/~elmurphy/emurphy/cle4.html

2. Albeit in a qualified manner. For example, low levels of discipline may be indicative of poor teacher quality. But they may also be attributable to the behavioral patterns students bring from their family and community environment.

3. That result should be interpreted with care, as we have only one independent (private paid) school in the sample and it is combined with private subsidized schools.

CHAPTER SEVEN

1. The typical argument is that the three Anglo-Saxon countries with increasingly unequal income distributions have averaged higher growth than continental Europe, which has kept its income inequality more or less constant for the past twenty-five years. Yet Korea, Singapore, the People's Republic of China, and Taiwan, all with fairly equal and only slightly rising inequality in income distributions, have had more rapid economic growth than Latin American countries, with their much greater and rising inequality (see Bourguignon, 2004).

2. When the Chilean government became democratic again in 1990, it recognized the harmful effects of growing inequality in the school system, as evidenced by the so-called Brunner Report (Comisión Nacional, 1995).

3. Brazil has long required fifth- to eighth-grade teachers to have a university degree, but only recently is it beginning to require lower-grade primary teachers to be university trained. As we discussed earlier, most lower-grade teachers are only secondary school trained, and in low-income regions, an overwhelming majority have secondary teacher education or less.

4. From an evaluation perspective, it would be easier to assess the quality of particular teachers if they had one cohort of students over several years. Given the highly developed testing system in a country such as Chile, if a single teacher were responsible for a cohort, results of student performance could be translated into a "true" measure of how effective a teacher is with a given cohort. Principals could estimate the effects on student performance of weaker and stronger teachers, and

test whether these effects are cumulative over the primary school years. Supervision would also be a great deal easier when data are available for teachers teaching the same cohort over a longer number of years.

1. One of the "mysteries" of the Cuban results was the small difference between third- and fourth-grade test scores (on the same test but with different students taking the test). One possible explanation is that the test was sufficiently easy for Cuban students that a high fraction of both third and fourth graders achieved perfect scores, so that it was difficult to achieve much higher average scores in the fourth grade. This is called "topping out." We observed the same phenomenon in Bolivia, but the "topping out" explanation is highly unlikely in that case.

2. We also estimated how much Cuban students' scores would change were Cuban student, school, and school social context characteristics equal to the means in other countries, but the "payoffs" (estimated coefficients) for those estimated for Cuba remained the same. However, we do not report these results because they are far less interesting, policywise, and difficult to interpret.

3. We did not differentiate between different types of private education because this was not possible with these data, but it is evident in other studies, such as in McEwan and Carnoy (2000). That research examined differences in student achievement among public, private subsidized secular, and private subsidized religious schools.

1. Reprinted by permission of the publisher from M. K. Stein, M. S. Smith, M. A. Henningsen, and E. A. Silver. 2000. *Implementing Standards-based Mathematics Instruction*. New York: Teachers College Press, © 2000 by Teachers College, Columbia University. All rights reserved, p. 16.

References

Abelman, Charles, and Richard F. Elmore. 1999. *When Accountability Knocks, Will Anyone Answer?* Philadelphia: Consortium for Policy Research in Education.

Alcazar, Lorena, et al. 2004. *Why Are Teachers Absent? Probing Service Delivery in Peruvian Primary Schools.* Washington, DC: World Bank.

Amsden, Alice. 1989. *Asia's Next Giant: South Korea and Late Industrialization.* New York: Oxford University Press.

Amsden, Alice, and Wan-wen Chu. 2003. *Beyond Late Development: Taiwan's Upgrading Policies.* Cambridge, MA: MIT Press.

Aronson, Julie, Joy Zimmerman, and Lisa Carlos. 1998. *Is It Just a Matter of Time?* San Francisco, CA: West Ed. http://www.wested.org/wested/papers/timeandlearning/2_history.html. Downloaded March 2006.

Bahro, Rudolph. 1990. *Die Alternative: zur Kritik des real existierenden Sozialismus.* Berlin: Verlag Tribüne.

Baker, David P., Cornelius Riordan, and Maryellen Schaub. 1995. The Effect of Sex-Grouped Schooling on Achievement: The Role of National Context. *Comparative Education Review*, 34(4): 468–482.

Benveniste, Luis. 2003. The Political Structuration of Assessment: Negotiating State Power and Legitimacy. *Comparative Education Review*, 46(1): 89–109.

Benveniste, Luis, Martin Carnoy, and Richard Rothstein. 2002. *All Else Equal.* New York: Routledge.

Betts, Julian, Andrew Zau, and Lorien Rice. 2003. *Determinants of Student Achievement: New Evidence from San Diego.* San Francisco: Public Policy Institute of California.

Bonjorno, José Roberto, and Regina Azenha Bonjorno. 2001. *Matematica: Pode Contar Comigo 3.* Sao Paulo, Brazil: Editora FTD.

Bourdieu, Pierre, and Claude Passeron. 1977. *Reproduction.* Beverly Hills, CA: Sage.

Bourguignon, François. 2004. The Poverty-Growth-Inequality Triangle. Washington, DC: World Bank (mimeographed).

Bowles, Samuel, and Henry M. Levin. 1968. The Determinants of Schooling Achievement: An Appraisal of Some Recent Evidence. *Journal of Human Resources*, 3(1): 3–24.

Brookover, Wilbur. 1979. *School Social Systems and Student Achievement*. New York: Praeger.

Brown, Michael K., Martin Carnoy, Elliott Currie, Troy Duster, David B. Oppenheimer, Marjorie M. Schultz, and David Wellman. 2003. *Whitewashing Race*. Berkeley: University of California Press.

Bryk, Anthony S., Valerie Lee, and Peter Holland. 1993. *Catholic Schools and the Common Good*. Cambridge, MA: Harvard University Press.

Bryk, Anthony, and Barbara Schneider. 2002. *Trust in Schools: A Core Resource for Improvement*. New York: Russell Sage Foundation.

Burns, R. B. 1984. How Time Is Used in Elementary Schools: The Activity Structure of Classrooms. In L.W. Anderson, ed., *Time and School Learning*. London: Croom Helm.

Carnoy, Martin. 1994. *Faded Dreams*. New York: Cambridge University Press.

Carnoy, Martin. 2001. *Sustaining Flexibility*. Cambridge, MA: Harvard University Press.

Carnoy, Martin, Amber Gove, Susanna Loeb, Jeffery Marshall, and Miguel Socias. 2006. How Schools and Students Respond to School Improvement Programs: The Case of Brazil's PDE. Stanford, CA: Stanford University School of Education (mimeographed).

Carnoy, Martin, Cristián Cox, Gustavo Cosse, and Enrique Martinez (eds.). 2004. *Las Lecciones de la Reforma Educativa en el Cono Sur Latinoamericano*. Buenos Aires: Ministerio de Educación.

Carnoy, Martin, Iliana Brodziak, Andres Molina, and Miguel Socias. 2005. Do Teacher Pay Incentives Improve Student Achievement Gains? The Case of Chile's SNED. Stanford, CA: Stanford University, School of Education (mimeographed).

Carnoy, Martin, and Jeffery Marshall. 2005. Cuba's Academic Performance in Comparative Perspective. *Comparative Education Review*, 49(2): 230–261.

Carnoy, Martin, Jeffery Marshall, and Miguel Socias. 2004. How Do School Inputs Influence Math Scores: A Comparative Approach. Stanford, CA: Stanford University School of Education (mimeographed).

Carnoy, Martin, and Joel Samoff. 1989. *Education and Social Transition in the Third World*. Princeton, NJ: Princeton University Press.

Carnoy, Martin, and Jorge Werthein. 1980. *Cuba: Cambio económico y reforma educativa, 1955–1978*. Mexico, D.F.: Editorial Nueva Imagen.

Carnoy, Martin, Richard Sack, and Hans Thias. 1977. *The Payoff to Better Schooling: A Case Study of Tunisian Secondary Schools*. Washington, D.C.: World Bank.

Carroll, J. B. 1963. A Model of School Learning. *Teachers College Record*, 64: 723–733.

Coleman, James S. 1988. Social Capital in the Creation of Human Capital. *The American Journal of Sociology*, 94, Supplement: S95–S120.

Coleman, James S. 1990. Choice, Community, and Future Schools. In W. H. Clune and J. F. Witte, eds., *Choice and Control in American Education, Volume 1: The Theory of Choice and Control in Education*. London: Falmer Press.

Coleman, James S., E. Campbell, C. Hobson, J. McPartland, A. Mood, F. Weinfeld, and R. York. 1966. *Equal Educational Opportunity*. Washington, DC: U.S. Government Printing Office.

Coleman, James S., and T. Hoffer. 1987. *Public and Private High Schools. The Impact of Communities*. New York: Basic Books.

Coleman, James S., T. Hoffer, and S. Kilgore. 1982. *High School Achievement: Public, Catholic, and Other Private Schools Compared*. New York: Basic Books.

Comisión Nacional para la Modernización de la Educación, Comité Técnico Asesor del Diálogo Nacional sobre la Modernización de la Educación Chilena. 1995. *Los Desafíos de la Educación Chilena frente al siglo XXI*. Santiago: Editorial Universitaria.

Evans, Peter. 1995. *Embedded Autonomy: States and Industrial Transformation* Princeton, NJ: Princeton University Press.

Fagan, Richard. 1969. *The Transformation of Political Power in Cuba*. Stanford, CA: Stanford University Press.

Fernández, Tabaré. 2004. *Distribución del conocimiento escolar: clases sociales, escuelas y sistema educativo en Latinamérica*. Unpublished Ph.D. dissertation, El Colegio de México.

Fuller, Bruce, L. Dellagnelo, A. Strath, E. Santana Barretto Bastos, M. Holanda Maia, K. S. Lopes de Matos, A. L. Portela, and S. Lerche Vieira. 1999. How to Raise Children's Early Literacy: The Influence of Family, Teacher, and Classroom in Northeast Brazil. *Comparative Education Review*, 43(1): 1–35.

Gasperini, Lavinia. 2000. *The Cuban Education System: Lessons and Dilemmas*. Washington, DC: World Bank Country Studies in Education Reform and Management Publication Series, 1(5).

Glewwe, P., and H. Jacoby. 1994. Student Achievement and Schooling Choice in Low-Income Countries: Evidence from Ghana. *Journal of Human Resources*, 29(3): 843–864.

Gonzalez, Pablo. 2001. Estructura Institucional, Recursos, y Gestión en el Sistema Escolar Chileno. Santiago: Ministerio de Educación (mimeographed).

Gove, Amber K. 1997. Neoclassical Economics and Higher Education Policy Formation in Chile and Britain. Master's Monograph, Stanford University School of Education.

Gove, Amber K. 2005. The Optimizing Parent?: Household Demand for Schooling and the Impact of a Conditional Cash Transfer Program on School Attendance and Achievement in Brazil. Unpublished Ph.D. Dissertation, Stanford University School of Education.

Hanushek, Eric A. 1986. The Economics of Schooling: Production and Efficiency in Public Schools. *Journal of Economic Literature*, 24(3): 1141–1177.

Harbison, Ralph A., and Eric A. Hanushek. 1992. *Educational Performance of the Poor: Evidence from the Rural Northeast of Brazil*. New York: Oxford University Press.

Heyneman, Steven, and W. Alexander Loxley. 1982. Influencs on Academic Achievement across High and Low Income Countries. *Sociology of Education*, 55(1): 13–21.

Hirschman, Albert O. 1977. *The Passions and the Interests*. Princeton, NJ: Princeton University Press.

Hsieh, Chang Tai, and Miguel Urquiola. 2002. When Schools Compete, How Do They Compete? An Assessment of Chile's Nationwide Voucher Program. New York: National Center for the Study of Privatization, Occasional Paper No. 43.

Jencks, Christopher, and Michelle Phillips, eds. 1998. *The Black-White Test Score Gap*. Washington, DC: Brookings Institution.

Jencks, Christopher, and Susan E. Mayer. 1990. The Social Consequences of Growing Up in a Poor Neighborhood. In Laurence Lynn and Michael Mc-Geary, eds., *Inner-City Poverty in the United States*, pp. 111–186. Washington, DC: National Academies Press.

Jimenez, Emmanuel, and Yasuyuki Sawada. 1999. Do Community-Managed Schools Work? An Evaluation of El Salvador's EDUCO Program. *World Bank Economic Review*, 13(3): 415–441.

Karoly, Lynn, M. Rebecca Kilburn, and Jill S. Cannon. 2005. *Early Childhood Interventions: Proven Results, Future Promise*. Santa Monica, CA: Rand Corporation.

Karweit, N., and R. E. Slavin. 1981. Measurement and Modeling Choices in Studies of Time and Learning. *American Educational Research Journal*, 18(2): 157–171.

Knight, John, and Richard Sabot. 1990. *Education, Productivity, and Inequality*. Washington, DC: World Bank and Oxford University Press.

Kremer, Michael, Karthik Muralidharan, Nazmul Chaudhury, Jeffrey Hammer, and Halsey Rogers. 2004. *Teacher Absence in India*. Washington, DC: World Bank.

Krueger, Alan. 1999. An Economist's View of Class Size Research. Princeton, NJ: Princeton University, Department of Economics (mimeographed).

Laboratorio Latinoamericano de Evaluación de la Calidad de la Educación (LLECE). 1998. *Primer Estudio Internacional Comparativo sobre Lenguaje, Matemática y Factores Asociados en Tercero y Cuarto Grado*. Santiago: UNESCO.

Levin, Henry. 1980. Educational Production Theory and Teacher Inputs. In Charles Bidwell and Douglas Windham, eds., *The Analysis of Educational Productivity: Issues in Macroanalysis, Vol. II*. Cambridge, MA: Ballinger Press.

Levinson, Bradley. 2001. *We Are All Equal: Student Culture and Identity at a Mexican Secondary School, 1988–1998*. Durham, NC: Duke University Press.

Lockheed, Marlaine, and Adrian Verspoor. 1991. *Improving Primary Education in Developing Countries*. Washington, DC: Oxford University Press and World Bank.

Lockheed, Marlaine, and Henry M. Levin. 1993. *Effective Schools in Developing Countries*. London: Falmer Press.

Loeb, Susanna, M. Bridges, D. Bassok, B. Fuller, and R. Rumberger. 2007. How Much Is Too Much? The Influence of Preschool Centers on Children's Development Nationwide. *Economics of Education Review*, forthcoming.

Luschei, Thomas. 2005. In Search of Good Teachers: Patterns of Teacher Quality in Two Mexican States. Unpublished Ph.D. dissertation, Stanford University, School of Education.

Marshall, Jeffery. 2003. Build It and They Will Come. Unpublished Ph.D. dissertation, Stanford University, School of Education.

Marsico, Maria Teresa, A. Coelho de Carvalho Neto, M. do Carmo Tavares da Cunha, and M. E. Martins Antunes. 2004. *Caracol 3, Matemática 3ª Serie*. Sao Paulo: Editora Scipione.

Mathematics Learning Study Committee, Center for Education, Division of Behavioral and Social Sciences and Education, National Research Council, J. Kilpatrick, J. Swafford, and B. Findell (eds.). 2001. *Adding It Up: Helping Children Learn Mathematics*. Washington, DC: National Academy Press.

McEwan, Patrick. 1998. The Effectiveness of Multigrade Schools in Colombia. *International Journal of Educational Development*, 18(6): 435–452.

McEwan, Patrick, and Martin Carnoy. 1999. The Impact of Competition on Public School Quality: Longitudinal Evidence from Chile's Voucher System. Stanford, CA: Stanford University, School of Education (mimeographed).

McEwan, Patrick, and Martin Carnoy. 2000. The Effectiveness and Efficiency of Private Schools in Chile's Voucher System. *Educational Evaluation and Policy Analysis*, 22, 3:213-239.

Ministerio de Educación, Unidad de Curriculum y Evaluación, Seguimiento a la Implementación Curricular. 2002. *Escuelas Testigo: Implementación Curricular en el Aula. Primer Ciclo Básico (NB1 y NB2)*. Documentos de Trabajo No.23 a No. 27. Santiago: MINEDUC.

Ministry of Education, Brazil. 1997. *Parametros curriculares nacionais*. http://www.mec.gov.br (accessed December 2005).

Mizala, Alejandra, and Pilar Romaguera. 2001. Regulación, incentivos y remuneraciones de los Profesores en Chile. Santiago: CRESUR.

National Council of Teachers of Mathematics. 2000. *Principles and Standards for School Mathematics*. http://www.nctm.org/standards/ (accessed March 27, 2006).

Oaxaca, Ronald. 1973. Male-Female Wage Differentials in Urban Labor Markets. *International Economic Review*, 14(3): 693–709.

Ogbu, John. 1978. *Minority Education and Caste: The American System in Cross-Cultural Perspective*. New York: Academic Press.

Ogbu, John, and Margaret Gibson, eds. 1991. *Minority Status and Schooling: A Comparative Study of Immigrant and Involuntary Minorities*. New York: Garland.

Organization for Economic Cooperation and Development (OECD). 2003. *Literacy Skills for the World of Tomorrow: Further Results from PISA 2000*. Paris: OECD.

Organization for Economic Cooperation and Development (OECD). 2004. *Reviews of National Policies for Education: Chile*. Paris: OECD. http://www .oecdbookshop.org/oecd/display.asp?sf1=identifiers&st1=142004091P1 (accessed March 2006).

Parsons, Talcott. 1977. *Social Systems and the Evolution of Action Theory*. New York: Free Press.

Post, David. 2002. *Children's Work, Schooling, and Welfare in Latin America*. Boulder, CO: Westview Press.

Program for International Student Assessment (PISA). 2004. *Learning for Tomorrow's World: First Results from PISA 2003*. Paris: OECD.

Putnam, Robert D. 1993. *Making Democracy Work: Civic Traditions in Modern Italy*. Princeton, NJ: Princeton University Press.

Putnam, Robert D. 2000. *Bowling Alone: The Collapse and Revival of American Community*. New York: Simon & Schuster.

Rivkin, Steven G., Eric Hanushek, and John Kain. 2005. Teachers, Schools, and Academic Achievement. *Econometrica*, 73, 2: 417–458.

Rogers, F., Halsey J. Lopez-Calix, N. Chaudhury, J. Hammer, N. Córdoba, M. Kremer, and K. Muralidharan. 2004. *Teacher Absence and Incentives in Primary Education: Results from a National Teacher Tracking Survey in Ecuador*. Washington, DC: World Bank.

Rothstein, Richard. 2004. *Class and Schools*. New York: Teachers College Press.

Rumberger, Russell. 2003. The Causes and Consequences of Student Mobility. *Journal of Negro Education*, 72: 6–21.

Rutter, Michael, B. Maughan, P. Mortimore, and J. Ouston. 1979. *Fifteen Thousand Hours: Secondary Schools and Their Effects on Children*. Cambridge, MA: Harvard University Press.

Salgó, Irena, Constanza Ripamonti, and Maria Teresa Pascual. 2001. *Aplica las Matemáticas. Tercer Básico*. Santiago: Ediciones Cal y Canto.

Santibañez, L. M. 2002. Why We Should Care if Teachers Get A's: Impact on Student Achievement in Mexico. Unpublished Ph.D. Dissertation, Stanford University School of Education.

Sarquis Soares, Eduardo. 1997. *Matemática Com o Sarquis, Serie 3ᵃ*. Belo Horizonte, Brazil: Formato.

Schmidt, William H., C. C. McKnight, R. T. Houang, H. Wang, D. Wiley, L. S. Cogan, and R. G. Wolfe (eds.). 2001. *Why Schools Matter*. San Francisco: Jossey-Bass.

Sennett, Richard, and Jonathan Cobb. 1973. *The Hidden Injuries of Class*. New York: Vintage Books.

Skocpol, Theda. 1979. *States and Social Revolutions: A Comparative Analysis of France, Russia, and China*. New York: Cambridge University Press.

Smrekar, Claire, James Guthrie, Debra Owens, and Pearl Sims. 2001. *March toward Excellence: School Success and Minority Student Achievement in Department of Defense Schools*. Washington, DC: National Education Goals Panel.

Stein, M. K., M. S. Smith, M. A. Henningsen, and E. A. Silver. 2000. *Implementing Standards-Based Mathematics Instruction: A Casebook for Professional Development*. New York: Teachers College Press.

Stigler, James, P. A. Gonzales, T. Kawanka, S. Knoll, and A. Serrano. 1999. *The TIMSS Videotape Classroom Study: Methods and Findings from an Exploratory Research Project on Eighth Grade Mathematics Instruction in Germany, Japan, and the United States*. Washington, DC: OERI, NCES.

Villalón Incháustegui, Miriam, R. L. Peña Gálvez, L. Garea Alonso, M. Bello Domínguez, L. Varela Piloto, N. León Figueras, and C. Rizo Cabrera. 1991. *Matemática 3, Tercer Grado*. Havana, Cuba: Editorial Pueblo y Educación.

Willis, Paul. 1981. *Learning to Labor*. New York: Columbia University Press.

Willms, J. Douglas. 1989. Patterns of Academic Achievement in Public and Private Schools: Implications for Public Policy and Future Research. In Edward Haertel, Thomas James, and Henry M. Levin, eds., *Comparing Public and Private Schools: School Achievement*, Vol. 2, pp. 113–134. London: Falmer Press.

Willms, J. Douglas, and Marie-Anne Somers. 1999. *Schooling Outcomes in Latin America: A Report for UNESCO*. Santiago de Chile: Laboratorio Latino de Evaluacion de la Calidad de la Educacion, UNESCO.

Willms, J. Douglas, and Marie-Anne Somers. 2001. Family, Classroom, and School Effects on Children's Educational Outcomes in Latin America. *International Journal of School Effectiveness and Improvement*, 12(4): 409–445.

World Bank. 2001. *Brazil: Teachers Development and Incentives. A Strategic Framework*. Washington, DC: World Bank, Human Development Department, Report No. 20408 BR.

Wright, Eric Olin. 1977. *Class Counts: Comparative Studies in Class Analysis*. New York: Cambridge University Press.

Index

Italic page numbers indicate material in tables or figures.

voluntary associations, 52
voucher schools, 24, 81
Vygotsky, Lev, 31, 93

wages. *See* salaries
wealth, collectivizing, 53
Werthein, Jorge, 29, 187n1
whole-class activities, 118
Willis, Paul, 50
Willms, J. Douglas, 55, 59, 186n1, 188n4
Wilson, Pete, 33

Workers' Party (Brazil), 38
World Bank: Brazil, teaching in, 104–105; research, 10; and rural absenteeism, 108; teacher evaluation programs, 99
Wright, Eric Olin, 186n3 (chap. 3)

youth culture, 53

Zau, Andrew, 14
Zimmerman, Joy, 110